Fo

In your head you are for ever young. The photo page in your passport states a fact, but it doesn't tell the truth. When some of your best friends die, however, you have at least to give a nod to the arithmetic.

I never wanted to write a memoir because I didn't think my life remarkable. But at some point after the pandemic I became aware that people of a younger generation were struggling to understand what I was saying. It was as if the stars by which I'd always steered now belonged in a different sky.

The only dividend of the years' vanishing, as far as I can see, is that it makes aspects of the past appear more interesting or humorous than they felt at the time. So I thought I'd put together some essays on the things that had meant the most to me, to fix in print my gratitude or pleasure; and if some of what emerged would seem quaint to younger readers that would be part of the deal. When they'd looked at these thirteen enthusiastic pieces, randomly ordered, my publishers asked me to leave out the least autobiographical and to rearrange the rest in a more chronological sequence. So as I'd tried to steer away from memoir, they shunted me towards it. The result is therefore a hybrid. But we are all mongrels, I suppose, so maybe that's not such a bad thing.

I was also asked to remove some of the many names of friends or colleagues to whom I felt indebted, for fear that parts might read like the credits at the end of a film. So I did. However, I think these people know who they are and how much they have meant to me. Whether or not they find their names here, this book is dedicated to them. Also to those, much missed, who have already braved what lies ahead.

FIRES WHICH BURNED BRIGHTLY

ALSO BY SEBASTIAN FAULKS

FIRES WHICH BURNED BRIGHTLY

A Life in Progress

Sebastian Faulks

HUTCHINSON
HEINEMANN

HUTCHINSON HEINEMANN

UK | USA | Canada | Ireland | Australia
India | New Zealand | South Africa

Hutchinson Heinemann is part of the Penguin Random House group of companies
whose addresses can be found at global.penguinrandomhouse.com

Penguin Random House UK,
One Embassy Gardens, 8 Viaduct Gardens, London SW11 7BW

penguin.co.uk

Penguin
Random House
UK

First published 2025

004

Copyright © Sebastian Faulks, 2025

The moral right of the author has been asserted

Set in 13/16.5pt Fournier MT Pro
Typeset by Jouve (UK), Milton Keynes

Printed and bound in Great Britain by Clays Ltd, Elcograf S.p.A.

The authorised representative in the EEA is Penguin Random House Ireland,
Morrison Chambers, 32 Nassau Street, Dublin D02 YH68

A CIP catalogue record for this book is available from the British Library

ISBN: 978–1–529–15465–8

For William, Holly and Arthur
with apologies

Il n'y a qu'une vie, c'est donc qu'elle est parfaite
Paul Éluard (1895–1952)

Contents

I.

Mayonnaise

Everything is fine. We're alive. We live in England. It's all good. From a fog, faces and words emerge. Mum. The kitchen table with a metal mincer clamped to the edge. Willy, the friendly Dalmatian with his thumping tail. A bowl of dripping. Wet washing on a rack above the range. But who we really are and what it's all about . . . That'll come into focus when I reach the age of six or seven — by which time we'll have reached the unimaginable, space-age date of 1960.

To start with, though, it's all about things. Hard surfaces and not falling over. Chairs and tables. The texture and smell of different woods. Marmalade on fried bread at breakfast. The awful cold mutton at lunch. As a toy, I have a 'farm': a piece of hardboard painted green with a blue splodge for a pond and a balsa wood 'house' with straw thatch that's been glued to the board. There are some plastic Friesians that can be placed at the edge of the pond. It's a present from our grandmother, on Mum's side. We never meet her, though, and when we ask why, a pained look comes into Mum's eyes and she says it's better that way. Dad's mother died of cancer in the War. Mum's father was killed by the Germans. Dad was wounded by them and they thought he'd die. But he didn't.

So Edward, who was born in a local hospital in 1950, and I, who was born in 1953 (in the bathroom for some reason), are part of a new project. Pioneers in a landscape that's been through a bad time but on which the sun is now set to shine. We're not rich, but we're not as poor as the people in the cottages next door; for a start we have an indoor lav. Mum is tall and fair, Dad is handsome and has tweed jackets and striped ties; they know what they're up to.

The world beyond our house at the village crossroads is filled with other people, who to my mind are either frightening or ridiculous. Everything I need is here in the house and in the garden that surrounds it, with its brick steps, wrought-iron gates and musty wooden sheds. Edward is an inventive playmate, introducing me to pirates and cowboys and armies and dressing up. I trot along behind, an Apache in the old garage, a lookout in the walnut tree. Ship ahoy!

Everything seems to be old or second-hand. My clothes are cast-offs or bought from jumble sales, bazaars or 'bring-and-buy's. Likewise, the Dinky and Corgi toy cars are battered, flaked and missing tyres. But there are plenty of them, enough to have races down the wooden corridor that leads to the telephone (we share a 'party line' with the people opposite) and ample, when you add the lorries and the vans, to build a traffic jam round the gate-legged table. Some of the toys must have been bought as a job lot because even though Edward has had two more birthdays and three more Christmases, he couldn't have been given *this* many Vanwalls and Sunbeam Talbots. Next door, visible through the fence, is Abberbury Close, an almshouse for old ladies, who donate the occasional knitted golliwog or cock-eyed teddy bear.

As well as Willy, there is Bumble, a miniature dachshund with a kink in his tail. He walks on three legs because as a baby I rolled off the bed and fell on top of him. We don't talk about his broken leg because it doesn't reflect well on whoever was meant to be doing the childcare. (Many years later a hypnotherapist in Wimpole Street will try to persuade me that a suppressed memory of falling is at the root of my fear of airborne turbulence. It doesn't work.) Where Willy is all eager affection, Bumble is halitotic and difficult. Mum insists that the little dog accompany her and Willy on their daily walks up to Donnington Castle, where the long-legged Dalmatian bounds over the fields. Bumble limps along the path, his prodigious male organ smacking him first on one flank, then the other. He has a thin, handsome face, with a long nose and whiskers.

In the morning, Mum comes in and wakes us up. There's no heating, but we're allowed to have the gas fire on briefly while we get dressed. I like sitting in the bathroom while Dad has his bath. In vest and boxer shorts, he then shaves in front of the mirror and anoints his hair with something called 'Honey and Flowers', combing it back in

3

the candid, nothing-to-conceal style of the reliable man. 'How old are you, Daddy?' 'Thirty-nine.' 'You've got a paunch.' 'No, that's relaxed muscle.' The routine never varies. He holds his trousers out in front of him back-to-front, puts in one leg, then flips the trousers round deftly to get the other leg in the correct hole. When he dies – in February 1998, when he's eighty and I am forty-four – I will put my own trousers on the same way for a time, as a tribute; but I lack Dad's snappy wrist action.

When Edward goes to school, I'm quite happy to play alone. I saddle up with an old towel over a wheel-back chair and canter off across the prairie. Even though we live between the racecourse at Newbury and the training yards of Lambourn, I'm so allergic to real horses that I can't get closer than twenty feet without having a fit. So the polished pine of the chair will have to do. Luckily I have acquired a magnificent gun called a Buntline Special, which is my permanent companion. I drill a hole in the bottom of the holster with Dad's corkscrew, push some string through and tie it to my thigh to make me faster on the draw. I urge the chair on across the dusty plain.

Cowboys are on television most days. We like *The Lone Ranger* and *Champion the Wonder Horse*, though we puzzle over the theme song and the line 'He can take a whitton from a bone', though a close listening today suggests it was actually 'like an arrow whizzin' from a bow'. Not at Horne Mead House in 1957, though. Later comes *Bronco* with Ty Hardin. The theme song lyrics are on the trite side, I admit: 'Bronco, Bronco, tearin' across the Texas plain / Bronco, Bronco / Bronco Layne.' But Ty Hardin is tough. Probably uses a Buntline Special. Then there is sport, for which our appetite is huge. Horse racing, swimming, athletics ('atherletics' to me) and, best of all, the slow, intoxicating drama of Test cricket with our national honour depending on the courage of Fred Trueman and Colin Cowdrey. Lunch at Old Trafford is not until one-thirty, but reluctantly we are dragged from the screen at one for whatever cold-meat horror awaits. In theory I'm not allowed to leave the table until I've finished, but this rule is seldom enforced and at a pinch I can get Willy to help out. He has absolutely no problem with cold mutton; fat and gristle are fine. I love him and his soft black ears with white hairs showing through.

Our own versions of sport are half-formed. I'm too young for cricket, though I like running. We've watched enough atherletics to know that in long-distance races you don't just sprint all the way: tactics are important. From the early days, there's a dramatic commentary, provided by Ross and Norris McWhirter. I'm usually Vladimir Kuts, the Russian 1956 Olympic champion. As I round the apple tree for the third time and wait for the sound of the bell, I collapse in an asthmatic fit ('He's down, he's down! Kuts is down!') and bang my fists on the grass in an attempt to get some air into my lungs. The real Kuts never seems to have this problem.

The outside world makes a move on me at last when I'm sent to what I think is called a kindergarden. Miss Barton's is in Speen, in a sort of prefab down a track. It's full of other people. Children, to be precise. Around the walls are pictures of apples, bicycles, cats, dogs, elephants . . . all the way through to zebras. I have no interest in this or in the silly squiggles that are written on them. I don't know what to do with plasticine and I can't wait to go home, because there's a level crossing on Station Road where I persuade Mum to linger until the gates close and a train comes clattering past on its way to Kintbury. That's more like it. I love trains, though a model set is beyond our means, apparently. When we get home, it may with any luck not be cold mutton for lunch but my favourite – tinned tomato soup on grated stale Canadian cheddar.

One day at Miss Barton's I have a pain in the lower abdomen and am allowed to go home. There's a suspicious lump down there. Mum, who used to be a nurse, thinks this is not right. In Newbury hospital I'm operated on for a hernia, though how I've ruptured myself is unclear. Too much shot-putting in the Soviet cause, perhaps. I come home swathed in bandages with a huge scar in the groin that will be the subject of curious comment over the years. I'm spending a lot of time in bed anyway, since I contract every virus in southern England. Colds, coughs and all manner of chest infections keep me between the sheets with *Housewives' Choice* and *Workers' Playtime* on the wireless. Back in hospital, I have my tonsils and adenoids removed on the grounds that if you have no tonsils you can't get tonsillitis — and you really can't fault the logic there. Thanks to the new National Health Service, this is all done for free.

In the early evening, after work, Dad comes upstairs for a game. Perched on his shoulders, I can see a single star out in the night. Perhaps it's the very one in the song 'Twinkle, Twinkle' that's hanging in the sky over Abberbury Close. Though neither of our parents is a believer (they never go to church), we have to kneel and say prayers, including a dodgy one in which we ask God to 'make me a good boy tomorrow'. There is often a French song called *'J'ai perdu le "doh" de ma clarinette'*, which goes on for ages, as you also lose the re, the mi, the fa and the rest of them. The chorus goes 'Oompah, camer-a, oompah, camer-a, oompah, oompah, oompah.' (It's many years before I discover that it's actually *'en pas, camarade'*.)

Dad, it turns out, is a 'solicitor', a lawyer who gives people advice in a dark back room of a Georgian brick building in Cheap Street, Newbury. He has 'clients', who pay for his knowledge, and sometimes he appears in the local magistrates' court to plead the case of a housebreaker or local rough. He is the junior partner in Pitman and Bazett. Pitman is deceased and Bazett rides to work on a moped, which he parks in the office corridor. The best clients are the local landowners, for whom Dad does 'conveyancing', the fee for which can run the office for another month or so; though when he gives advice to a stable lad about his tenancy agreement I think he 'forgets' to send in a bill afterwards. He works for five and a half days a week. On Saturday mornings, he wears a sports jacket rather than a suit; he stays home after lunch, though, and does some gardening. He has two weeks' holiday a year. I'm not sure if he 'enjoys' it. I suspect he doesn't ask himself that question.

The adult world is one of obligation. People seem to expect nothing from it except survival. Peace is a continuation of the War by other means. Many years later I will read in novels and memoirs of how grown-ups experienced this decade. Ted Hughes described it as 'a Tundra that we had to cross'. Doris Lessing's novel *The Golden Notebook* depicts a London intelligentsia all at sea over Ban the Bomb and masochistic sex; the deeply confused main character goes to a meeting (I'm not inventing this) 'to discuss Stalin on linguistics'. *Lucky Jim* by Kingsley Amis evokes the austerity of re-used razor blades and 'the smallest drink he'd ever been seriously offered'.

For a village child in 1959, however, it's all fine. We don't mind being cold, and the size of an alcoholic drink is not a problem. I know nothing of Soviet tanks in Budapest, supertax or contraception; I pray only for a mutton-free lunch and a Ted Dexter half-century. I am even starting to make exceptions to my fear of 'other people'. Once a week a man comes to help in the garden. He rides a heavy bicycle with a huge chain guard; he has hobnail boots and cycle clips and thick sandwiches, wrapped in grease-proof paper, that leave a pile of crumbs, like sawdust, in the tool shed. He's a very good gardener. His vegetable crop is so prodigious that Mum gives some surplus beans and marrows to the people in the row of cottages next door. When he finds out, the gardener ticks her off and Dad sacks him for being rude. I'm disappointed because I've never got to try his crumby sandwiches. The milk-man is all right, too. I like the pencil tucked behind his ear at an angle and the way he hands the bottles through the kitchen window. He has orange juice on his float as well, though we're not allowed to have this fancy stuff. Then there's Mrs Taylor, who comes and does the rough work — banging a hoover into the skirting boards and polishing the grate. She gives us Everton mints from a paper bag and calls your hand a 'pud' (rhymes with mud); she says 'mankelpiece' and 'acrost' and 'five and twenty past'. One evening, Mum and Dad go out (a rare event) and she babysits for us. When our parents get home they find a note by the telephone that says: 'A lady rung.' I think this is helpful of Mrs Taylor, but Dad is mysteri-ously amused for days and days. Mrs T takes a shine to me because I 'put her in mind of the little one I lost'. Our names are quite beyond her, however, and she refers to us as 'Edwin and Bonny'. When a thrilling new food called yoghurt arrives in the shops, the closest Mrs Taylor can get to the word is 'vulgar'. 'Oh yes,' she says, 'Edwin loves a raspberry vulgar.'

Well . . . What's this all about? What's going on? Is this 'happiness', perhaps? Pealing ignorance and tinned tomatoes on toast. Shirley Abicair on the wireless and 'Sugartime' by Alma Cogan. I can maybe stay in this village house and its garden with its books and dogs for ever, looking out of the window, thinking about horses and cars, particularly my favourite, the beautiful Citroën DS with its sloping headlights and airy suspension. Perhaps things will never change. Perhaps they don't need to.

Then, in the summer of 1958, when I'm five and Edward is nearing his eighth birthday, we go to a place called Elstree, in Woolhampton, a village about twenty minutes' drive towards Reading. This is a 'boarding school', into which my parents, looking serious, disappear with the headmaster and his wife. There's a grass semicircle in the drive in front of the forbidding house, round which Edward and I chase each other for half an hour until the grown-ups re-emerge.

That September, Edward vanishes. He has gone to be a 'boarder' at Elstree. I catch Mum crying in the garden.

I'm sent to a tiny village school in the corner of a

field in West Woodhay. It's called Greenwood, and we fifteen reluctant boys in green ties, shorts and sandals are its first pupils. The junior class is taken by Mrs Sexton and the senior by her husband, the fearsome Mr Sexton, also known as 'Sir'. He carries his right arm tucked away, loose, inside his jacket; his right leg is attached to a surgical shoe by a spring that disappears up his trouser leg. He has been shot in the head while fighting in a tank in Sicily and shipped back to England with life-threatening injuries. He has had to learn not only how to walk on one good leg and to write with the wrong hand, but how to speak again. He has a deep voice and a grave manner and we're in awe of his injuries and his stoical bearing.

Every morning I wait in Dad's office to be picked up by Mr and Mrs Sexton and driven to Greenwood. There are two or three of us crammed into the back of a maroon van, whose controls have been adapted for Mr Sexton, though not extensively. There's a notice on the back window that says, 'Disabled. No hand signals.' A round knob has been attached to the steering wheel to enable him to turn it with his one good hand, and that's about it. I close my eyes when he has to change gear.

At Greenwood, I learn to read. There's a mobile library that comes to Donnington, or sometimes we go to the public library in Newbury, where there's a wider choice of bad men to be defeated by brave underdogs. Of the books we have at home, my favourite is *The Voyages of Doctor Dolittle* by Hugh Lofting, which I persuade

Mum to plough through several times, even after I can read for myself. I lose count of how many times I've read *The Hundred and One Dalmatians* by Dodie Smith, but I always fight back tears when Cadpig gazes rapt at the figures in a model nativity in church because it's the closest she can get to watching television. (We don't like the later Disney film, though, with its American accents and the two female dogs fused into one, which undoes the book's uneasy triangle of Pongo and his two bitches.) Sometimes Mrs Taylor reads to us, but she doesn't like it when I put her right on the longer words.

After school, Mum tries to make me play with other children. There's a date in a big house with a boy who has a 'nanny' and therefore barely sees his parents. I think this is ridiculous. Luckily I have an asthma attack and have to be taken home. There's tea in a bungalow with a boy whose mother is from Venezuela, though I react so strongly to the long grass in their garden that this date also comes to an early end. And then there's poor Danny Grant, a little boy with specs and a leg iron, who lives on a modern estate. We give him a lift home every day after school; and every day he gets his caliper caught on the door sill and sends his small bundle of books flying. His father drives a Humber Hawk, a car which for some reason I despise, and give as my excuse for not going to play there. Mum has no idea about cars, so eventually I'm made to go — and stay the night as well. The Grants do everything the wrong way. Instead of thrashing a football about in the garden, they want me to do advanced Meccano with Danny. I've been given a stage one Meccano set myself, but have managed to build one thing only, the beginner's bench, which wobbles. Danny's bedroom is like an engineer's workshop. And then, when it's time for bed, Mrs Grant asks me if I'd like a 'tinkle in the toilet'. A what?

At Greenwood there's a system of stars for good work that appeals to me; the trouble is I can never get far on the star chart because I'm off school so much. I have to leave early on a Wednesday to go to the hospital to have injections that are supposed to cure my allergies — and so once more that smell of gas and antiseptic in corridors painted only halfway to a horizontal line and carrying their puzzling signs, 'X-Ray', 'Pathology', 'Out-Patients'; the waiting area with its torn magazines; and then the iron ache of the injection as it fills the arm and the glucose sweet from a tin for not making a fuss. In summer, they open the French doors of the men's ward and push the old boys out to lie in the sun.

I miss most of my last term for a more exciting reason. In the Easter holidays, Edward and I have been watching horse racing on television, culminating in the Grand National, where the grey Nicolaus Silver recovers from a jumping error to forge ahead on the run-in. As soon as it's over, we naturally go out into the garden to rerun the race ourselves. Becher's Brook is a low yew hedge which Edward tells me to take on all fours, like a real horse. I obediently fly head-first over the jump, grazing the top with a trailing foot, and land on my left elbow. There's a peculiar sound — and the sensation that my lower arm is falling off, remaining attached only by skin to the rest of me. It hangs useless by my side. So it's back to those pungent corridors and into the children's ward, though it feels like slipping into another century. My plastered arm is held vertical and attached to an overhead bracket. That evening (when the call is cheaper, after six o'clock) Dad telephones an old doctor friend to ask what's going on; the doc unwisely speculates that the arm is being held up to keep the blood flowing back to the heart and so avert the risk of amputation. There's probably no such danger, but Mum is alarmed by the news. Meanwhile, there's no specialist bonesetter available. The nearest surgeon thought to be up to the job is a Mr Squire, who's based in Reading. He's much in demand, it seems, and day after day I ask the nurse if Mr Squire might be in that day. The worst thing is the bedpan and having my bottom wiped not with paper but with something that looks like a horse's tail. Dad visits after work and looks at the table in the middle of the ward where the children who can get up are being fed. 'It's like a chimpanzees' tea party,' he says, cheerily. To hell with chimpanzees. Where's this surgeon?

Eventually the bone is set and I go home with a hefty plaster cast in a sling. I at once contract whooping cough, with spasms and projectile vomiting. For some reason,

I decide this is the ideal time to learn how to ride a bicycle — something I've long believed to be beyond me. With one arm in a sling, I manage to complete a circuit of the lawn on a child's Raleigh from a jumble sale before being sick into the flower bed.

The Raleigh's too small, it has return handlebars and is painted a sissy red; it's a girl's bike, really. Along the streets of Newbury and Thatcham I gawp at the different bicycles that go by: drop-handlebar racing bikes and shiny machines ridden by Brylcreemed youths whose handlebars are swept up in a V shape, allowing their riders to sit back and whistle. But we can't afford a new one, so I switch my yearning to the accessories. I spend hours in Halford's on Northbrook Street looking at saddlebags, which range from the tiny toolkit to the multi-compartmental tourer. I long to have one — so I can put things in it and carry them. Even a medium-size bag costs something insane, like seventeen and six. Anyway, it wouldn't go on my little Raleigh because it doesn't even have hooks under the saddle.

Mr Squire's handiwork, an X-ray reveals, has not been quite all we hoped. So I have to go back to hospital to have the arm re-set. Up till now, I've rather enjoyed the attention due to a wounded steeplechaser, but this seems a bit much; it also rules out any chance of a late run on the school star chart.

About twice a year for the rest of my life (so far) my left arm will gently rise of its own accord while I'm lying in bed at night. I never know when it's going to happen, but it's a strangely pleasant feeling, as if the bones have their own memory.

In the holidays from school, Edward and I resume our old games. On the mantelpiece, there's still the blue papier-mâché egg with a coin slot in the top mounted on a base that reads, 'The League of Pity'. This is a charity that helps poor children, orphans, 'spastics', those with polio or leg irons or some other disadvantage too terrible to think about. We're meant to put spare coins in it. Unfortunately, Edward and I don't have any spare coins. My pocket money is six old pence a week, one penny for each year of my age; Edward is on nine. Six old pence is 2.5p in today's money and even allowing for inflation that leaves slim pickings for the poor children.

Apart from soldiers and cars, the main occupants of the toy cupboard are soft toys no longer needed for bedtime comfort — teddy bears of various sizes and states of wear; dogs and rabbits; a couple of monkeys and some foam-rubber characters with wire in the limbs that can be bent into various shapes. It seems important to find an activity that can involve them all and really there's only one thing for it: cricket.

The ground is the playroom; the wicket is the lino floor revealed by pulling back the rug. It's quick and slippy, with something in it for all the bowlers. The stumps are three narrow cylindrical wooden building bricks; the bats are small wooden rectangles from the same kit and the ball a large dice covered in sticking plaster. Its numerous edges give encouragement to the spinners.

Under the flag of the MCC, Edward selects his best eleven; my team is the CCC. We have to kneel down and, grasping the hapless toys, engage them in the game. The foam-rubber ones get cheap runs on the rebound but also give many caught-and-bowled chances. My stars are a rubber golliwog called Mr Swingabout, a genuine all-rounder who bats four and bowls first change; and a stylish batsman called Nana — a three-legged dog whom I had secured from Edward's squad in exchange for two erratic glove puppets. As a reward for not making a fuss about my arm, I've been given a small rubber Mexican with a sombrero and a poncho. I christen him 'Mexican' and he scores 112 not out on debut. It's the first time any CCC player has made a century and I only wish I could say it was the first of many for my little *amigo*, but in truth he struggles to hold his place after the return of Blue Bear from an emergency limb reattachment.

As we grow older, the cricketing aspect becomes secondary to the human drama, much of it taking place off the pitch and involving a seductive Siamese cat. At lunch one day, I stun my parents by telling them that Mrs Teddy is getting a divorce. The game expands to meet our need for psychological drama, becoming a mixture between *Test Match Special* and *Peyton Place*. I don't know at what age we finally put the toys back in the cupboard. Dad will merrily maintain that it was when Edward went to university. I believe it was when the CCC won their first and only test, when, on the afternoon of the fifth day, my opener (a Lenny the Lion puppet) cut the ball backward of square into the skirting board for four. It may have been in 1964 or '5; but whatever day it was, we both accepted that part of childhood then was over.

There's an age when your memory stops being episodic and becomes continuous. I think children enjoy this change, because it enables them to look forward to the high points and to endure those things that have to be borne. They know it's 'traditional' to have Coca-Cola on Saturday morning and have noted that Father Christmas is a stickler for dates. Repetition is power. *The Brains Trust* on television always ends eventually, giving way to Sooty and Sweep. You can even kid your parents that because they once bought a bag of crisps after a swim at the local pool, it is now their duty to do so every time.

When I try to remember being a child, I think mainly of struggle. But my memory, so adhesive when it comes to useless facts, is probably suspect on this bigger picture. The things that push themselves into your recollection are the ones that made your life different from that of others: that's just good narrative sense. These quirks also bulk large because other members of the family have teased you about them over the years: the day that Mum took you to the cattle market for a fun outing, but you cried because the calves' heads were tied up so tightly; or the time when you wept because you couldn't bear to see the roses being deadheaded.

The truth is that as a child I was usually cheerful and always had enthusiasm for the day ahead. Also, there was music. There was *Pick of the Pops* with Alan Freeman on Sunday afternoon as well as Radio Luxembourg. The first single I bought was 'Johnny Angel' by Shelley Fabares, a teen drama with a ghostly reverb. The explosion of excitement that came from pop music in the Sixties somehow expressed our own sense of coming change — the thrill of growing up and believing all things to be possible.

My own tastes were intense but narrow. They included: all the Beatles singles, but not so much the album songs — except 'All My Loving', which seemed to me then, seems still, the perfect pop song – anything with a wall-of-sound, Phil Spector production; one or two voices, like Roy Orbison and, a bit later, Dionne Warwick or Stevie Wonder.

One evening we went to a folk and skiffle concert in Oxford. Among the acts was a harmony group called the Springfields, who had two good songs, 'Say I Won't Be There' and 'Island of Dreams'. In the middle of each one, something odd happened. The girl singer, who had blonde hair and mascara, stepped forward and sang the middle-eight alone; a sort of charge went through the theatre before the washboard harmonies resumed. Her voice was hard, yet plaintive; it seemed to crack with emotion on particular chord changes; it made your scalp tingle. A year or so later, Dusty went solo, and her first single, 'I Only Want to Be With You' (on the blue Pye label), had a giggling sexiness added in just below the killer notes in her mid-range. We played it till our parents begged us to stop.

I've run ahead a bit here. I hadn't heard these acts at the age of seven, which is where I'm trying to stop and take stock. It's 1960. We are at that milestone now. And although style journalists will try to convince us that 'the Sixties' didn't 'really' begin until 1963 and will then quote the most-over quoted poem in history to support their case, we can safely stick to the facts. Things *are* changing. Food, for instance. Mum has ditched the cold mutton and the sponge desserts that no one liked. She's discovered '*le continent*': Constance Spry is being elbowed off the shelf by Elizabeth David. We've met a family called Johnson, who live in Bradfield, where the father teaches Geography. The glamorous mother is called Eliane, she's from Belgium, and she passes on some culinary tips. Out goes the salad cream, never to return. Meanwhile in the medicine cabinet the tiny bottle of olive oil, purchased every two or three years from Hickman's the chemist to be trickled into an inflamed ear, receives a surprise call-up. It's now to be dribbled, drop by drop, into beaten raw eggs to make something called mayonnaise. We've previously had offal because it was cheap (pig's liver was powerful; heart – not sure which animal it came from — was chewy); but now Mum is serving up mild sweetbreads and kidneys in rich sauces with rice, cooked not in pans but in coloured 'casserole dishes' bought in London. The dining room has acquired a rug from a shop called Casa Pupo. Blimey. The old roast beef, my favourite, is still pink inside but the gravy is enriched with home-made wine. The vegetable garden, of which Dad is now in sole charge, produces waxy new potatoes flecked with mint, mountains of soft broad beans, tiny fresh courgettes fried in butter (marrow is out) and fistfuls of baby carrots. These vegetables complement the new cuisine as efficiently as they rescued the old. The fruit cages, Mum's domain, are engaged in a constant battle with 'those blasted birds', but still produce more than we can eat in the summer, with the remaining raspberries and blackcurrants being bottled.

The sun has come out. We still don't have any money (nobody does) but it seems that somehow we can afford a Hornby Dublo train set. It's only a small circle, but it's so well made that Berkshire's most ham-fisted family can fit it together. It has a little green locomotive, two open wagons and a guard's van. There's a hefty trans-former with a dial that can make it go faster or slower or backwards. On Christmas Day, I sit on the floor entranced while the train goes round and round and round.

Our house is not as big as it had seemed to me as a tod-dler. There are three bedrooms — ours, our parents' and the spare room at the top of the staircase. The bathroom doubles as an Olympic swimming pool, where we work on tumble-turns while impersonating the Scottish swimmer Ian Black. During the 1960 Olympics, we discover that the fifty-kilometre walker Don Thompson trained in his own bathroom with kettles and heaters blasting steam to prepare him for the heat of Rome, where he wins the gold medal with a hanky tucked beneath his cap and hanging down his neck. I find it useful to dress this way when fast-walking to the shop, commentating on my progress up the village street, now the Appian Way.

So the house is quite compact — though there's a door we aren't allowed to open, beyond which lives a 'tenant', whose weekly rent is recorded in a threepenny notebook. For a long time it's a bachelor called Mr Buchanan, who has a built-up shoe, which makes a clunking echo as he walks about above our kitchen. 'Uh-oh,' says Mrs Taylor, 'Mr Bowman's coming through the roof.' The best tenants, though, are the last.

On his return from work in the summer, Dad has barely had time for a glass of milk before he's required to bowl to Edward and me on the lawn. Although he is still in his early forties, he's already stopped playing cricket regularly after a couple of seasons as captain of Newbury. He finds the bowling of an eight-over spell every evening a bit more than he fancies, and it's a great day when he asks the new tenant, a young man called John Kemp, if he fancies a trundle. I wouldn't say Mr Kemp has Dad's guile or variation of pace, but he's willing to put it there or thereabouts in his Bri-nylon

shirt. Edward's strong bottom-hand is severe on anything in the leg stump area, but Mr Kemp gamely sends
down another over of gentle outswing, keeping his wife,
Shirley, waiting with his tea.

The decade-defining change is dramatically clear when
it comes to holidays. A week by the icy sea at Bexhill in
1956 was no one's idea of fun. The Isle of Wight was a step
up, with better ice cream (Eldorado, not Wall's) and slip
practice with a tennis ball on the beach — 'What a catch!
Oh no! He's put him down!' — but the sea itself, in sight
of the container port at Portsmouth . . . Thick sweaters,
thermos flasks and running on the spot were essential after
the briefest dip. You should never ask a lady why she isn't
swimming, we'd been told; and whatever that reason may
have been, it got Mum off the hook for the full fortnight as
she sheltered from the north-east wind behind a sea wall.

Then in 1961, when I was eight, something momen-
tous was announced: a visit to France. Dad's elder brother,
Uncle Neville, was behind it. He'd booked several rooms
in a boarding house called Le Beau Séjour in Deauville,
a seaside resort in Normandy, purpose-built in the 1890s.
All I knew of 'France' was what I'd learned at Greenwood,
where I'd drawn coloured pictures of Madame Souris, Mrs
Mouse, a busy little housekeeper. I'd also been to Reading with my mother to see *Monsieur Hulot's Holiday* at
the cinema. There were two picture-houses in Newbury, the Regal and the Forum, but Mum liked to go to
Reading (lunch of liver and bacon in the Oasis café first)

because it was there, in 1948, when she had been working for Elizabeth Arden, that she first met my father. The smoky old brick town with its cloying smell of malt from the Courage brewery, so unlovely to everyone else, had happy memories for her.

Monsieur Hulot could hardly have been a better preparation for the Beau Séjour. There was a sandy tennis court nearby, a shaded terrace garden and a short walk to the beach. The bathrooms had little basins called 'bidets' that were the source of inexhaustible amusement to the grown-ups. The doors from the hall into the dining room were glass-panelled with half net curtains; a swing door led into the kitchen from which came the *plat du jour* borne in by white-coated waiters. Round the room were respectable French couples, the level of whose wine bottle was marked off on the label with a coloured pencil at the end of dinner. Lapdogs were fed by their owners with morsels of cheese at table.

Edward and I were allowed to sit at our own table for two, which made us feel grand, though my fear of what might issue from the kitchen was intense. It turned out to be all right — then better than that. There was usually some sort of green soup that held no horrors; the main course was free of mutton fat or fish bones; and for pudding there were things we had never had before — fresh peaches, bunches of grapes and Petit Suisse, a small cylinder of soft cheese in a thin cream sauce.

We had flown over in a propeller plane, which was less exciting than I'd expected, but had then taken a taxi, which to my delight was a Citroën DS 21. I had now actually been in the car of my dreams. Uncle Neville's wife, Aunt Bridget, found me, for some reason, hilarious. Mum thought it was something to do with watching me jump grim-faced from the top board at the local swimming pool. She had given me the *Rothman's Illustrated Guide* to the touring Australian cricket team under the captaincy of Richie Benaud, which I had read about sixty times, and in Deauville took me out to buy some shoes for the beach. She was not much of a linguist (*oui, non* and *comme ça* about covered it), but we got the job done and the beach shoes, while uncomfortable, were at least new. I think it was Aunt Bridget who first bought me a fizzy drink called *Pschitt!* – so named, I was told, because that was the noise made by the bottle when it was opened. The grown-ups were amused, bidet-style, by my frequent requests for a *Pschitt!*

In the evening, when the adults were gratifying their appetite for cigarettes and foul-tasting drinks (no *Pschitt!* for them) in the garden, Edward enlisted Judy, our same-aged cousin, to prepare a play to be performed at the end of our stay. It was to be based on the story of Bonnie Prince Charlie and his escape across the sea to Skye. Written and directed by Edward, it starred him as the Prince and Judy as Flora MacDonald. The play lasted about fifteen minutes and was set to take place in the Beau Séjour's largest bedroom, so that as many people as possible could cram in.

My job was to turn on the bidet. The noise of the water gurgling gave a very lifelike imitation, we thought, of the seas in the Outer Hebrides. The key moment came when the Prince arrived, disguised as an Irish maid, at Flora's cottage to make his escape. The voiceover, provided from the bathroom by Edward, ran: 'Prince Charlie knocked . . .' At this point, Judy, in islander's shawl, was meant to open the door of her humble croft. Unfortunately, there was something about the phrase 'Prince Charlie knocked', or perhaps the way in which Edward declaimed it, that always reduced her to giggles. We had tried rephrasing it and making her think of sad things, but it was no good. The play went swimmingly until that point, the bidet was terrific if I say so myself, but Judy's giggles were not only hysterical but infectious. The curtain, alas, had to be rung down early − though I have to admit the grown-ups put a brave face on it as they went downstairs to resume their smoking and drinking on the terrace.

Back in England, life seemed charged with possibilities. A friend of Dad's took Edward and me to see Richie Benaud's Australians in the final Test against England at the Oval. The characters from my *Rothman's Guide* came to flickering life in front of us: Neil Harvey, Alan Davidson, Wally Grout, right there on the green grass. My

England heroes (Trueman was absent injured, replaced by Jack Flavell) laboured in the field against the immovable Peter Burge (born, I knew well, at Kangaroo Point, Queensland, 1932).

Never mind. I still liked the look of this space-age new decade, with Yuri Gagarin and Duane Eddy and for me, it seemed, no more asthmatic seizures. I was pretty sure it was going to be good. But then we hit a wall. And a time machine hurled me back a hundred years.

2.

Break or Make

Twelve days after his eighth birthday, he goes to a new school. A trunk has been found in a loft and clothes (grey corduroy shorts and windcheater, grey shirt and pink tie) bought from the school second-hand stock. The head-master's wife has written to his parents to say that his locker number will be 13 and that she hopes it will be a lucky one. He is given a new Bible and prayer book and a block of Basildon Bond on which to write home.

It is a very large house of the kind he's heard described as 'Queen Anne'. The headmaster is a tall, craggy, grey-haired man called Commander Sanderson. He stands with his back to the fireplace, opposite a grand piano and a mangy lion skin on the floor. There are said to be more than eighty boys, aged from eight to thirteen, known by their surnames and, in the case of brothers, by an initial as well. He's told that his dormitory will be 'Number Five'. While his parents stand talking uneasily to Commander Sanderson, his brother is dismissed; then he's led away by Mrs Sanderson up an enormous oak staircase, through a baize door and down a long passageway to a room where he meets Halliday, Newcome and Bagge, three other new boys. He has now lost any clear sense of what is going on.

The others are about his size; they look tense. They are invited to play Kim's Game, a memory test in which a dozen objects — a thimble, a cotton reel, a playing card — are shown to them on a tray and then removed. They have to remember what has been on it, or taken away, or something. They look at one another, smile, grimace. It isn't difficult. But it's strange. Everything is strange. The size of the place, the surnames, the uniforms, the overheard names of the dormitories for the big boys — Chatfield, Wellington, Nelson — the not having any idea of what's going to happen next.

When Mrs Sanderson has run out of small items to put beneath her cloth, he thanks her and says he would like to go back and see his parents now, please.

'Your parents have gone,' she says.

It is odd, but until that moment he has been so keen to follow in his brother's footsteps that he hasn't paused to think what 'boarding' means. No parents, no dogs, no Bronco Layne, no 'Oompah, camer-a' and being hoisted on Dad's shoulders to see the single star in the night.

He looks at Halliday, Newcome and Bagge. They look back. They're not smiling any more.

There is tea downstairs, at long refectory tables with all the boys gathered, chattering — tall boys, fat boys, dark boys, little boys, gingers, cowlicks and curlies, all with surnames, all of them bigger and knowing what comes next, while the four new ones look about them, eyes wide, trying to stop the flood of the unknown. He will remember nothing of the next few days, except a sense of falling and of waiting to hit the ground, both longing for it and fearing the impact. Every sensation is unfamiliar. Rough red blankets, iron beds, plastic chamber pots beneath them, bells ringing, enormous Miss Buddle, old bald Mr Hewitt with his gold-rimmed glasses who has been there for ever and carries the keys to the school's mysteries; plump Mrs Sanderson, now vanished after the treacherous Kim's Game; and the terrifying Head with his iron-grey hair, a man who has instilled fear into grown men at sea.

The trouble with Elstree is not that it is stricter or harder than home; the problem is that it bears no resemblance to any life he has known. The door has slammed on the new decade and he is now back not just in the Fifties but something more like the 1850s. 'Have you learned the Collect yet? There's a test on Sunday after "Letters".' 'A test? On a *Sunday*?' 'Yes.' 'What's "Letters"?' 'Writing to your mater and pater . . .' Lavatory paper that's hard and shiny, 'Now Wash Your Hands Please' printed on each sheet; porridge at breakfast and a strip of bacon served by 'simple' maids in overalls, out on parole, they say, from some institution even odder than their own; morning 'buns', in fact a half-slice of bread with margarine and sugar; silent 'Collections' before lunch and tea to learn the Latin grammar for tomorrow's test . . . The reading out loud, by the Head, of the School Rules. 'Rule One: Every boy must have a book to read, a game to play or be otherwise suitably employed . . .' Locker doors banging, a boy shouting, 'Landslide!' as his books and possessions slither from his over-crammed locker onto the floor; 'What's your occupation?' 'I don't know, I just . . .' 'You're on report. Go and report to Mr Hewitt'; a plastic washbasin set in a wooden stand, cold water in it, a tube of Signal toothpaste, the last connection to home; Friday fish with bones and cold skin to be forced through a closed gullet because you have to finish everything; two church services on Sunday and no games, but a walk in crocodile in grey herringbone cap and coat . . . and the 'early boys' back to Number Five; too much rustling of the jacket of a book, 'Go and stand outside the Head's study,' 'I was just turning a page, Miss Buddle,' 'You were making a noise,' and the wait to be beaten and the reprieve when the Head has still not returned by lights out; and a Methodist hymn in bed, 'Glad that I live am I, That the sky is blue, Glad for the country lanes, And the fall of dew. After the sun the rain, After the rain the sun, This is the way of life, Till the work be done.'

But *why* is it all suddenly a toil – an alternation of rain and prayers and Latin till the 'work' be done? No one explains. But it's as if we all need straightening out, correcting.

There is a postcard from his mother by his breakfast plate one morning; it shows a small boy in uniform blowing a tin whistle in a painting by Manet: *Le Fifre*. He is confused. Is it meant to be him? Is he her little soldier, or is this something he might grow up to become? Not waiting till 'Letters' on Sunday, he goes to his locker to find the Basildon Bond. Since locker 13 is too high for him, he's been assigned Edward's locker, 83, at ankle level until he can grow tall enough to reach his own. Then he sits on a bench in the big schoolroom where they have prayers twice a day and begins to write. Pens are banned until the top form, so he writes to his parents in pencil, expressing his dismay at what has befallen him. The writing paper proves unreceptive to the press of the pencil; no marks appear and it seems his plea for help will go unheard. He lowers his head into his hands until some passing boy stops and asks him what the matter is. The stranger points out that he's trying to write on the sheet of blotting paper attached to the top of the pad. He thanks the boy for his help, but finds that the blotting paper proves receptive to the tears that drop on it. Perhaps now he has finally stopped falling.

After three weeks, all the boys are allowed a visit from their parents or to go home for the day — all except the new boys, who have to wait four weeks, a full month, to allow them to 'settle in'. He watches the stalled hands on the clock in the big schoolroom. The Fourth Sunday before Advent, the 75th Sunday after Trinity. Perhaps the time will *never* pass.

Make your bed with 'hospital corners', stand by your bed for inspection . . . Music with Miss Davis, who is eighty-five, and Elstree is famous for its music; tonic sol-fa, crotchet, minim; Kennedy's *Latin Primer*, *mensa*, a table; *mensa*, o, table; a long line of lavatories with no door which you have to queue to visit after breakfast, your name and regularity checked by a prefect with a clipboard and lying to him daily, 'Yes, Turner'; blocks of red carbolic soap, no talking in the corridor, no talking in the classroom, prayers and urgent bells . . . Until finally, one day, some sense of pattern begins to emerge: not every experience is new; some are repeated; and even the most unpleasant are better for being familiar.

Then, one bright Sunday morning in early June, when he has been at the school for half his life again, he walks in Sunday suit and black tie at the tail of the school crocodile with Halliday, Newcome and Bagge, from the back door of the school, down the drive — no talking — through the kitchen gardens and up to the rear gate into the village churchyard. The path leads between the yews and leaning headstones, then turns to show the flint angle of the church wall, in which, lit by the summer sun, his parents are standing.

They are waiting for me still, I sometimes think, my mother in a cotton dress, my father in a gingery tweed jacket and striped tie, smiling nervously. I break ranks from the crocodile and run to them. In a flurry of awkward embraces, I notice that I'm crying, which seems strange, because I'm not sad at all. After church, there's a dash back to the dormitory to change from Sunday into 'ordinary' clothes before finally rejoining our parents outside.

We're home in time for a glass of fizzy lemonade before lunch. I haven't talked to Edward in the four weeks of term; I have only glimpsed him once or twice in a corridor down which each of us was silently making our way. And there are Willy and Bumble to catch up with as well.

There's a great deal to say and I don't want to own up to having cried (or 'gone on blub' as it's called at Elstree); so I tell them instead how Newcome and I, who have both been assigned to East, the losers' house, have scored so many stars in Maths that East has won the fortnightly house competition for the first time since . . . since even Mr Hewitt can remember. The result is a Milky Way chocolate bar to every boy in East at Saturday break time. I have picked up an Elstree convention by which you're allowed to boast of your achievements provided you say 'non-swank' before you start. Edward lets me go on a bit before telling them about the first match of the season in which he has played for the school Under-11 side. The hours in the garden working Mr Kemp's medium-pacers through the gaps have paid off.

Lunch is roast chicken, a dish for special occasions only, with frozen peas, roast potatoes and bread sauce, then orange jelly with tinned mandarin orange segments set in it. There's then a lengthy visit to the bathroom, to compensate for the days of doorless cubicles, and the chance to use soft paper. Next, there's time for some playing, but by about three o'clock it's starting to seem futile. We try some indoor cricket, some cowboys or whatever, but we're only going through the motions now, as the clock hands speed onwards. There's tea, with biscuits, but it's hard to swallow. Let's get the whole thing over with.

On Edward's advice I fix in my mind an image of our mother as she stands waving goodbye in the brick passageway outside the kitchen, the place where only about five years earlier I had first become aware of being alive, gazing at the lizard-tongue leaves that poke from the mortar. 'Take a picture in your mind,' Edward had said, 'then you'll find it easier to remember.' Dad alone is charged with the return journey; it seems too much for Mum. The drive coincides with *Pick of the Pops* with Alan Freeman on the radio, but the timing is tight. If we're late back to school, we'll be sent to bed with no tea; not even a puncture or a cancelled train is considered an excuse. Equally, we need to know which song is number one that week.

Dad likes to leave plenty of time, for this and every other appointment. If we're ahead of schedule when we reach Bucklebury Common, about three quarters of the way, we pull over on a bit of hard standing on the edge of the wild bracken and listen to a couple of the top ten. Some of the most poignant songs of the 1960s will enter my head for the first time at this odd place — the heart-breaking 'It's Over' by Roy Orbison for one: 'Golden days before they end / Whisper secrets to the wind . . .' We time it so the last song is finishing as we turn off the Bath Road and begin the climb to Elstree. *Pick of the Pops* is followed by *Sing Something Simple* with the Mike Sammes Singers, a harmony group who do old-time favourites. Their dirge-like signature tune is the tincture of despair.

It's considered bad form to embrace your father, so we make off quickly through the hall into the big school-room, where the others are gathering for Evensong, the second service of the day. I bite my lip when the groaning harmonium confirms: 'The day Thou gavest, Lord, is ended . . .' Afterwards there's brown soup, bread and Marmite and a knob of cheese.

When I go to my iron bed in Number Five that night, I find I have one of Mum's handkerchiefs in my pocket. I put it under my pillow, scared of what might happen if I'm discovered with a woman's handkerchief unidentified by a Cash's woven nametape, but beguiled by its scent — now, along with the Signal toothpaste, a second physical connection to what's been lost. When I tell Edward this story, he says the same thing happened to him once and he too had found it helpful. In his first term he had also brought with him a small teddy bear (a handy off-spinner, as it happened), but under the eyes of other boys had asked for it to be packed away in his trunk to be sent home at the end of term. Miss Buddle turns off the lights.

Because all his efforts are needed to keep going, to find a way of getting through the next stretch of Latin and rules and Friday fishbones, he never pauses to think what his being away for two thirds of the year might mean to his parents. In any event, Dad, as a man, is invulnerable. He's been a soldier, he and his friends helped defeat the Nazis; he's a 'solicitor'; he's almost six feet tall and can drive a car; he can hit sixes at cricket, heaving a ball clean over the house: he has long ago closed the door on sadness, or on any feeble 'feelings' at all — feelings being the province of childhood. Women seem to have a softer side, it's true, but the fact of being grown up surely means that Mum is almost equally invulnerable. In any case, they have television and nice food and the dogs: they have home.

Although he can tell from the glances that Halliday, Newcome, Bagge and he shoot each other from time to time that they too are struggling, he can't imagine they have an inner life as all-consuming as his own. At that age he looks on other people as the sum of their physical attributes; he responds to them in proportion to how much they threaten his well-being, or survival. Although he can be made to cry by characters in books or films (the death of Bambi's mother) or moved to pity by an obvious physical misfortune like Danny Grant's caliper, he has no empathy for other people. It doesn't occur to him that every human is a flailing mixture of fear and want, more or less mastered. And if someone were to explain to him at the age of eight that this is the case, he would refuse to believe it — partly because it seems so unlikely, but mostly because the knowledge would be unbearable.

He finds grown-ups frightening and other children 'silly' or 'stupid'. He has managed to rebuff all his
mother's attempts to make friends for him after school at
Greenwood and has thus lived entirely within the cocoon
of Horne Mead House and its garden. His shyness is
glossed by his parents — rather unkindly, he thinks — as
his being 'antisocial'. At Elstree, surrounded by others day
and night, he has to figure out a way of living with them.
Work seems to be a possible path. He likes the appreciative nods in the corridor from older boys in East when
Newcome and he secure the chocolate Milky Ways again.
More 'stars' could be the way forward.

So he gets a grip on things. Newks, Halli, Bagge and he are
all bright enough and good enough at games; he has *settled
in well*, a postcard from Mrs Sanderson tells his parents.
To keep on top of the thousand different ways in which
you can go wrong or be found wanting in the course of
a day, he has to concentrate, to plan ahead. So he does.
He spends a fair amount of time in the sickbay, naturally.
He has grown out of asthmatic seizures, but still catches
every available chest virus and has developed a new line
in excruciating ear infections. The sickroom, which for
some reason is known as Egypt, has some jigsaw puz-
zles with missing pieces and a big plug-in wireless. He
finds that if he turns the dial a fraction west of Hilver-
sum there's a pirate station that plays pop music. In the
course of a later stay he tries to decide if 'Be My Baby' by

the Ronettes is the greatest song ever, or if it's 'Then He Kissed Me' by the Crystals.

He's right on his own there, up in the roof behind the Queen Anne parapet, cut off from home or company, or anything at all, living only in his slightly fevered mind. And German measles, chickenpox, measles . . . All that, naturally. Then one spring term there's a mumps epidemic — or 'plague' in Elstree parlance. The school is in quarantine, and you aren't allowed home on leave until you've had it. He tries everything to catch it, but it seems he's finally found a virus to which he is immune. This is pleasing in a way, though it means that he passes an entire term at school, three months, without seeing his parents.

He seems not to mind. In some ways it's easier. He pushes on with Maths and Latin and Scripture and forces his way into the Under-11 football team as a busy if unskilled inside-right. He has come to understand how all the Elstree systems work, and in such a tightly organised society he doesn't feel that shy; he's a cog that's found a wheel. It's true that he gets beaten by Commander Sanderson for raiding the school strawberry beds in a gang robbery one summer day after swimming. The Head tells the eight Strawberry Thieves to go and wait for an hour downstairs because if he beats them there and then they'd never sit down again. It is a long hour. He gets beaten on another occasion for talking in the wrong place or perhaps at the wrong time; but the beatings, administered with a rectangular 'butter pat', don't hurt that much. The terms and the years begin to roll by.

He is being changed, re-moulded into something — though he doesn't quite know what. A hopeful, credulous little boy is being unpicked and discontinued. He's like a creature in a science-fiction story that's been sent back to have its factory settings altered.

At Elstree, he has perfected the art — begun at Miss Barton's, refined at Greenwood — of switching off completely. Half-hours can pass without his having an idea what the teacher has been saying as he gazes out of the window and wonders whether either Mick Norman or Brian Reynolds, who open the batting for 'his' team, Northamptonshire, will ever get selected for England. Northants are not a fashionable county, like Surrey or Yorkshire, but there's a young fast bowler called David Larter, who is six feet seven and a half inches tall (important, that half-inch, he feels), who is 'knocking on the selectors' door'.

Intensive daydreaming can be tiring and it makes him yawn — to the irritation of Mr Raven, the Maths teacher, who marches him out of the room and unloads him, mid-term, on the next class up, run by Mr Cooper. This is a good move, because Mr Cooper's fractions turn out to be a doddle compared to Mr Raven's long division, which no one likes. Mr Cooper, however, also becomes irritated by his staring out of the window and threatens him with a 'report card', which is something you have to have signed after every lesson and can lead to a beating from the Head if not satisfactory. Even more annoying for Mr Cooper are his marks. At the age of ten he comes top of the school (non-swank) in a Common Entrance arithmetic paper, scoring 100 per cent, reduced to 98 for having rounded down, not up, a fourth decimal place.

But he isn't a 'swot', let alone 'clever'; he just has an ability to remember things. He listens to what the teacher says and thinks, 'OK, got that,' so he can revert to thinking about cricket. He has no real feeling for Maths, unlike Newks, who has a flair for something pure and algebraic; in English he isn't naturally as fluent a writer as Fali Vakeel, a new arrival from Bombay, who's obviously read more and better books. But coming top in any subject secures you five shillings in the shape of two half-crowns in a small sealed envelope at the end of term.

Is this more than a silly contest, is it an education? The hours of Maths and Latin grind into them a logical way of thinking. He enjoys the process of geometrical proofs and writing 'QED' emphatically at the end. In the top form they spend two nights a week on Latin verse, which means learning about scansion and metre, rearranging jumbled words into the right order and, finally, composing their own verses in Latin. He becomes obsessed by this exercise; the mechanics of it give him the sort of satisfaction other boys seem to get from car engines or Meccano.

By the age of twelve he can translate almost any English poem into Latin hexameters.

Yet of science, there is not a word: no lessons are offered. He knows a spondee from a dactyl, but not an atom from a protein. Other subjects, French, History, English and Geography, are covered in a half-hearted manner. Maths and Latin are all-important; then Greek is introduced. There's only one way to describe Ancient Greek as far as he can see: difficult. In addition to the passive and active voices, Greek has a third voice, the middle. In addition to indicative and subjunctive moods, it has a third: the optative. It has an extra past tense, too, the aorist. The funny script is the least of their problems.

They begin Greek in the year South Africa tour England, bringing the Pollock brothers, Colin Bland and Eddie Barlow. Bland has made fielding more than a weary picking up and chucking back to the keeper; he's made it vital and athletic. In one Test match, he runs out Ken Barrington in the nineties with a direct hit from cover point. But all this Greek means he's not able to give the touring South Africans the attention they deserve.

One other subject is important at Elstree: Scripture. In Mrs Sanderson's evening Bible class on Tuesday they study the Old Testament and on Friday the New. He has never forgiven Mrs Sanderson for the Kim's Game deceit, but he has to admit she is a captivating teacher. The stories of the Old Testament are more exciting than any of the adventure books he's borrowed from the school library (even *The Man-Eating Leopard of Rudraprayag* by Jim Corbett). The expulsion from the Garden of Eden, as poignant as the loss of childhood; Cain's murder of his annoying younger brother, Abel; Abraham unbelievably commanded to sacrifice his own son, Isaac; Daniel in the lions' den; Shadrach, Meshach and Abednego in the fiery furnace. The warlord Jephthah and his vow to God to sacrifice the first living creature he sees if he is successful in battle . . . only to find that the first thing that meets his eyes, running out to greet him, is his beloved daughter. These stories are so stirring, so full of drama, sex and adventure, that he is surprised they are 'allowed', let alone taught by the headmaster's wife.

The Jewish God is a vengeful old party who won't even let Moses into the promised land after all he has done for the Children of Israel. His son, on the other hand, is quite emollient. Paradox is His thing. Love your enemy. Blessed are the meek. This is puzzling and a bit suspicious. Yet His life is told in stories that are as gripping and as moving as those in the Old Testament. The raising of Lazarus, the madman and the Gadarene swine; and the Garden of Gethsemane, which they come to at the end of the Easter term, culminating in his words on the cross, 'My God, My God, why has Thou forsaken Me?' But it's the kindness of strangers that is the last straw: Simon of Cyrene bearing the cross to Golgotha and Joseph of Arimathea, who gives up his own tomb to bury Him before the Sabbath.

He knows it's coming, but still has a surreptitious flick with a finger at the corner of his eye.

The most exciting event in any week is the cricket or football match against another school; and since there are fewer than twenty boys in any school year, the chances of getting into the side are better than even. A grim camaraderie develops in the minibus as it drives through the back roads of Berkshire; they are on a mission like the men in the 'Dambusters', under-armed against superior firepower, with no expectation of success. He has become an opening batsman (he must have volunteered at some point, thinking that way he was sure at least to get a go) and eyes up the opposition with his fellow opener, Nick Bramall, wondering which of these huge boys will be their fastest bowler. Their coaching has been all about defence, and it has an ethical dimension. The forward defensive is the mark of a good Christian gentleman; a cross-bat shot of any kind, unless to a long-hop well outside leg stump, is frowned on. Bramall and he make Boycott and Edrich look expansive as their left elbows point skyward and the half-volleys drift by unpunished by their exaggerated 'leave'. One false move and your day is over. Cricket offers only the faintest chance of glory; it has no 'let' or second service, no chance of redemption after the rattle of ball on stump or the raised finger of death.

Football matches are less stressful. A wickerwork laundry basket is carried up and dumped in a dormitory.

45

Inside, the crimson shirts are new and the boots have been cleaned, dubbined and re-laced by blinking Jim Campion, a friendly old chap who apparently lives in a burrow beneath the boot room. If a boy has won his 'colours' for playing well he wears red-and-white hooped socks to differentiate him from the foot soldiers.

A glimpse into the life of another school makes them think Elstree is not so bad. The corridors at St Andrews smell more cabbagey; the boys at Horris Hill walk round naked and have 'showers', like Americans (at Elstree they just scrape the mud off their legs in a trough); Ludgrove is frightfully posh; the pupils at Hawtreys call each other by their first names, the weedy wets. They win about half the matches, though never against Horris Hill. He plays at right wing-half (defensive midfield in today's terms) and is sometimes told to man-mark, but against Horris Hill he's wheezing after shadows because they pass the ball so early, calling out to each other all the time. Their centre forward is a boy called Gammill, who scores at least three times. He feels better about his failure to nail Gammill when, fifteen years later, he sees him play wing three-quarter for the Scotland rugby team at Twickenham. He's still quick.

In the summer term of 1965, he is happier than he's ever been. At the age of twelve he's just old enough to be a 'prefect', which means he's expected to keep order and occasionally read the lesson at morning prayers.

Specifically, it means he has charge of a dormitory. He is given Romney — a small room at the end of the second-floor landing, well away from the patrols of the dormitory master. He feels like a young Hornblower in his first command. It's a dream commission: his bed at the window overlooks the park on sunny evenings, the eight other boys are lively company and he sets a rota to keep watch at the door while they sing and wrestle and pillow-fight.

To his intense surprise, he is appointed captain of cricket. The obvious choice is Jonathan Halliday, who is a much better player than the rest but is about three weeks younger so hasn't quite made prefect. Halli lives in Beckenham in south London and has had coaching in the holidays from a young local pro called Derek Underwood. Unusually for a twelve-year-old, he can make the ball turn sharply; he also has a command of length that a club player might envy.

As captain, he puts himself on to bowl the first over, half a dozen pies, and watches as their batsmen confer at the end of it: if this is the best Elstree has to offer, what easy pickings might be next? Their wary optimism turns to delight as they see that the other opening bowler, Halliday, is coming in off only four paces.

An hour later, they aren't smiling any more. These twelve- and thirteen-year-olds have never faced a left-arm spinner who can make the ball turn and lift off a length. As wicketkeeper, Newcome collects endless stumpings, his oversized gloves raised high in appeal. In the course of a thirteen-match season, Halli takes eighty-four wickets.

The source of most of what's exciting in their lives is a young master called David Cooper, known always as Kipper. They long to be selected for the First XI cricket and football teams he oversees, yearn to be awarded three house points after a school match (two is regulation, one is poor; only Halli ever gets four) or to feature in his 'comments' in the minibus on the way home. 'We come now to the right half. A rather slow start, but stuck to his job. Arguably out of position for their first, but an excellent through-ball to the centre forward for the last goal.' A warm glow then spreads through his limbs on the plush of the coach seat, to go with the well-being instilled by the sausage and beans of the match tea. They yearn for a ride in Kipper's bottle-green Morris 1100, partly for his cheery conversation ('No, I don't "stick up for" any particular county side, though I take a friendly interest in Sussex') and partly for the bag of toffees in the glove compartment. The classroom is not really Kipper's milieu (he teaches Geography from a green book by someone called Pickles, which tells you that Port Sunlight is famous for making soap and Redditch for pins and needles); his strengths are in sport and competition, in providing light in a grey world.

When his parents drop him back at Elstree in September of his final year, they stop for the usual word with Commander and Mrs Sanderson in the hall; this is so that Mrs Sanderson can tell boys which dormitory they're going to be in. 'Nelson,' is the answer, which is a disappointment, because he has so loved Romney, and a surprise — because it means that he's been made head boy. This is not because of any leadership qualities (his lack of which on the cricket pitch has been ruefully pointed out to him by Mr Cooper), but because the two boys ahead of him in the pecking order have both been beaten in the course of the previous term, while he has led the riots undetected in distant Romney. Nelson is the largest dormitory, first-floor and gloomy, probably the 'master bedroom' when the place was a private house; it's so big that he has to have a second-in-command at the far end to help keep order. He takes his new duties solemnly and becomes a disciplinarian, not much liked by the troops. It will be the only time in his life he is ever able to exert control over anyone.

In the end-of-term carol service, Miss Wood, the glamorous black-haired music mistress who has replaced old Miss Davis, tells him he'll be singing a solo verse during 'In the Bleak Midwinter'. He's been in the choir for a long time, and Miss Wood has taught him to listen to his own voice while singing, to adjust for a tendency to go flat. This he has managed; and although his speaking voice is low, his twelve-year-old vocal cords can, in song, reach very high notes (the something above middle-something-else, for one). He isn't sure how it's done, but the mixture of conscious effort and blind faith is interesting: different parts of the brain spontaneously connect as you breathe in and aim for that distant note — with only a millisecond to fine-tune the sound you hear emerging.

The carol service of six lessons is of a good standard, better than the school's football or rugby. It begins with 'O, Come All Ye Faithful', sung in Latin with a descant on the penultimate verse that, in a phrase of his father's, 'makes the welkin ring'. Mr Raven, once of the long division, has a fine tenor, in which he also gives a solo. Lessons from the King James Bible are read by the boys, all of them exhaustively rehearsed by Mrs Sanderson since early November. The final solemn lesson is read by Commander Sanderson: 'In the beginning was the word . . .'

No excitement in his life will ever match these evenings. He loves the descants and the language of the readings, but it's more than that. In the coming of Christmas, it's as though the world of Greek verbs, bony fish and grey shirts has been forced to join hands with a place of light and laughter — somewhere that in the long days of term they sometimes found hard to believe could still exist. The birth of the child has overcome even the naval discipline of Commander Sanderson; and after the religious hymns, the later carols — 'Torches, torches, run with torches! All the way to Bethlehem!' — express their yearning for liberation, home and coloured wrapping paper. It's victory, we've won, it's joy, we've beaten Horris Hill ten–nil! He can't quite believe that in the school hall itself — the rows of benches crammed with excited faces and the choir installed in tiers up the huge oak staircase — the day has finally come and that such emotions are allowed.

In the spring term, he's told to sit the scholarship exam for Wellington College. Other schools are possible, and various suggestions are made; but he wants to go where his brother is and he finds it odd that people seem reluctant. Looks are exchanged, as if . . . Something he isn't being told. He doesn't care. He just wants to get through the exam — though it's a bit daunting to think that he's up against boys from all over the country. His teachers warn that neither his Greek nor French is up to much. Too much window-gazing, apparently.

On the given Monday morning in March, Mrs Sanderson takes him down a remote corridor upstairs to a part of the building he's never been to before, perhaps an old footman's bedroom. He's given a glass of milk and a Mathematics paper of fantastic difficulty, full of weird signs and elements of differential calculus, which they haven't yet reached. He hopes his neat handwriting will make up for the fact that he's guessing the answers. Maths 2 is supposed to be harder, but in fact has some approachable logic and number-grinding in it.

So the week wears on. On Wednesday afternoon, he looks out and sees the others going off to play a rugby match while he wrestles with Latin composition. The clatter of their studs on the paving is hard to bear, especially since he's missed the previous match for the usual bronchitic reasons. The English paper offers, among other things, a passage from 'The Lady of Shalott' with some obvious metrical tricks; by pure chance the Greek Unseen turns out to be a story he already knows. It's a mixed week, but he enjoys the milk and biscuits and it ends in time for him to resume the fly-half shirt on Saturday.

Shortly afterwards, he is summoned for interview. His father can't be away from work, so his mother is detailed to drive him there, a journey of about an hour, or — since she is afraid to drive on main roads — a bit more. It's snowing and she is very anxious. They're twenty minutes early and have to wait on some common ground on Finchampstead Ridges, just above the long descent down 'Wellingtonia Avenue'. These extra minutes, with the blow-heater fogging the windows, do nothing for the nerves.

What he doesn't know is the financial background. Dad's office in Newbury, Pitman and Bazett, has a partner firm in Reading, where a rogue employee has embezzled the funds. This man has been found, tried and sent to prison; but the partnership is jointly insolvent. Many panicky negotiations have ensued and Dad's elder sister, Aunt Sheila, has had to lend him money; but without a scholarship the fees will be beyond them.

They drive down to the school and up the long tarmac drive, through rhododendrons. Inside the Porters' Lodge his rivals are assembled, warming their hands at a coke brazier, their school caps thrown on to a chair, presumably unable to contain their giant brains. Eventually it is his turn to be escorted to the Headmaster's study. Mr Stainforth is of his grandfather's vintage, with a heavy waistcoat and chain and gold-rimmed glasses. He calls him 'sir' every other word in a shaky voice. Also there is his deputy, Mr Wort, a rubbery-faced old gent who asks if he likes the theatre. He says he's seen Laurence Olivier as Othello at the Old Vic, with Maggie Smith as Desdemona. He isn't sure how to pronounce the great actor's name, though. Most people said 'Oliviay', but Dad pronounces it 'Olivia'. He tries to cover both bases. They soon run out of things to talk about and it is a mercy when he's told he can go.

After an early lunch in the empty dining hall, they are all free to leave and he waits at the main gate for his mother's car — an under-powered grey Mini-Minor estate with wooden slats on the back. He has no idea how well or otherwise the day has gone, but tells Mum that after the debacle of Maths I he's not hopeful. She looks disappointed. She seems to care a great deal.

They eventually get back to Elstree, by which time it has stopped snowing. They park beside the semicircle of grass round which Edward and he had chased each other almost ten years earlier and go up the steps. Commander Sanderson comes out of the double front door to meet them.

The Commander looks, unusually for him, most disconcerted — as though the first officer has told him they are holed below the waterline. 'I've just had the Headmaster of Wellington on the telephone,' he says. 'You've won the top scholarship.'

This is hard to take in. The Head is now rocking slowly back and forth, still evidently in shock. He rallies. 'Well done. On Latin Unseen you took alpha plus, which means—'

But they never do discover what it means, because at that moment his mother lets out a strange cry and clasps him to her. Gently, he disentangles himself and goes into the school before anyone can see that his mother has 'gone on blub'. In the corridor, Mr Hewitt's squeeze of congratulation almost breaks his ribs.

By tradition, a boy who wins an award to his next school can ask Commander Sanderson for a 'half-holiday', which means that the afternoon's lessons are cancelled and everyone can go outside and play. From being a figure of fear and dislike, he has become suddenly popular. Out in the chilly afternoon, he strides among the grateful, smiling faces, trying to make it look as though the outcome is nothing less than he'd expected all along.

In a recent book *Sad Little Men*, Richard Beard analysed a child's emotional upheaval in the boarding school experience. There were some telling quotations from Erving Goffman's book *Asylums* on the management of the moment of abandonment itself, when the child/patient/prisoner is admitted to the 'total institution' for the first time. Reading it made me think about my own Kim's Game episode all those years ago.

How traumatised were we? How damaged? The truth is that I have never wanted to know. A writer is before all else a person who strives to avoid the known or familiar. The starting point of every sentence is not to imply or say, 'You know what I mean, he was the sort of man who, it was one of those things where . . . ', but to suggest: 'You have no idea what I mean because this is all new to you, and vital. So listen.' The last thing any writer wants, therefore, is actually to *be* a cliché. Fali Vakeel told me nearly five decades later, in Bombay as he still called it, that at the time I'd seemed more emotionally open than most boys, so that's something. Fali, by the way, thought Elstree was unremitting barbarism with no saving features; but then he had come from a wealthy ship-building family, doted on, I suspect, by numerous aunties and *amahs*. No wonder he didn't want to be second man into my dirty water on bath nights.

I suppose what I think now is not so much how barbaric it was, but how bizarre. What a staggeringly strange childhood, so extraordinarily and unnecessarily intense. We were told it was all normal, a 'privilege', just the ticket, off you go. But you could *see* your mother weeping from the corner of your eye. And then there was the clear assumption, from the start, that there was something unregenerate about you: that your much-loved parents had somehow got it all wrong for the first eight years of your life and now you needed to be broken and re-made.

But I bent to the world I found myself in. In fact, I seemed, by its strange lights, to flourish. After a few weeks, there came an approving postcard from the Head: 'It did not take Sebastian long to become an Elstree boy . . .'

Fine. I don't know what happened to the Donnington boy, though. Did he vanish? Die? Or did I meet up with him again in later life? At the age of seventy, I still enjoy the smell of summer hedgerows, hawthorn and cow pars-ley, the sound of poignant pop songs, dramatic news from Trent Bridge or the MCG. These pleasures are perhaps intensified for having been rationed in childhood; but they're touched with sadness, too, for having been first glimpsed through institutional bars. Just to hear a Beatles song on the radio I had to press my ear to a maid's bedroom door and risk being beaten.

I was a curious (in both senses, I suppose) boy from a loving family who might have been expected to enjoy the unrepeatable experience of childhood. Yet between the ages of eight and seventeen I spent most of the time wish-ing that each day (in term at least) would burn and vanish as fast as possible. At the time I more or less accepted this, but now that my aching back limits what I can do it seems sad to have longed for the speediest possible passage of those days of carefree energy.

Occasionally I meet Newcome and Bagge for a Straw-berry Thieves reunion dinner. Baggie seems pretty well and youthful-looking: he doesn't twitch or look wounded. He ran a vigorous campaign in the General Election of 2024 as an anti-Liz Truss independent in Norfolk. After school, he spent some years in a cavalry regiment before becoming a barrister, then a solicitor with a firm in London. It seems as though he's had a happy life. Halliday, alas, doesn't make these dinners. The most able of the four of us, he has suffered terrible mental health problems: schizophrenia, I believe, which afflicted him from a young age.

Newcome became Bishop of Carlisle. He and I chanced to meet in Westminster Abbey during a service to mark the centenary of the November 1918 Armistice. James was there on bishop duty, I as part of the Government Advisory Group on the commemorations. My interest in the 14–18 war had first been sparked when, aged twelve, I had had to read out on Remembrance Sunday the list of Elstree boys who had died in it. I ended speechless, my throat raw with all those names.

After the service, standing by the tomb of the Unknown Warrior, I had a long chat with the bishop, my old partner in pursuit of the Milky Ways. Then I walked alone across Parliament Square in the dark, feeling the churn of time past and wondering – even at the age of sixty-five – if Newks and I had made Commander Sanderson proud.

3.

Liberté!

When I was just fifteen I ran away from school. I didn't have a bike of my own, so I took my best friend David's from the racks and headed off, down the long tarmac drive between the cricket and athletic grounds and out through the big iron gates with their motto '*Heroum Filii*'. Sons of Heroes . . . Of soldiers killed in action, to be exact. No hero me. More of a deserter. Down the village street, over the railway bridge, up to the roundabout and I was gone — pedalling to freedom.

What I was escaping was a cubicle with a chair, an iron bed and a small table that acted as a desk. It was one of forty identical rooms opening off a seemingly endless corridor. The partitions between the cubicles stopped half-way to the ceiling. Opposite ours was an identical wing and on top of us were two more. A third of the way down each was a small table beside which were plastic dustbins with sliced, spongy white bread from which all trace of wheat had been processed out and slabs of margarine with wrappers stamped 'Not for retail sale'. There was also a paper bag full of crystals, though it was hard to know if they were intended as a scouring aid or a food. Someone thought they might be diluted to make a drink, but I never saw anyone try — and anyway there were no glasses. With the forty boys on the corridor above we shared a lavatory.

During the day, there were lessons in rooms that opened from the stone quadrangles. The teachers wore black gowns and lace-up shoes with huge welts, on which they rolled down the colonnades. When you walked past one you were meant to raise your right forefinger parallel to the ground as a sign of respect. Most had grey hair and many were unmarried. Some smoked pipes and had yellow Labradors. One was attached to each corridor and was supposed to concern himself with the well-being of the boys there. In fact, these places were run by the inmates themselves on a 'top dog' basis and some masters-in-charge were reluctant to venture on to 'their' wings.

These men were not figures of authority. They were more like performers in a ritual of which the rules, once known and enforced, had been forgotten. Two of the older ones shared a holiday house in Andover where they used to hold hands on the sofa, still in their grey flannel trousers.

In the pungent science rooms there was a huge chart behind the teacher's desk. I presumed it was the lesson timetable, but could never figure it out. All those funny subjects people did. H was History, I supposed. But Ag. What was that? Fe presumably was French. But Cl, Na? I'd arrived in a summer term at the end of a school year and the other boys had been doing Chemistry for two terms already, or five terms — or even eight terms, some of them. They probably knew what those letters meant, but none of them spoke to me.

For two years I had tried to understand what the school was about or what it wanted from me.

Then I gave up and got on David's bike.

It was a beautiful afternoon in June. I rode through one village after another. From the hedgerows came the scent of hawthorn and cow parsley. This was the smell I remembered from another life.

From the borders of Hampshire and Surrey, I crossed back into Berkshire and kept on pedalling. There were schoolchildren going home to tea, boys of about my age on bikes with swept-up handlebars, listening to transistor radios and calling out to one another. On a recreation ground, some men in white were going out to start an early-evening game of cricket. On the outskirts of the next large village, workers were clocking off at a factory, lighting cigarettes as they walked towards the bus stop. In a Wheatsheaf inn, I saw the first electric light of evening going on inside the public bar. This was ordinary life, something I recognised, though I'd barely been exposed to it.

High on the smell of the hedgerows, I had no idea where I was going. My legs felt no fatigue as twenty miles, then thirty miles went by. I just wanted not to look back, to put more distance between me and the corridor I'd left behind.

Eventually, I came to a main road, and it was one I recognised. At this point I became a little scared. I had no money and had never stayed in a hotel. And anyway, after tonight there was the rest of my life to think about, years and years of it, presumably. I needed a plan.

At the junction, I looked left and I looked right. Lorries were thundering along the tarmac, their sides shaking. I turned left and kept pedalling. When, half an hour later, I came into the outskirts of a town, I gave up struggling and allowed my legs to carry me. Before long I had turned down the main street of the village where my parents lived.

This was a disaster. I had wanted to make a break for freedom and had ended up going home. It was dark by now and David's bike had no lights. I wheeled it up the drive and hid it in the shed, but I was too ashamed to ring the bell.

So I went to the end of the garden, where it bordered a field, and sat in the long grass. My parents would be furious, I knew. I was on a scholarship to a place that might otherwise have been beyond their means. Even so, they lived frugally so that my brother and I could enjoy what they believed to be the advantages of the school.

What these were remained unclear. The place seemed, in an incoherent way, to want to change us all. But I had been broken and re-made once before − turned from a village boy into a little man who kept his left elbow up when cover-driving and could spout Latin verses. That had all been weird enough, but at least I had understood the deal: you were asked to do well, 'come top'; then you could be rewarded by silver cups and chocolate bars and half-crowns in sealed grey envelopes.

This new place, by contrast, had no clear idea of what it wanted you to be. It distrusted achievement, offered no encouragement or praise, though it approved of people who didn't make a fuss. So far as I could understand, it wanted to turn me into a duffer in a tweed jacket who was not much cop at anything but enjoyed rifle drill and listening to the Mike Sammes Singers on Radio 2. The older boys were free to make up rules as they went along. One of them had proposed to beat me with a cane, but I declined his offer and took some other punishment. He looked unstable.

Meanwhile, it was starting to get cold and wet where I was sitting in the long grass at home. So quite late, perhaps getting on for ten o'clock, I slunk down the garden and knocked at the back door. The light came on. To my amazement, my mother seemed not angry but relieved. My father smiled rather less, but didn't actually tell me off. They had been telephoned by the school when I had not been present at a roll call. It was agreed that we would talk about it in the morning, which meant that I would be allowed to spend the night. I slept pretty well after that bike ride.

After breakfast, I went to the village shop and bought some cigarettes, which I smoked in a field until I felt sick. I was allowed to spend another night, but disappointed my parents by not being able to explain myself.

Among the things we'd never talked about was sex. There were no girls at school, but during the holidays a couple had let me kiss them at parties in the village hall. Although I'd once also kissed a boy and quite enjoyed it, I knew that girls were my thing. The act itself, I was obliged to accept, belonged to grown-ups, film actors and the people whose diseased parts we'd been shown in biological 'sex lectures'. It would have to wait, because it couldn't be integrated into the rest of one's existence. This didn't mean I couldn't fantasise on the iron bed in the cubicle at night, when the lights on our wing had been switched off. I often seemed to be a valet or manservant to a demanding older woman who lived in Beverly Hills (or possibly Bel Air; I wasn't fussy).

More pressing than sex was the need to find some way of living with the situation my parents had dropped me in. None of the boys in my class spoke to me, because they regarded me as an intruder who should have been in lessons with people of his own age. I didn't blame them. In a place where standing out from the crowd was the only thing that everyone agreed was wrong, their attitude seemed fair enough. Such confidence as I had had on arriving had evaporated, leaving me self-consciously exposed.

On the third day, I was driven back to school, dreading what the other boys on my wing would say. Spaso, wanker, poof would be some of the terms they'd use. My brother had reassured me on the telephone. 'It's OK. Some of them quite admire you. But basically, they don't care. It'll be fine.'

Edward was right. It was a lesson in what other people think of you. They don't think of you. They have better things to think about.

It was a hot June and my first lesson back was Greek: Thucydides Book VII, a set book for A level, due next summer. Because of the heat, the class (only five of us) met on a lawn outside. The others said nothing to me, as usual. The teacher was quite civil, if a little amused. In my end-of-term report, he wrote, 'I think his path to happiness lies in a renewed application to his studies.' More Homer, then: that was the way forward. And after that Lucretius, Plato, and the *Aeneid*, Book IV.

Oh well. There was always music. Edward and I had been obsessed by pop music since we had discovered Radio Luxembourg, on 208 metres in the medium wave. When we were children, pop had seldom been allowed on to the BBC. By June 1968, however, there was Radio 1 – and pop was turning into rock. Following 'A Whiter Shade of Pale' the year before, Procol Harum had released a fascinating album called *Shine on Brightly*, which I listened to every day. The words, by Keith Reid, seemed to chime with what I felt. 'My eunuch friend has been and gone, He said that I must soldier on . . .' There were thick chords on the Hammond organ, melodic piano lines and a lead guitar buzzing like an angry wasp; there were stuttering drums and a white soul voice.

The English teacher had meanwhile given us a book called *David Copperfield*. It was very long and there was moaning in class when it was handed round. I joined in with the rest, so as not to stand out, though I was in fact a little curious. Television existed, but we weren't allowed to watch it. Music was permitted only during a twenty-minute lavatory break at 8.15 p.m. and erotic fantasies were not a runner until after dark. So a long book was something with which to pass the time.

I had read a lot as a child, but after a brief Agatha Christie jaunt had not recently found anything I liked. The time was right for a bridge. I opened *Copperfield*. Within a few pages, I had forgotten where I was and, for an hour or so, even who I was. This boy was like me, only further up shit creek. Dead father, lovely but defenceless mother, Peggotty the nurse and then . . . Murdstone! I can remember seeing the chapter heading 'Changes at Home' with dread and a kind of anger. Steerforth, Micawber, Heep . . . New people kept on appearing, each more astonishing than the last, their lives a matter of more interest to me than those of anyone I knew. And when I reached the end at last — 'O Agnes, O my soul!' — I was distracted by a strange bellowing sound in my cubicle. It took me a moment to figure out where it was coming from. If you are sobbing but keeping your eyes open to see what happens next, that's the noise you make.

My essay on the book received a lukewarm comment from the teacher (I may have referred to Dickens as 'the old maestro'), but I began to take books from a shelf in the classroom. One of them was a green hardback called *Pride and Prejudice*. It was a challenge to take on a title so off-putting. It seemed full of the kind of people I disliked — clergymen and toffs and hypocrites. But I was only a few pages in before I saw that Jane Austen disliked them even more than I did, and was going to skewer them for my delight. As a writer, Miss Austen seemed to be up there with Keith Reid. I set about sharing my enthusiasm on paper and although it was only a couple of weeks on from *Copperfield*, it turned out that somehow, in the interim, I'd found a way to analyse or explain. And this time the essay came back with several lines of excited red ballpoint, as if the poor man had waited a long time for a pupil to respond in such a way.

After that came *Sons and Lovers* and what seemed to me a different way of looking at characters. Instead of pushing them around to illustrate or entertain, Lawrence seemed happy just to spend time with them. And then there was the question of his tenderness towards Paul and Miriam. He actually *loved* them. People he'd invented. And he seemed able, magically, to share that concern with the reader. It was a long way from Alistair MacLean.

Then I sped through others of Lawrence's books, sitting in my cubicle, where the sun came in, through those silent summer evenings. And there I walked along the river with Will Brangwen in *The Rainbow* and felt there was going to be a life for me after all — in a version of a Nottinghamshire coalfield, with a curly-haired daughter, and a connection to a vital force that had been stifled by the mechanised society and the mines that scarred the landscape of old England.

I had not previously given much thought to what I would do when — or if — I grew up. I quite liked the idea of being a taxi driver with my own car or, failing that, a surgeon. After reading Austen and Lawrence, however, it became clear that I would have to be a novelist. That way I could be artistic and rebellious, yet respectable and perhaps revered one day as well. The drawback was that there seemed to be no way of learning how to do it — no pathway, college or course. And the careers master, who had spent his own life at the school, boy and man, generally advised Sandhurst or local government.

Had I somehow emerged in the wrong skin? Bob Dylan, I read, had been born in Duluth, Minnesota, a city famous for having the first covered shopping mall in America and for inventing 'pie *à la mode*', a fruit tart with a splodge of ice cream on top. Questioned about these unpromising roots, Bob had replied, 'I was set down a long way from where I was meant to be.'

Schoolboy angst seems comic from afar, but for a pubescent boy to fight for air in a mighty institution — physically huge, militaristic, broadly indifferent, occasionally cruel — does take some ingenuity. You can't as a child 'see things in perspective', because you are defined by your resentment. There was also the complication of my continuing loyalty towards, and love for, my parents. But at least by now I had a good friend. I'd first met David Jones-Parry outside school because our parents knew each other from dinners over flagons of Peter Dominic's blended 'Carafino' wine. In the holidays, I was also close to David's older sister, Caroline. Their father was a chicken farmer, a charming man who had once delighted us by explaining the secret of poultry breeding: 'You have to get your cock and pullet from the same place.' He had a beaten-up Mini Cooper which Caroline and I used to thrash up and down the farm track. It had no first gear, but could start in second if you revved it hard enough.

Sometimes at school David and I acted out short plays or skits, improvising into his tiny cassette recorder. We'd imagine we were characters at a teenage party, which included being girls in the ladies discussing the boys they'd been dancing with (plus sound effects of running water). We also formed part of a little troupe that went round old folks' homes and village halls on Wednesday afternoons performing sketches and songs, some of which we wrote ourselves. David had unfailing good manners and sometimes felt I laid it on too thick about 'the system'. 'But one thing you have to understand, Dave,' I countered, 'is that all this will one day be held against you as being privileged. This bread and margarine, this lack of fun and basic hygiene. Even the teaching.' We didn't argue any more because we were both laughing too much at the idea of Plod Foskett's grind through 'Physics to O level' being called a 'privilege'.

In Victorian times, the school had set up a 'mission' in a then slum area of London, Walworth. In the 1960s, volunteers were still asked to go and visit the 'Wally Boys' and play ping-pong with them in their youth club off the Old Kent Road. One day, there was a return visit and half a dozen dressy London teenagers found themselves on our wing. One of them offered me a Benson & Hedges King Size and I explained that we were not allowed to smoke, although I did have ten Number 6 hidden behind my small record collection. We chatted about music and football ('You're not West Ham, are you?') and when it was time to leave, the baffled young Londoner tucked the remains of his Bensons into my jacket pocket. 'Here, mate, you'd better have these.'

In the summer of 1969, David's family asked me on holiday with them to the Costa Brava. This turned out to mean paella, Ducados cigarettes, dancing to '*Je t'aime . . . moi non plus*' and kissing English girls on the beach. Caroline refused to join in the fun on the grounds that before coming to the Costa Brava she'd fallen in love with a

Frenchman on another beach somewhere. She was very sad, so I used to take her for a walk before dinner and sing to her. 'Though I know the night has fallen / And the sun's sailed out to sea . . .' Side two, track one of *Shine on Brightly*. Caroline had dark eyes and freckles and a passionately engaged way of talking. Perhaps I was a little in love with her myself at this point. I liked to think so, because it made the situation so novelistic.

I hadn't managed to grow my hair as long as Jimmy Page's, but had made a fair effort and had acquired a weirdly muscular physique, perhaps from the tennis team or swimming in the sea (it can't have been from reading Lawrence on the window seat). This, and the successful fumbling with the teenage girls, had given me back some confidence. What had really made the difference, though, was literature. Through reading, I felt I had joined a freemasonry of like-minded people, alive and dead, all round the world. It was true, I admitted, that e .e. cummings didn't have the same view of life as Jane Austen; Dickens and Donne might not have seen eye to eye; but all of them were drawing on a ghostly paradigm of things that was more valuable than anything on offer from the institution that was trying to constrain me. Until I read these books, I had found life and 'other people' incomprehensible. Now it all began to make a kind of sense, because I'd been shown that everything important lay beneath, visible only to the initiated. I knew I could draw on this knowledge and on the brotherhood of these people for ever. The old taxi business was going to have to wait.

Back at school in September, I went and told the bad-tempered teacher who was meant to look after us that I'd had enough. I wanted to go to the local technical college and meet girls and grow my hair long and listen to Procol Harum and Pink Floyd. The teacher was not pleased. He sent me off to see the Headmaster, who asked me what the problem was. Why couldn't we have girls and television like normal people, I asked, and edible food and better teaching? I was sent home, again, to discuss the matter with my parents. This time they were not so sympathetic. My father placed a call to the local grammar school, who said they'd find a spot for me. I was a bit sad to say goodbye to David and the others, but I was excited about starting a new life.

However, the counter-arguments — for 'sticking it out' — were then made to me. Edward, who had also disliked school and not given much thought to lessons, being too busy playing lead guitar in a band, now found himself at Oxford. It had been a circuitous trip (there'd been talk of Sociology at Hull) but he had ended up in a charming Welsh college called Jesus and was having a good time. He had 'stuck it out' and prospered — and that was something to consider.

I was meant to go to Cambridge, where my father had been before the War. If I were to win a scholarship, I was told, I would be allowed to keep the money it carried on top of my student grant (tuition was free). This was a second good argument. The trouble was, I pointed out, that it was too late to enter the Cambridge exam this autumn and the next one was four terms away; added to which, I had no chance of winning an award. But apparently the teachers thought I was in with a chance (news to me) — and a year would pass in no time. Well, that was absurd because I knew how slowly time passed on that awful wing. Four terms was a life sentence.

Their best argument was the last one. Mum told me that Dad had been more upset than she had ever seen him; she suggested he might even have shed a tear. This was conclusive. Dad was a hero to Edward and me. So, sulkily, I caved in. The deal was that if I agreed to knock off another A level, I would be liberated from the wing and sent to live with an old English teacher, Mr Letts, in the garret of his house in the woods. I was to have one tutorial a day with either of the two teachers who had been asked to prepare me for the Cambridge exam, plus the occasional French class. No one ever needed four A levels, but we shook on it. There was also something called S level, which involved further hours in the exam hall. I marched out of the French one, leaving a blank page as some sort of protest, though against what I can't remember. Encouragement? Education?

In English, things began to look up at once. I now had two teachers to myself. Michael Curtis had been at the fall of Singapore as a young private soldier in 1942. He was taken prisoner and made to work on the Siam–Burma Railway. He had contrived to carry a complete Shakespeare with him in captivity and to improve his chess by playing against Dutch prisoners of war. Somehow he had survived the Death Railway. In his late forties, he seemed physically twisted and diminished, but he was not bitter. On the contrary, he was filled with enthusiasm, especially for Shakespeare, and had a joyful urge to share his knowledge. Together, Mr Curtis and I also studied Keats, Hopkins and Eliot; I'd sometimes go to his bachelor lodging in the evening for coffee and biscuits to talk over Orwell and Kipling and Peter Brook's ideas about theatre. Then he took a few of us to see Brook's *Midsummer Night's Dream* at Stratford. I don't know how he managed to get the tickets, even up in the roof, but no one there would ever forget what they saw that night. I believe Michael Curtis died quite young, as did most veterans of what he had endured, but he had told me he wouldn't mind being dead because 'I'm going to spend the first hundred years of eternity sitting in a corner with Bill Shakespeare discussing exactly how to stage those difficult late plays.'

Mike Fox was in his mid-twenties, in his first proper teaching job. We studied Chaucer and Jane Austen, Donne and Marvell; I pretended to read Richardson and Fielding while eating Ritz biscuits on the bed and skimming *Melody Maker*. Mike was informed, humorous and friendly – a natural. He was also the first teacher in the school to have an English degree; previously the subject had been taught by others with time on their hands. As well as a passion for literature, he brought a longer perspective; he saw the school for what it was and recognised that some boys needed help beyond the classroom. Many years later, when he was eighty, I visited him and he said kind things about my teenage literary awareness, adding, 'But you were guarded. You were not someone who was going to give your trust easily.' I think the reason I was 'guarded' was that I couldn't believe my luck in having stumbled on the Curtis–Fox Experience. Here at last was 'privilege' — something I acknowledged with a faint unease, because such teaching was not available to everyone, but mostly with a dazed gratitude.

Up in my garret I played *The Turning Point* by John Mayall, softly, so as not to annoy my landlord, Mr Letts. Johnny Almond's melodic saxophone was almost too sad, as was Mayall's homesickness for Laurel Canyon, Saw Mill Gulch Road and other dusty, mythical places that were more real to me than the damp woods in which I was sequestered. I listened repeatedly to Soft Machine's suicidally introspective *Third* because I was interested to see how deep into darkness music could take me, how long I could hold my breath before coming up for air. Good practice — for something, one day, I felt sure.

In the time left over from *Melody Maker*, I read Wordsworth, though it was less like reading than living. I had never been to the Lake District — and there seemed no reason to go now, since I had trodden every blade of grass, climbed every fell and seen Grasmere glitter under evening sun before a 'huge peak, black and huge' pursued me home. The words, like Eliot's, remembered themselves in your mind, as if they had always been there, waiting only for their time to come.

Sometimes I wrote poems in black ink on orange paper and sent them to Susanna, a brown-eyed girl with a Julie Driscoll hairstyle who I'd got quite far with in the village hall at Inkpen. I was influenced by Harold Norse and others of the New York school I'd discovered through the Penguin Modern Poets series. It never occurred to me to ask if I could take a train to Reading one day and actually meet up with Susanna — go to the cinema or something. I was lost in a haze of fag smoke and poetry and longing. And imagine if Susanna had had no views on Donne's later, religious poems or John Bonham's drumming. That would have been awful.

In the summer, David and I joined up with Rob from school, who'd borrowed an old Renault 4 with the gear shift in the dashboard, and drove off to the Isle of Wight to see Jimi Hendrix. Caroline arrived later, in love with a new French boyfriend, this one being the son of the family she'd stayed with outside Paris. She'd left school early, I don't know why, and this new guy, who was called Hugues, though he spelled it 'Hughes', was pretty cool and smoked a lot of Gauloises, from which, as David and

I watched wide-eyed, he tore off the filter before chucking it away. He was at art college, also good news in my world. David and I agreed not to mention French pop music (Mireille Mathieu, Johnny Hallyday) in case it put him at a disadvantage.

Joni Mitchell was annoyed with the crowd because they made too much noise when she was trying to tune her dulcimer. She played some new songs that would be on her next album, which she said was going to be called 'Clue', or possibly 'Blue'. It was hard to catch all the words of these songs from so far away, but David and I felt that with this new record she could definitely be on to something.

We saw the Who, the Doors, Miles Davis and Chicago Transit Authority, from a certain distance, and then got hold of a cube of hashish. We smoked it near our tent, but it didn't seem to work, so I ate half of it. And then it worked so much that I couldn't stand up. So I did get to hear Hendrix, but lying down among the stars.

Next day, we went to clean up in the sea but found that soap didn't work in salt water, though luckily a Swedish girl with sunburned breasts emerged from the waves to wash our hair in Fairy liquid. For David, it was then back to the wing in September, while for me there was one last term in Mr Letts's garret. Eventually, the day arrived for the big exam. It was rather solemn. Cambridge was, rightly or wrongly, believed to be harder to get into than Oxford, with the result that I was the only one sitting an arts subject, though there were three or four trying in science. We sat, braced, beneath the gaze of a sombre man in an academic gown, who looked down from the stage of Old Hall.

My questions came on orange-gold paper. Practical criticism was eight short lines of Wordsworth, a 'Lucy' poem, on which you were asked to write for a couple of hours. Next day, there was, for some reason, a French exam, also quite easy. In the eighteenth-century paper, I banged on about various long novels that my close study of *Melody Maker* hadn't left me time to read. A few weeks later, I was summoned for an interview by Emmanuel, the college of my teachers' choice (someone had once known a don there, though he wasn't there any more), and this was thought to be a good sign. We didn't know that it was to be a freakish year in English for the college and that they would award fourteen places as opposed to the usual three.

One December afternoon, I walked over the rugby pitches to the railway station and took a train to London. At Cambridge, I got on a bus at the station but was too shy to ask where Emmanuel was. I hoped I might recognise the pillared facade, perhaps from an old print or a table mat. About an hour or so later, having made a tour of the city, we were back at the railway station. Somehow, in the end, I got there and was despatched by a man in a bowler hat to a distant room that smelled of old gas fires. I was interviewed the next morning by two men with beards. I knew, because he'd told me so, that the bad-tempered master in charge of my wing at school had written to Emmanuel telling them they'd be better off without me, but neither of them mentioned the letter.

A few weeks later, I left the school at last, feeling happy that I'd managed to avoid being shaped by it. On the contrary, I'd found two fine teachers and, by refusing to cooperate with the authorities, had in the end contrived a proper student life. I thought little more about the place for half a century – until 2017, to be precise, when an email invited me to return and open the new English faculty building, which had been named after me. What? I drove down from London anyway, expecting some sort of Nissen hut in the woods, but found a large and well-equipped learning centre. More to the point, I saw a co-educational school with energised staff and academic ambition, offering lessons in happiness and yoga, with girls and boys playing and working together. It was the kind of place we had been reviled and even punished for imagining; but any sense of grievance I may have had towards the school was for ever buried by the sight of it.

Back in December 1970, I was in an attic in Gloucestershire, listening to Traffic's *John Barleycorn Must Die* and cautiously puffing on a joint, when someone from the party downstairs stuck his head through the hatch and said I was wanted on the phone. It was my father to say that I had won a minor scholarship, an 'exhibition'. Some picky don had rumbled the fact that I hadn't actually read *Clarissa* but I'd done OK on the other papers. Dad seemed pleased when I got back the next day and I hoped I'd made amends for the upset I'd caused him.

In January 1971, everything in England was dark or on strike or shut down, but somehow I got over to Paris, where I was met at the Gare du Nord by Hughes's mother, Madame d'Achon, and driven to their house in Herblay, a small town north of the city. '*Crache-la, ta Valda,*' I said to a red traffic light. A Valda was an orange-coloured cough sweet. The equivalent might be if a French exchange boy had said, 'Show us your Strepsil, then,' on his way from Victoria to Epsom. It was only something I'd learned by rote from a 'List of Idioms' in class, but Madame d'Achon looked a bit taken aback.

She was a very good cook, I soon discovered, though Monsieur d'Achon didn't look that pleased to have a paying guest in his house when he came home in the evening and gazed over his *côte de veau* at the hunting prints on the wall. I guessed he was pining for an aristocratic life that had been lost to his family as a result of all those revolutions. Madame d'Achon and I read Saint-Exupéry together, listened to Beethoven's Ninth on the old family gramophone and went to Versailles, where we saw the Hall of Mirrors and walked through the gravelled parterres. She was very kind, but I was desperate for something a bit more rock'n'roll, and after a couple of weeks got myself a room in a flat off the Avenue de la Grande Armée, not far from the Arc de Triomphe.

The trouble was that, for all my knowledge of its past participles, I couldn't actually speak French. Still less could I understand it. I'd asked for '*vingt Gauloises*' in a bar and the bloke had given me twenty *packets*. I'd soon finished all the books I'd brought with me from home, even *Ulysses*, and was glad to spot a library on the Boulevard St Michel. There seemed to be no limit to the number of books you could borrow and they were all new as well. This was a lot better than England. It was only when I went to check them out that I understood that a *librairie* was not a library. I was of course too ashamed to put them back, so paid for them all and reconciled myself to not eating for a week.

Impressed by my grammar (and perhaps the Valda), Madame d'Achon had booked me into an advanced literature class, taught in French by a priest, at the Institut Catholique, near the Jardin du Luxembourg. Some of the other students were French and some were Americans in their junior year, therefore about twenty years old. I was still only seventeen and couldn't bring myself to speak to any of them. At some point, a boy asked me to a party down in some dingy place in the 13th, near a raised railway track. I found myself late that night escorting an American girl back to her room near Odéon. I may have kissed her. We arranged to meet again, but she was much less stoned the second time and wanted to talk only about her boyfriend back in Wichita or Wyoming or Saw Mill Gulch Road. She gave me *Trout Fishing in America* by Richard Brautigan, but we never got round to discussing it because the conversation always went back to Jim and what a bastard he was and how much she missed him and all the things he'd said and done, or hadn't done.

After the *bibliothèque* incident, I discovered the American Library on the rue du Général—Camou, in the shadow of the Eiffel Tower, and carried home armfuls of books for a student fee of only a few centimes. Hemingway was the first canonical writer I had failed to respond to — my discovery that I had some resistance to pared-down writing. 'In my younger and more vulnerable years . . . ', however, the opening of *Gatsby* — just to think of it and I'm lying on the bed in that room, letting Fitzgerald's words push back the lonely walls of my existence.

My landlady was a small woman of extreme old age called Mademoiselle Alexander. She had a wrinkled face, a stick and possibly a wig, but she liked me on the grounds that I was so studious — '*Pas du tout comme ce monsieur japonais avec ses disques,*' she used to say, referring to my fellow lodger, whose little record player I terrifically envied. I could never break it to her that the only reason I read all night was that I had no friends. Mlle Alexander used to make black tea and bring it to my room at about five o'clock each afternoon with an arrowroot biscuit. To begin with, I was appalled (not just by the lack of milk), but after a time I caught myself coughing loudly in the corridor on re-entering the flat so she'd know I was back, and open to room service. I couldn't afford a launderette, so washed my clothes in her bath and hoped she didn't mind.

Occasionally I would venture out after dinner to the St Michel area, into the narrow rue St André des Arts, and find a cheap glass of red wine, which I would drink at the bar with a Gitanes *filtre*. I was desperate to meet people, but terrified of doing so, knowing I would either be too shy to speak or, if they were French, would understand little of what they said. I think it was about this time, incidentally, I read that shyness, as well as being a handicap, was a function of exaggerated self-regard. I could see the possible truth in this, though I can't say I found it much help to feel sinful as well as lonely.

By day, I loved the Métro and became an expert on the different lines. I mainly used Vincennes–Neuilly with its new, rubber-wheeled rolling stock, whose pneumatic doors let out a ripe farting sound when they closed. Porte de Clignancourt–Porte d'Orléans had rattling old carriages like cattle trucks, with wooden seats and slatted floors. There were notices asking you to give up your seat to *mutilés de guerre*, presumably from the Marne or Verdun (there were still plenty of these old men in Paris), and everywhere people smoked. There was one first-class carriage and one for the handful of weird non-smokers, but no longer a Jews-only *wagon*, as there had been during the Occupation. Any reference to 'recent events' was to the street riots of 1968, not to the *années noires* of 1940–44, which the country was now doing a sterling job of making out had happened to someone else entirely.

What was most enchanting about the Métro was the smell. Tarred rope, garlic, Gitanes, oil, soot . . . I couldn't work out exactly what the components were, though I knew what they added up to: nostalgia. But how could you feel homesick for something you've never known? Taken with the suggestive station names — Sèvres-Babylone, Filles du Calvaire, Mairie des Lilas — the aroma seemed to be an intimation of immortality.

In the evenings, I went upstairs to another apartment where a doctor's widow, Madame de Manet, had paying guests for dinner. They included a young Swede who played me Crosby, Stills and Nash on her cassette machine, two Japanese businessmen and a bullet-headed Marseillais of about sixty. Madame de Manet was an admirer of Tchaikovsky and I persuaded her to see the Ken Russell biopic, *The Music Lovers*, which had just come out. She went, and gamely thanked me for the tip, though I don't think she can really have enjoyed a naked Glenda Jackson writhing on the floor of a railway carriage.

The key to Paris was a student card, which offered reductions on everything worth having, though it took a lot of form-filling and attendance at a seldom open office on the Quai des Grands Augustins. Once I had the little *passe-partout* in my pocket, I spent hours at the Jeu de Paume in the Tuileries Gardens, which housed the Impressionists. I didn't like Renoir's rosy-cheeked women or Degas's ballerinas, but found Monet almost overwhelming. And Pissarro, Sisley . . . and this place Louveciennes that they'd painted – under snow, in sun, at dusk, the Suicide's House – in such a way as to make it seem essential, not just to itself but to all of France and to the world. I had to limit it to two or three visits a week and force myself to the Louvre, the Grand Palais or smaller galleries I discovered in *Pariscope*, the weekly guide that even I could afford to buy from a news-stand.

Much as I loved the Métro, walking was cheaper and a good way to explore. On my way to the American Library one day, I discovered a café on the windy Avenue Rapp that did a *sandwich Camembert* (*sans beurre*) for ten centimes less than the going rate. Other days, I went to a large café at the top of Avenue Wagram where the black-waistcoated waiters were all brisk efficiency, shouting back their orders to the bar – '*Deux express, DEUX!*' – and I was flattered that they accepted me with my *sandwich jambon*, *vin rouge*, *café* and Gauloise to follow, leaving a manly twenty-centime tip spinning in the saucer.

Once or twice I met Hughes for a glass of rum in a place called La Rhumerie on the Boulevard St Germain. He was a lovely man, I was discovering – complex, sensitive, yet robustly humorous – and he later became one of my greatest friends, though at this stage he was frustrated by his inability to express himself in English and by my failure to follow him in French if he went faster than five kph. But there was goodwill between us, a growing *entente*, and endless cigarettes whose filter tips I also now threw contemptuously to the floor, while forcing down another nauseating *rhum*.

Having no record player, I had invented a six-man rock group of my own, which played improvised songs in my head. I had read that John Coltrane had recorded an extended version of 'My Favourite Things', so it was natural to let my tenor sax play a solo that lasted the entire length of a walk down the Champs-Élysées or that the pianist should do a thirty-five-minute extemporisation on the theme to *Love Story*, just out in the cinema, while I trudged back from another fruitless encounter with my American girl at Odéon. It was always going to be hard to know which songs to put on the album, but that didn't stop me designing the cover. The saxophonist eventually turned up as a session man on Anya King's first album in my novel *A Possible Life* forty-one years later.

One day when I was looking for something I could afford to eat, I saw a tumbledown building off a side street near the Place Saint-Michel. A small blackboard outside advertised dinner, with wine, for ten francs (there were fourteen francs to the pound). It would mean not having lunch for a few days, but the bargain was irresistible.

Inside, it was not so much a restaurant, more a front room with half a dozen unmatched tables that might have come from a country *brocante*. The lower half of the window on to the side street was covered with a curtain on a rail; the upper panes were too grimed with cooking fumes to let in the light. A sad-looking man with an apron asked me what I wanted. It was easy: *escargots*, steak (*à point*), Camembert. As for the wine: '*Rouge ou blanc?*' *Rouge*. The waiter went through a door into a dingy passageway that led . . . God knows where. I pictured an old crone at a stove, perhaps his mother, while Père Goriot sat at the table.

I waited. On one wall was a faded poster for a show by Mistinguett at the Casino de Paris in 1910. On another was a reproduced landscape in a thin brown frame of what may have been the Auvergne. The room was drenched in a dream of the past. It was someone else's dream, but I felt it could be mine as well.

I was free, free at last. Free from wholesale margarine, military haircuts and the exaltation of the second rate. But freedom wasn't all that I'd expected it to be. It was true that I had only one class a day at the Institut and that I could get up when I wanted, go where I wished; there were no restrictions on my movement or on my overheating imagination.

But I was lonely. I had swapped the companionship of David and the others at school for the solitude of the big city. I bought a sketchbook and made little drawings to illustrate the books I'd read — a huge whale crunching a small boat (*Moby-Dick*) and Malamud's Fixer, pounding the floor of his cell. In a green exercise book I wrote free verse expressing my hopeless longings.

In the midst of all this, something strange had happened. I could speak French. I had already known the grammar and after a few weeks found that speech was a matter of . . . well, of daring, mostly — of holding your breath and jumping in. As for the accent, it was easy: you imitated a Frenchman. It was an act, but a fairly convincing one that led the natives to believe I could understand what they were saying. In fact, it was still a noise to me, in which the vowel sounds were indistinguishable variations of '*ont*' or '*en*' or '*ans*' and more.

Still determined to make amends for my misbehaviour, I wrote long, newsy letters home. I wanted my parents to think I was happy, that I was putting the money they could hardly spare to good use. So I took to describing fun-sounding things — parties, picnics, excursions to Fontainebleau — and I suppose, when I come to think about it, these were my first attempts at fiction. They were certainly inventions.

There were some exams to take at the Institut Catholique, but I had understood almost nothing of what the priest had said over the months, so wrote dismissively about Verlaine and Rimbaud, comparing their superficialities with the '*complexité boulversante*' of Wordsworth and Keats. I suppose I thought that news of my cavalier attitude would leak out and that some of the American girls would then want to become my lovers. It would have been simpler to ask them out to a café.

My visitor's idea of France, meanwhile, diverged by quite a long way from France's idea of itself. The public lavatories were a hole in the ground with footholds either side. The telephones barely worked and you had to dial a prefix (was it 14 or 16?) to speak to 'the provinces'. Their word for 'ninety' was 'four times twenty plus ten'. The flimsy two-pin electric plugs fell out of the socket. The plumbing was not ventilated. They had no rock music. The country seemed, in a word, primitive. They had been overrun by Germany in the War and as a matter of policy had cooperated with the conqueror, viewing British resistance, twenty miles away, as idiotic. They appeared to live in a world of make-believe. They were odd.

On the other hand: their painting, their wine, their landscape and their cuisine . . . These were mitigations, surely. To say nothing of the Citroën DS, and the *nouvelle vague* films that still showed in the rue de la Harpe and other Left Bank picture houses I found in *Pariscope*. And Paris itself. Although I was unhappy there, it had the Métro and the Jeu de Paume for heaven's sake. The Parisians themselves seemed permanently indignant and lived life by a series of obscure little formulae, but their city was undeniably beautiful. The boulevards and *rues* were variations on a theme, their proportions determined in a famous re-design a hundred years before. Such uniformity in the buildings raised exciting questions, I felt, about the individuality and conformity of those who lived in them. Seeing widows bend over to pick their vegetables from the boxes outside small *épiceries* at close of day and push them in their shopping bags to the apartment building at the end of the street, where a tiny elevator had been squeezed between the chopped-out banisters, and imagining the dinner they'd be making on the fourth floor with a glass of wine from a re-corked bottle . . . It made bits of Balzac swirl round in your head. I didn't like Paris, but that was beside the point. You weren't meant to *like* it; you were meant to be inspired by it.

English people of my parents' generation had been appalled when the Prime Minister Paul Reynaud took flight in 1940 — shocked both by his weakness and by the fact that he announced his escape to the press with his mistress, Madame de Portes, on his arm, *in a fur coat*. I felt I had a mission to explain. You could start with Chardin. Or Corot. Or Courbet. Or Camembert. Or Cézanne. Just the glories to be found under the letter 'C' would convince any reasonably fair-minded person to think again. It was decades before I understood that most French people saw no need for special pleading since they believed that France led the world in every aspect of life. They knew that the Revolution was the greatest event in human history (the greatest since the birth of Christ, anyway, according to Victor Hugo) and that the efforts of other countries in science, art or discovery were at best playful bagatelles to be indulged with a smile. At worst, such foreign claims were frankly mendacious attempts to pretend that anything had actually been made, discovered or achieved outside France.

Back in 1971, long before I understood any of this, I had a letter from Jonny Chadd, one of our beach gang on the Costa Brava, suggesting we go to Turkey in the summer. It sounded like a plan, but I had no money. 'We'll hitch-hike,' he replied. Right. But we'd still need to eat, wouldn't we? Yeah. Bummer. To get some cash, I signed up to work for an English company called Canvas Holidays at £15 a week putting up tents in a pine forest in Vendée on the west coast. At some point we decided to install electric lights, clipping fluorescent tubes to the metal tent frames, and laying cables beneath the pine needles. My electrical know-how stopped at changing a plug, so there was the potential to join twenty-eight frames in one glorious short circuit, frying the campers and setting fire to the forest. But my fellow courier, a Lancastrian called Martin Livesey, and the campsite owner's two sons were more resourceful.

When I'd saved £80, I figured I had enough. These interstitial months were not yet mocked as a 'gap year' and before cheap flights or mobile phones, getting to Asia Minor on foot was thought to be quite enterprising. I had no idea what would actually be involved. Jonny was already in Italy, so I left the campsite and blew several francs on an overnight train to Genoa. It was hot in Italy, and I had emptied my army water bottle by the time a red

Alfa Romeo gave me a lift all the way to Jonny's *pensione* in Sestri Levante. Jonny produced a fat paperback called *Europe on Five Dollars a Day*, which was roughly three dollars a day more than we had to spend. My contribution was a couple of army maps that my father's company had used in the Italian campaign of 1944, when they were being supplied by mules in the hills north of Florence. The maps had nothing to offer in the way of *autostrada* or youth hostel, though I'm sure they'd been handy for siting Bren pits.

Florence, Rome, Naples . . . We were determined to see it all − every gallery, every church − so the trip became more cultural than I'd foreseen. In Naples, we slept on a dock, where a lonely man propositioned me (I declined). We carried a two-man ridge tent as well as a change of clothes and a tiny Camping Gaz cooker; we also kept a bottle of wine in a side pocket of my rucksack. Now I had freedom *and* company. I was happy at last, truly happy, as we gazed at the pillars of the Parthenon and drank draught retsina poured from battered copper jugs.

When I lay down on the ground in the campsite at night I did sometimes worry about the future. Was solitude a condition of freedom? Would the warm and reassuring company of others kill my ability to live the kind of artistically pure life that Donne and Eliot (not to mention Keith Reid) would have approved?

And loneliness. How much of my adult life would be spent alone in bare hotel rooms with a notebook in my hand? Would that be the price I'd have to pay? Or could I have it all — purity and fun — by switching in and out of different lives? Too soon to say, at just eighteen. And anyway, a few minutes later, the afterglow of retsina and Karelia cigarettes would usher me into a procrastinating sleep.

On Corfu, we hired mopeds and went to what was said to be the prettiest beach, at Palaiokastritsa. There was no one there. We swam out and looked down at the sea bed, visible twenty feet below us through the clear water. When we walked back up the beach we were stopped by an angry man in a frayed straw hat. It was obvious that my fair hair was part of the problem; maybe, I told Jonny, he was not a Robert Plant fan. And then it became clear: he thought we were German. When we had assured him that nothing could be further from the truth, he led us to his small taverna, with the Greek hand signal that looks like 'Go away', but in fact means, 'Follow me.' He sat us down and brought cold beer, then lunch, on the house. 'English,' he smiled, 'English.' Twenty-six years, I understood as I dug into a second helping of moussaka, is not long in the memory of war.

On Samos, we found another deserted beach, with a single vine-covered taverna. With three or four other backpackers, we took all our meals beneath the vines and slept on the beach. Then we were in Izmir, Turkey, on an overnight bus. I didn't fall asleep until we were crossing the Bosphorus. On our arrival at the youth hostel, I discovered that my passport had been stolen and there followed a day of shuttling from the police station to the consulate and back. A piece of paper was eventually produced, but needed to be stamped in Izmir, where I had entered, after which I had only forty-eight hours to get out of the country. We found a lift on the message board at the hostel, offering a ride in a VW camper van if we were willing to 'share gas'. The van belonged to two Americans who talked a lot about hashish, and I nodded wisely, though since the Isle of Wight I'd hardly touched it. We were stopped at the border by the Turkish police. To begin with, this was only a passport inspection. I proffered my scruffy piece of paper, stamped as it was by both consulate and police, but they were not impressed.

The driver and his pal were questioned in an aggressive way while the interior of the van was searched. Jonny and I were ordered out. 'Don't worry,' I said. 'It's nothing to do with us. We'll be fine.'

Where my faith in the Turkish justice system had come from, I'm not sure. This was nine months after the events dramatised in *Midnight Express*, in which the American Billy Hayes received thirty years for drug smuggling.

Jonny pushed his foot back and forward in the dust. I smiled a lot at the sweating police, but they didn't smile back. The Americans were taken inside a kiosk for further questions. The sun climbed higher in the sky and I began to wonder how difficult it would be to get a call through to Dad's office in England.

Eventually, the Americans reappeared and climbed into the van. 'Get in,' said one. 'Don't look back.'

We drove off fast, heading for Greece, birthplace of taramasalata and democracy. Apparently the Turkish police had said, 'We know you have drugs in there, but we can't find them without dogs, so just get out of here fast.' I never knew how much hash we'd been carrying. Quite a lot, I think.

Soon we were back in Italy — in Venice — and we breathed more easily. A week later, after another gas-sharing lift, we reached Paris. I rang Madame de Manet, who invited us both to dinner. In London, I said goodbye to Jonny, who had been such a superb companion, and hitch-hiked along the M4. In the cab of a lorry I listened to a Test match commentary, which seemed to come from a different life. I walked the last bit of the journey, up the village street to our house at the crossroads. With my filthy rucksack and sun-bleached hair to my shoulders, I must have looked like a tramp, but there was no one there to see me from the rows of little cottages on this hot August afternoon. I went up the drive, past the shed where I'd dumped David's bike when I ran away from school. The front door of the house was open and I found Mum in the garden, deadheading some late roses.

4.

Whisky, Syrah, Cab and Ale

I began to drink alcohol in earnest when I arrived at university. I hoped it would banish the shyness that was limiting my enjoyment of, and participation in, life. This tactic was successful up to a point, though I rather overdid it. And in the aftermath I came to rely on alcohol not only to bring me up to the functioning level of a normal person, but to make sure I could sleep.

The fear of insomnia has kept the habit in place for more than fifty years now, though there is another reason I've continued drinking: I enjoy the taste and effect. Booze doesn't make me belligerent or melancholic. Drink to me is friendship, love, laughter — life raised to the level of jollity its creator might once have envisaged.

The pub opposite my college in 1971 had a barman who wore women's clothes and sold unpleasant beer called Younger's Tartan, one of the new 'keg' brews into which carbon dioxide had been forced, to make it last longer. Although it was not strong in alcohol-by-volume terms, two pints made me dizzy (as well as gaseous). I determined to improve my tolerance, on the grounds that if being mildly drunk lifted me to the level of other people, being a bit more drunk would be better. Cambridge was renowned for this kind of inductive logic. My determination was reinforced by the chaplain's sherry party, after which I was sick into the metal wastepaper bin in my room. This small container, given away free at supermarkets, was decorated with reproductions of the drawings in the caves of Altamira and was well up to dealing with a pint of recycled amontillado.

My best friends in college were Ian Black and Paul Carling, neither of whom shared my enthusiasm for drink, and in fact diverted me down the path of marijuana. Ian was from Leeds and had a fantasy that he and I represented North/South, dark/fair, gritty/privileged, Jewish/gentile and other slightly false but, to him, hilarious antitheses. On seeing me in a student photograph, Ian's mother remarked, 'He's very *blond*, your friend, isn't he?' Ian was keen on Dylan and Dvořák, which he played on a small mono record player; but his true passion was for Jefferson Airplane and 'White Rabbit', which he sang along to with his head thrown back: 'Feed your he-e-ad, feed your he-e-ad!' I told him that a different Ian Black had been a hero of the bathroom in my childhood as we tumble-turned beneath the taps, but he was not a big sports fan.

Ian and I made each other laugh and, in our fourth term, we were on the Emmanuel College *University Challenge* team together. Ian was having trouble reconciling his left-wing political beliefs with his attachment to the state of Israel, where he had been on a kibbutz. This dilemma and the possibility of a two-state solution became his lifelong interest, through many years as the *Guardian*'s Middle East editor, speaking both Hebrew and Arabic; it found its full expression in his book *Enemies and Neighbours: Arabs and Jews in Palestine and Israel, 1917–2017*. To believe, as eighteen-year-olds, that Ian would eventually publish something so authoritative would have made us both laugh; though beneath the hilarity, Ian was ambitious. So was I, though not ready to confront the fact.

Paul Carling was a gentle soul, who spoke with the murmurous voice of a late-night DJ on an FM station that only he and Donald Fagen knew how to find. He was reading Theology, so his conversation often had the words Bonhoeffer or Durkheim dropped in between the names of Little Feat or Sneaky Pete (on pedal steel guitar). I never discovered if he had any religious belief, but he liked to disappear to remote places in the summer, and I'd receive postcards from crofts and bothies on storm-drenched islands where there seemed to be only him and his maker, a few sheep and a little tin of Afghan Black. Like Ian, Paul was a man of the Left and joined one of the many sit-ins of the university buildings with a home-made placard demanding RAT, or Radical Alternatives to Theology. Paul and I occasionally wrote record reviews together for a student magazine. One of them, I think, was of *Goodbye Yellow Brick Road*, Elton John's new double album. Paul was a connoisseur of the liner note as well as of the chord change, at one point enthusiastically calling through the smoky fug of a student room, 'Gus Dudgeon on rhino whistle!' I loved Ian and Paul.

It had been Elton's *Madman Across the Water* that was the backdrop to our early friendship, and the opening piano chords of 'Tiny Dancer' still find me pulling a Rizla from the packet, looking round my modern room in South Court where we gathered because I had the best stereo system (Garrard manual deck, Sansui 2x30 watt amp and Wharfedale speakers). The record itself belonged to Dave Roberts, another sweet-natured young man, always happy to put his maths to one side, make you a Nescafé and let you hear his new Yes triple album. I was able to persuade the boys that *Home* by Procol Harum was also worth their while and Robin Trower's guitar solo on 'Whaling Stories' could be timed to match the marijuana high as we went off to dinner in hall.

Considering I had been to only one lecture, my first-year exam results were puzzlingly good. For a moment that summer I thought I should try working hard, aim for a First, and take it from there. But I couldn't see how I would manage the fact that there were other people at lectures – a lot of them. Maybe I could get what I needed from critical books: after all, I could just about negotiate the faculty library. But then again I wasn't sure what an English undergraduate was supposed to be doing in his essays. Finding out new things about the authors? No, that would be considered journalistic. At Cambridge, literature was a 'closed system', wholly aesthetic; to suggest that a line of verse or a character in a novel was drawn from the author's experience was thought to miss the point — which was that art should *transcend* the personal, not ploddingly reproduce it. Was I therefore meant to describe my own emotional response to Yeats or Donne? That hardly seemed academic. Close reading and practical criticism were acceptable, but they had their own dedicated exam papers, which I enjoyed. It was what to put in my weekly essay that I couldn't get the hang of; and neither of my supervisors offered suggestions. Perhaps, to be fair, I didn't pose the question clearly enough. Emmanuel was a fierce college with a puritanical history; its student exam results turned out (when such things were finally published, years later, in the derided academic 'tables') to be among the best. I never felt my simple questions about what we were supposed to be doing would receive a sympathetic ear. So at the start of my second year, I gave up the struggle and devoted myself to drinking.

The college bar allowed you a free pint if you could drink your first one in under five seconds, something I found quite easy, especially since keg beer was best drunk without touching the sides. By now, I had a head for it. It came quite suddenly. One day I was not wobbly after two pints; next day I was still all right after five. So with the stomach lined by a couple from the college bar, one free, I ventured out into the night; and, boy, did Cambridge have pubs. Almost every building that was not a church seemed to be a bar. I soon discovered that ale was better without an injection of CO_2 and that Greene King, based in Bury St Edmunds, made the right stuff. In addition to its own IPA, Greene King made Abbot Ale, a powerful glass that tilted the world to a better angle. Today their website confirms: 'A 5% ABV premium ale for the beer connoisseur, brewed longer for a distinctive full flavour. Warming, malty and fruity.'

Abbot also makes you feel like a god, but I suppose they can't say that on the home page. It certainly makes you feel both warm and fruity. The Bath hotel in Bene't Street (another place, oddly enough, where the barman wore women's clothes) was congenial for a short stop, but the back bar of the Eagle next door was my usual destination, made better by the fact that it was too louche for most undergraduates. The regulars were council office workers, primary school teachers and people on a break from life: not unfriendly, quite congenial in fact, but not from the mainstream. The ceiling of the bar was scored with squadron numbers burned into it by air crews stationed nearby in the Second World War. It was into this room that Watson and Crick had burst one day in 1953 to explain that the structure of the DNA molecule, which they had just discovered in the labs opposite, was *only a double helix*! It amused me to think of the response from the regulars as they looked up from their midday pints.

One of the English dons whose lectures I had not

attended was called Barrell; another was Beer. In fact there seemed to be two Beers. My own director of studies in Emmanuel was called Derek Brewer. Who was I to resist such nominal guidance? The Free Press, the Anchor, the Mill, the Fort St George, the Three Horseshoes at Madingley, the Green Man at Grantchester . . . The Fens were alive with the sound of brewing.

In a bar on King's Parade I met James Ruscoe, who ran a course at Wolfson College. James was nearly thirty and a good deal more worldly than I was, but he shared my impatience with the puritanical atmosphere of the city and, to a large extent, my thirst. While Ian and Paul got on with some work in the evenings, James became my regular playmate. He had been a friend of Edward's at Oxford when completing a postgraduate degree and came recommended. Cambridge was a brief stop for him before he forsook England for mysterious jobs in Rome, where he lived in a large apartment overlooking the Tiber.

In my second year, I took part in the King Street Run. This short back street behind Sidney Sussex had eight pubs, a not unusual density for Cambridge. To win your spurs, you had to drink a pint in each one and complete the course in under two hours. If you went to the gents for any reason you had to go back one pub and start again. Each of us had a 'jockey', someone who had successfully done it himself and would look after you in case of mishap. Mine was called Kevin, an Irishman in the year above, and he told me to eat dinner in hall first, putting plenty of salt and pepper on the food but without drinking water, so the first pint would be simple hydration. Seven to go. It was a genial couple of hours, not too demanding, and the last pub on the street was full of singing and laughter. If only every night could have been like this, I thought, as I walked back to Emmanuel and dropped into the bar for a nightcap.

Many years later, I returned to my college to find that my old director of studies, Derek Brewer, had become Master. We had always got on well and I had been lucky enough to have one-to-one supervisions with him on Chaucer in my last year. Talking to Derek, I began to feel uneasy about how I had wasted my time as an undergraduate; specifically, I felt guilty that I had taken a place from a more deserving student. I then got to know and admire Richard Wilson, who was elected Master in 2002, a time when student tuition fees were becoming a difficult issue. By then I was in a position to pay the fees for one or two of a new generation who might otherwise not have been able to go there – an arrangement that helped my guilt hangover.

All the grown-ups I knew drank. My parents always had a couple before dinner, sitting either side of the fire while they did the crossword. Dad drank whisky. He favoured paler brands such as J&B because you could pour yourself 'an absolute zonker' while people looking at your glass would think it was mostly water. Mum had variations of

Dubonnet, Cinzano or Martini — sometimes with what Dad called 'a small introduction' (gin).

They were good advertisements for alcohol. It made them optimistic and jolly. They never drank too much or behaved badly and neither became dependent, even if Dad did seem to get through a lot of Alka-Seltzer in the morning. ('Well, I may be an alcoholic,' he ruminated once in old age, 'but at least I'm not a dipsomaniac.' An important distinction, we agreed.) As well as being self-controlled, they were a bit lucky because both came from families of epic boozers and could easily have succumbed. Mum's mother, not that we ever met her, was an alcoholic and her father was a big drinker, too, but in more of a rugby club sort of way, I think; and in any case the Germans got him before his liver could.

Dad's family tree was complicated. His father was one of seven brothers, many of whom had had a weakness for drink, in some cases a fatal one. One hot evening on holiday, Uncle Neville, Dad's older brother, talked us through the entire history. Many a potted biog of Great-Uncle So-and-So ended with a baleful look and the gesture of a glass being raised. Uncle Neville himself had a large capacity, though it didn't affect his legal career; only in his retirement did he move the bar opening time forward from six to half-past five, the clock watched fiercely with one eye as he finished a hand of bridge – 'The rest are mine, I think.'

Everybody drank, and perhaps the knowledge that

there were dangers made it taste all the sweeter. The 'zonker' was the king of drinks, designed to make the world a better place, and fast; it might be followed by a 'freshener', slightly smaller, and then the derided 'just a pub one' — a reference to the bare moistening of the bottom of the glass you got in the saloon bar (only a fool ordered spirits in a pub). A Sunday morning might begin with a mid-morning 'heart-starter' or, if the night before had been demanding, a 'phlegm-cracker'. Sometimes after a long country walk or a game of golf, two or three pints in a pub (always drunk standing up, never sitting), my father would enjoy a brace of pink gins before lunch and, just as we were about to sit down to eat, would treat himself to a 'palate-cleanser' — a glass of dry sherry. He made it sound a sort of duty — a politeness to the chef while the roast beef rested. There was often a snooze in front of the fire after lunch, but the bar reopened on the dot of six.

I was too young to witness the cocktail craze of the Fifties, though I enjoyed writing about it in *On Green Dolphin Street* and in the Wolfenden section of *The Fatal Englishman*. Dad told me that Berkshire people never mastered the American art of mixing; he recalled (not without a hint of admiration) one bluff host who opened a bottle of gin, poured a good measure down his throat, replaced what he had drunk with grapefruit squash, re-capped it, gave it a good shake and poured it over ice for his guests. By the Sixties, things had settled down to whisky and soda for men, gin and tonic or variations of vermouth as above for women; with port, brandy and liqueurs to follow food. Wine was not much in evidence.

Wine for me is about place. Where it comes from. Or, sometimes, where I drank it. There are few things more irritating than chefs going on about *terroir*, or wine being an 'expression of the soil' — but place does make a difference.

After I'd been made redundant by my last employer, the *Independent on Sunday*, in 1991, my wife, Veronica, and I decided that we wouldn't return from holiday, but just carry on . . . well, living abroad and not having a job. Veronica and I had met five years earlier at the launch of the *Independent*, for which we both worked. Through an old friend, David Dallas, a London picture dealer, we'd been offered a small place down a rutted track in a very remote part of Tuscany, near Seggiano — in so far as it was near anywhere at all. We set off in the car from the shadow of Mont Ventoux and headed for the Ligurian coast. In the back seat was William, our first child, who was eleven months old. While his parents believed him to be the most perfect infant ever to have walked the planet, obviously, they also knew that ten-hour car journeys were not his strong point. A grizzle that began somewhere near Marseille had, by the time we reached Siena, become a constant, nerve-shredding whine.

We had no directions to speak of and it had grown dark. The owner of the little farmhouse, whom we'd never met, was a man of few words, and we were not inclined to press him, since he was letting us have the place for free, as house-sitters. After much map-reading and many false turns, we found a steep downhill track. The car was a Saab 900 which had come with my old job and which I'd been allowed to carry on using for a few months. It was a great car, with heated seats and a 16-valve turbo kick; but it was very low-slung. Halfway down the track, with the sub-frame already scraped, it got stuck, suspended between a rut and a hard place. I left Veronica with the wailing child and went on by foot. A building loomed. We had had no instructions about how to get in, but with a cigarette lighter I found a key beneath a stone and managed to open a door. The electric light, as so seldom in such places, worked at once. By its dim glow, I could see back up the hillside to where the Saab was stranded. It was about sixty yards; and within half an hour we had rescued anything we needed for the night.

We looked in the fridge for the chance of dinner, but there was only anti-viper serum. Dinner was milk for William and for us the remains of the picnic lunch, rescued from the boot after another climb up the track.

'I've got to have a drink,' I said, and went off to explore the house and stone-built shed. Nothing.

Then, in a remote corner of the kitchen, I saw a bottle and held it up in triumph.

'You'd better not,' said Veronica. 'It might be something special.'

'I don't care how bloody special it is,' I said, drawing the cork and sloshing it into a large glass.

I was halfway down before I stopped and said, 'I tell you what. This actually is . . . Wow . . . Not just "special", it's . . .'

'We'll have to replace it.'

'That's fine. Try it.'

(I may not actually have said 'Try it'; but I like to think I didn't hog it all.)

Anyway, this was my first taste of Brunello di Montalcino (Biondi Santi, 1985, in fact). We did replace it. We found the exact bottle in a wine merchant's in the town of Montalcino itself. I forget how many tens of thousands of lire it cost, but the string of zeroes on the price tag was not a surprise. I was just glad that even in such frazzled circumstances, I'd been able to register its quality. It was like drinking an essence of Tuscany — hillsides, poplars and Renaissance painting — in one long draught.

Living at the end of an impassable track had its challenges. In a hillside trattoria, I found a man with a rope who towed the Saab off the rut where it was stuck. I learned how to rev up the engine to max before attempting the climb, with white stones shooting out from under the back wheels when I finally let in the clutch. Veronica closed her eyes; William was strapped firmly into the back. Any spare moments I had were spent trying to fill in the worst ruts with bits of spoil and loose chippings from the surrounding scrub. We bought quantities of bread and milk and froze them in case we were marooned again.

The nearest town, Castel del Piano, had a narrow main street lit by low-wattage lamps that gave it the air of a justly overlooked neo-realist film set. From the local butcher, Veronica, who spoke fluent Italian, learned of an inn halfway up Monte Amiata. A plain refuge, it served tagliatelle with shaved truffles that were almost other-worldly in their headiness when washed down with wine from the local vineyards, with their explosive cherry-and-Giotto rush.

A short time later, Anthony Lane, a friend from the *Independent*, came to stay with us and joined me in exploring some of the Brunello properties. Our aim was to find something as good as Biondi Santi but at half the price. The closest we came was an estate that belonged to a family called Neri. The daughter of the house, whose name was Anna, showed us round the vineyard and allowed us to taste some of her family's vintages. I bought a few bottles to take back down the track and urged Anthony to do likewise; but he was too bewitched by Anna to concentrate on the wine and could only talk about how he might tempt her back to his bachelor flat in Islington.

For all the joy of Brunello, the sangiovese grape tends to give me a headache, especially as made in Chianti. And it's not always connected to the quantity consumed. There are some wines you are never really going to get on with, though in my experience this can change. I thought Orvieto was a very second-rate drink until I had a cold bottle in an Indian hotel after two wine-free weeks. Even its admirers admit that sauvignon blanc has a bouquet of cat's piss and for many years I avoided it, but I have to admit I am slowly coming round to it, at least in its Loire valley incarnations. Perseverance.

I can't claim to have a great palate. I've met a few Masters of Wine, and their brains are wired differently. They have a superfast broadband link between sense and memory, bypassing reason. Sight and smell are almost as much involved as taste, I understand; but what neural connections allow them to come up with the maker, the vineyard and the year? That's a shortcut that no amount of courses can teach. One MW I know described her knack as 'like having perfect pitch'. My wine abilities could, by the same analogy, be described as being 'just about able to hold a tune'.

This means that to me some wine, red Bordeaux in particular, reaches a level beyond which it really can't be improved. In a blind tasting between a good third growth, costing about £40, and a first growth costing ten times that, I doubt whether I could taste a difference. The other disappointment of my wine life is that even in London it's sometimes hard to buy what you want. I once drank a glass of cold Franconian riesling in Rothenburg ob der Tauber, where I'd gone to see the Tilman Riemenschneider wood carvings as part of the research for *Human*

Traces. The taste was magnificent, but the Franconians don't export it. They drink it all themselves, I was told (I think that's what he said; my German isn't up to much), and who can blame them?

I had the same problem when Veronica and I visited the Ram's Gate winery in South Sonoma. Their chardonnay was as elegant and balanced as anything I'd had from Burgundy, but it's all pre-sold on subscription to their wine club members. We were lucky to be able to buy a couple of bottles and stick them in the back of the Jeep to drink while watching *Sideways* for the fifth time back at the hotel.

The greatest discovery of my wine life was the Rhône valley. It was in 1981, the summer of Botham's ashes, when I drove my Citroën DS through France with two friends, David Tucker and Tom Shields, in whose flat I was then renting a room. We had no particular plan, except to stay off the main roads and trust to luck. Our destination, for some reason, was Uzès, a walled town on the Gard side of the Rhône. I did most of the driving while Tucker (he always seemed to be known by his last name) navigated from the little yellow Michelin maps and Tom slept in the back. Since he was so well rested, we put him in charge of making hotel reservations. Calling ahead from a landline to book our next stop, he asked for a room with three beds, adding: '*Nous sommes trois garçons.*' We never discovered whether they needed more waiters.

If Tom's French was rudimentary, Tucker's was non-existent. At dinner in Burgundy one night, a waitress talked us through the cheese trolley. '*Celui-ci*,' she said, '*c'est du chèvre. Celui-ci, c'est un Coulommiers. Celui-ci, c'est un brebis* . . .' It went on for quite a long time. She stood with her knife poised and looked expectantly at Tucker. 'Well,' he said, with his imperturbable confidence, 'I must say the Celui-Ci looks rather good.'

We picnicked on the edge of a vineyard in Puligny-Montrachet and it was there, of all places, that we found we had no wine to drink. We looked longingly at the fat grapes on the vine. All three of us had fallen for the local white, beginning with the stony variants of Chablis, and going through the lusher versions of chardonnay, finding that spot where soft fruit meets hard backbone. The only red Burgundy we could afford was elegant, you might say, but thin and disapproving – almost governessy. This has ever since been my experience. While you can find a good Bordeaux for under £20 and a lovely Rhône for less, a comparably enjoyable Burgundy will cost five times as much. Its admirers say that of the best ten wines you ever drink at least five will be Bordeaux, yes, but the top two will both be Burgundy. That could be true, for all I know; but if I have a hankering for the taste of pinot noir, I look to Otago or Oregon. Heresy, I suppose; but I like the more jammy style of the grape in those far-off climates. At dinner one night at the hotel Casa del Mar in Santa Monica, California, I was confronted with a wine list as thick as an airport novel. I knew none of the growers or properties, so stuck in a pin, blindfold. It fell on Duckhorn 'Migration', Russian River Valley pinot noir, 2002. It was immense. Plummy, almost sweet; but complex, too. I still occasionally track it down to various importers in England, but it's hard to find.

Meanwhile, down in Provence, Les Trois Garçons explored the Rhône. I loved everything about it — the embossed glass of the Châteauneuf-du-Pape bottle, the richness, the pepper, the sense of abundant generosity and the feeling that one was absorbing some older, Roman, part of France itself. We didn't then know about the northern Rhône wines and we probably couldn't have afforded to drink them anyway, but I have a memory of gliding an extra hour from Lyon in the Citroën while Tucker navigated us to a village restaurant run by a Monsieur Jury, where the wine list featured many bottles from Condrieu and Saint Joseph. We took advice from the wine waiter and pooled our folded francs to buy a bottle of St Joseph Blanc, Domaine Pierre Gaillard. Made from the roussanne grape, it had a mixture of freshness, apricots and minerality that I can't really put into words without some sort of synaesthetic breakdown. Really nice, though.

Life in the Rhône valley looked up even further, when, in 1985, I started going to stay with Tim Saloman, whose parents had a farmhouse at the foot of Mont Ventoux. Tim was a barrister whom Edward knew from that world; I'd met him while playing cricket in India, when we became friends in the course of a long car journey. The Ferme à l'Étoile had a small vineyard, which was farmed by the local cooperative, an arrangement that gave Tim's family access to Côtes du Ventoux, a syrah-grenache blend delivered through a petrol pump into your plastic gallon container. Christened Château Saloman by its admirers, it was known to one visitor as the 'Red Infuriator'. It didn't infuriate me, but it made everyone sleep dreamlessly. Getting up at seven-thirty the next day to play tennis was like rising from the dead.

All the surrounding villages — Mazan, Flassan, Villes-sur-Auzon — had simple one-room restaurants where someone knew how to cook, even if my favourite, at Méthamis, had really only one dish, a powerful *soupe au pistou*. But with a *pichet* of red and a fifty-kilometre hillside view towards Forcalquier, it was enough. One of the local farmers put us on to Cairanne as a village whose wine was well worth the extra two francs. He also drove us to the top of Mont Ventoux before dawn with the local football team in a van pulling a trailer full of bicycles. We then cycled down the mountain, but off-piste, through the scrub. It was harder work than it sounds and took all morning, before lunch on trestles in the market square at Bédoin. Nowadays, I play tennis with two fanatical cyclists and occasionally drop in the fact that, 'Oh yes, I've done Mont Ventoux myself — the place where Tommy Simpson died during the Tour de France, isn't it?' Not sure I've ever mentioned that I 'did' it downhill.

Next to Mont Ventoux are the jagged Dentelles de
Montmirail and a good rule of thumb is that you will enjoy
any red wine made within sight of these mountains. I loved
the intense heat of those August days, driving through the
dusty villages in search of . . . I'm not sure what. Wine,
peace of mind, romance, inspiration, morning bread . . .
Caromb, hot and sleepy, whose name was like the toll of
a heavy bell . . . Beaumes de Venise, whose sweet muscat,
chilled to the point of freezing, was the accompaniment
of late-night boules on the gravel beneath the plane tree.

David became a regular visitor and joined me in making
barbecues on the tiny battered tin stand with a bit of broken
wire mesh as a grill. This kit made the challenge greater, as
did our purist refusal to use charcoal or fire-lighters. We'd
scavenge the borders of the vineyard for bits of kindling
and bigger logs to burn down into a white ash on which to
grill whatever had come back from the market at Carpentras. It was pretty rough, but tasted all right when washed
down with Château Saloman from a blue china jug.

The only testing occasion was the annual Beauvais
Lunch, when we would have to go to the nearest neighbours, with whom, Tim told us, it was essential to foster
good relations. Tim couldn't cook anything himself, but
encouraged the rest of us to make starters and puddings to
carry over as peace offerings to this formidable old couple.
I was despatched to Carpentras to scour the shelves of
the giant supermarket for a suitable wine. The Beauvais
were of an age to remember the German Occupation and

would therefore have had to make their choice of allegiance between Vichy and de Gaulle. After half an hour in Leclerc's chilly aisles, I plumped for a couple of bottles of Alsatian pinot blanc as a collaborative compromise. Monsieur B was a stiff old gent and Tim believed (though he wasn't positive) that his first name was Adolf. In the circumstances, it seemed safer to stick with 'Monsieur'.

Tim had an unshakeable reverence for the neighbours and anyone who fell into the holiest category, 'friends of my parents'. This deference extended to 'Monsieur Poulbot's dog', a dignified Pointer cross, who visited the Ferme à l'Étoile every evening at the hour of the aperitif — Pernod on ice — when he would approach the now-vacant swimming pool, go gingerly down the steps and swim two widths, before climbing out, shaking himself, and padding off back to his own house beyond the pines. There was an almost Proustian routine to this ritual, though so far as I know Monsieur Poulbot's dog never took the Guermantes way, sticking always to Du Côté de Chez Saloman.

One day when we're old, Veronica and I will buy a house in the hills, somewhere between Gigondas and Vacqueyras, in the shadow of the Dentelles, and I'll lie beneath an old walnut tree and drink myself into a final stupor, dreaming of all the friends and lunches and the books and hopes and history of this rugged yet sensuous region, feeling its essence run in my veins . . .

Or maybe we won't. I sometimes look at the places for sale in the Vaucluse and the Luberon, but the best are too expensive, or close to chichi villages, stunned by tourist traffic. I enquired about a more modest one the other day, near Uzès, but they told me the first thing it needed was a new septic tank and my interest faltered.

For some years we went to an old vineyard-owner's house near La Tour d'Aigues. It was an enchanting place, with a long view to the Luberon mountains and, below the gravelled terrace, a paddock in which a pair of retired horses grazed and snorted. 'Do memories plague their ears, like flies?' we wondered, as Philip Larkin had before us. For wine, we had only to stroll to the vineyard's off-sales counter across the yard, past the dozing dogs, who invariably came down to join us for dinner later on. The house itself had been intelligently restored, with the rooms largely untouched, and I borrowed something of it for the religious retreat entered by the main female character in a novel called *Snow Country*. Unfortunately, the whole place was sold; and we arrived one August to find the new owner had put plastic chairs on the terrace and flat-screen televisions on the walls.

Among our regular companions in the better days were Anthony Quinn and his wife Rachel Cooke. I had known Tony since the early days of the *Independent*, when he wrote to us from the bookshop where he was a junior assistant, to see if we had any reviewing work. So began his career in journalism, in the course of which he was for many years the paper's film reviewer. At some point he had managed to get himself a wine column on a magazine and was keen to do some fieldwork. So we drove off into the foothills of the Dentelles to see what we could find. We dropped in at Rasteau, my dark and muscular favourite, not for the faint-hearted, then went on to Gigondas, where the hotel-restaurant has a terrace so well protected by trees that you can eat outside even when it's raining. Vacqueyras has more places where you can sample and buy wine, however; and it was here we made our choice — a case of full-bodied but not overbearing red: friendly on the tongue but with spice and black pepper and the sense of Roman legions marching in the follow-through.

Our pleasure at completing this transaction reminded Tony of his childhood friend James Walton, with whom I'd had a long cooperation on the Radio 4 quiz programme *The Write Stuff*. When Jim was a child, his father took the family on holiday to France one year, to the town of Sainte Maxime. Ted Walton could speak no French beyond that of the half-remembered classroom, but needed to get some francs out of the local bank. With a combination of gestures and school vocab, he succeeded in securing exactly what he needed. He was so delighted that when he got to the door of the bank, now filled with a midday crowd, he turned to issue an expansive goodbye to the teller, calling out, '*Aujourd'hui!*' He knew there was an '*au*' in it somewhere.

The hardness of my head means that I don't misbehave or show the effects of alcohol in an embarrassing way. (I think . . .) I can remember only two times in my adult life when I've been incapacitated, and there were good excuses for both, I honestly believe. The first was in Antwerp, where I had gone for the wedding of a friend called Richard Lavers, who worked for the Foreign Office. There was a jolly pre-wedding dinner, heavy on wine, after which David Tucker and I thought we'd go and sample a few pints of Belgian beer. Neither of us realised that our ale of choice, something called Kwak, served in a sort of crucible held in a wooden retort, was almost as strong as wine. Several pints later, I tried to get back into my hotel room, but found that the key wouldn't fit the door. It was only after much wrestling and swearing that I discovered I was in the wrong hotel.

When I awoke the next morning I was incapable of moving and lay there thinking what a shame it was that having come this far I would now miss Richard and Brigitte's wedding. An hour later, I was somehow standing. I got dressed and made it over to Tucker's hotel. When he let me into his room, I gasped. He looked as if someone had tried to murder him. His detachable stiff collar and white shirt were spattered with blood where he had unwisely tried to shave with a new blade. 'How you feeling, Tucker?' 'A bit better than . . .' But I never found out what he felt better than, as he hurried back to the bathroom, from where terrible noises emerged.

The other occasion was Tim Saloman's stag party in autumn 1990. I was working at the *Independent on Sunday*, and Saturday was our press day. I had effectively sub-edited the entire paper, starting at nine in the morning, and was tense and exhausted when I eventually joined the others in a pub at seven that evening. They, by contrast, had been playing golf all day and were full of beery camaraderie. I made the mistake of trying to catch up, lowering three pints quickly. Nothing. I could still think only of Neal Ascherson's column, which it had been my final task to see safely away. We then went for dinner at the Polish Hearth Club in South Kensington, where there were many vodka shots on order. Lemon, pepper, raspberry . . . Nothing. In the course of dinner, red wine following white and more vodka on the side, something happened. I blame the two glasses of water, which washed the alcohol through in a tsunami. I had gone from nought to a hundred in five seconds.

I made my excuses and went outside, where I sat down on the pavement. Then I lay down and held on to a Royal Borough black-and-gold litter bin because I knew that if I let go I would float off into space. The answer was to cling on tight. I've no idea how I got home, but a fellow guest, Charles Nevin, told me that he later walked back to Brixton. When he got to Clapham Common he decided the only way he could be sure of the route was by following the traffic one-way system.

I mention these slightly sordid incidents in case anyone should think I'm encouraging others to drink. I am, of course: wine is one of the great joys of my life, and I would like to share my enthusiasm. But I know it's not for everyone and I'm sorry that some friends and former colleagues came to grief. Check your family history is my advice.

These days I seldom drink beer. I stopped going regularly to pubs when they banned smoking. Then I gave up smoking. But a pint of London Pride, fine drink though it is, was only half as good without the lift of nicotine to harmonise with it. Every evening of my life for thirty years was made of this up/down balance and I can't pretend that things have been the same with only alcohol; but I've done my best. My efforts have included dry Martinis made preferably with Berry Brothers No.3 gin, otherwise with Beefeater and the eponymous vermouth (the snobbery about how little Martini you put in — letting the sun shine through a closed bottle and so on — is absurd: you don't need much, but the drink has its name for a reason); negronis with a strict one-third split but never with the abomination of the alcopop Aperol, only with Campari (a splash of San Pellegrino is permitted on a hot day); dry cider, but only if completely still; whisky, Scotch or malt but not so peaty that it tastes like the bottom of your boots after a walk across the glens; vodka only as a Bloody Mary base; and never white rum, unless with Coke, a mixture which, as the philosopher A. J. Ayer discovered, made a good drink out of two unpleasant ones. Logical positivism at its best there.

A long-term project is to spend more time with sherry. The mention of the word in company promotes a blizzard of received ideas about vicars and great-aunts, even from normally cliché-free thinkers, so I think this will have to be a solo venture. Sherry is a secret delight: Protean, complex, subtle, with a heavenly aroma. You don't want to drink much of it at any one sitting; I sometimes think a single nip from a bottle of Palo Cortado in the fridge door is the best way, especially at those times when you're 'not drinking'.

Mostly nowadays it's about wine. I still have some reservations about drinking wine without food, but have gone with the popular flow here. And though I've been lucky enough to drink the odd glass of exquisite Montrachet or Latour, I remember more clearly the house white wine in a workers' restaurant in the busy port of Sines in northern Portugal in October 2023. It cost three euros fifty and it made us happy after a long morning at a difficult time. The best bottle I have ever drunk at home was Chateau Duluc Ducru 1990 from E. Leclerc supermarket, Villeneuve-sur-Lot, in November 1995. Even a less famous label can sometimes be extraordinary. Friends sagely — and just a little bit condescendingly — told me it was because I was in a good mood. But no. My palate is not that bad. And anyway, I *wasn't* in a particularly good mood. It was simply a rogue bottle, a miracle for about £9.

To end where we began, at Cambridge in 1972 . . . When Ian and I were asked to be on the *University Challenge* team, the Granada TV producer advised us to have a

nerve-settler before going on. This seemed like an excellent plan. We drove to Manchester in a car that belonged
to one of our team, John Cole, who was a postgraduate
and could afford a Datsun Cherry. His speciality was the
ancient world; Ian was politics and history; a boy called
Laurie Kirby was the scientist. And I . . . 'What's your
speciality, Seb?' 'Er . . . Not sure. But I've played golf a
couple of times for the college.' Golf? 'Yes. Last week I
eagled the eighth at the Gog Magogs against Fitzwilliam.'
Golf? The car grew glum.

Before the show, there was time to go to a pub. None
of the others was as nervous as I was, but they came for a
half. As a part-time barman in college, I had established
that the biggest bang for your buck came from a drink
called barley wine. It was sold in small bottles and was
drunk mostly by tramps in the market square. It tasted of
Marmite and teabags, but I managed to hold one down,
with the help of a Number 6 cigarette. Then another.

There were still twenty minutes before we were due
back in the studio. My teammates were nursing their
second halves, but I was beginning to feel confident.
Partly to take away the taste of the barley wine, I ordered
a cleansing pint of ale — Timothy Taylor's 'Landlord', I
think. Right. I smacked the empty glass down on the bar.

Our opponents were already in the studio looking
brainy and sober. They were from Glasgow University. Perhaps they had got wind of the fact that many
of Bamber Gascoigne's questions would relate to the

geography of the Western Isles. I didn't care. I was powered up. I was a Ferrari on the grid. Chemistry, astronomy, Shostakovich . . . Bring it on, Bamber.

The signature tune bong-boomed out noisily and my feet were tapping. I felt majestic. I lit another cigarette. I felt like a modern Renaissance man. I felt good.

'Fingers on buzzers. Your first starter for ten,' said Bamber. 'What was the military rank of the gentleman who gave his name to the standard score in golf before the arrival of the dreaded par?'

Golf!

Ian looked at me. John looked at me. Laurie looked at me. I jabbed.

'Emmanuel, Faulks.'

'Colonel.'

'Correct.'

I have seldom looked back. Why would I?

5.

Sand in the Gears

When I was about twelve, my godmother came to lunch with her son, Matthew, who was in his early twenties. She had telephoned my mother to say that Matthew was looking rather peculiar. But, my mother told us, we were not to be put off by his appearance; it was not his fault. He had been diagnosed with a condition that had a long and difficult name. It was a 'mental' illness, apparently.

Edward and I had never met anyone mad before. There was a boy in the village who was said to be 'simple' and we had a second cousin who was referred to as being 'a bit "off"'. Occasionally on a bus or train we must have glimpsed people with some obvious affliction, but it was none of our business and seemed best forgotten.

The first odd thing about Matthew was his hair. Although he wore a jacket and tie and spoke in an educated way, his hair was like Struwwelpeter's. He talked coherently, referring to potters and classical musicians; I think he had been a clever child, doted on by his parents. He was physically present, very much so with his hair and his deep voice, and he had some awareness of other people; but much of his focus seemed to be elsewhere.

Our rectangular lunch table with its water glasses and cold ham and baked potatoes didn't seem to engage him – with the exception of the manufacturer's name on the underside of his plate, which he held a few inches from his face to examine.

Mum was uneasy. Her sympathy for anyone in distress was tested by Matthew's appearance and behaviour. She may also have felt threatened. There was something superior in his manner, an implication that our reality was not worth his time. When Mum discussed the visit with my father that evening, she showed a degree of distrust, almost a suspicion that Matthew had been exaggerating. Apparently his diagnosis included the words 'paranoid' and 'delusions of grandeur'. These words didn't help. It was clear that no one understood what was really going on. Matthew's mother naturally showed signs of strain; but there was also embarrassment.

The conversation between my parents seemed to come down to the question: is it real or is it all in his mind? Even at that young age, I could see that there was a problem with this question; my vocabulary didn't yet include the phrase 'false antithesis', but I could spot one all right. The opposite of real, I thought, is 'not real'. The opposite of 'all in the mind' is 'all in the body'.

Isn't it?

Mental illness is a horrible subject. The words alone cause you to recoil. The jagged M and the familiar verticals of 'ill' summon the clang of a door locking on a back ward. We don't want to know about it. Although cancer may be more likely to kill us, we at least understand most of its processes. No one knows how psychosis works. We're appalled by the suffering we imagine; and 'imagine' is often the best we can do, because patients are not good at describing what it's like.

In the last few years, there have been efforts to shake off what's always called the 'stigma' of mental illness. Some well-known people have spoken in public about their own experiences, in the hope that their candour will 'encourage others to come forward'. There's not much provision in Britain for anyone who does 'come forward', but the point is well made: it's unfair to behave towards those suffering from mental health problems as if they have failed some citizenship test.

Perhaps the sting of social shame is starting to diminish. We've probably all met people who have suffered from depression or from anorexia. There's a second kind of shame, however, which is less obvious and may prove harder to shift. It's to do with dignity. 'What a piece of work is a man,' said Hamlet: 'How noble in reason, how infinite in faculty . . . In action how like an angel, in apprehension how like a god; The beauty of the world, the paragon of animals.' It's difficult to square that description with the sight of someone muttering, shambling, all gone wrong.

By the standards of natural selection, it's true we are

the most 'successful' current species. We've mapped the heavens, split the atom and are coming close to a single explanation of the universe and its workings. We've bent a watery planet and its resources to a single end, the service of *Homo sapiens*; we have by trade and cooperation made ourselves richer than the sum of our assets; and in our spare time we've created *Don Giovanni*, *Macbeth* and the *Ghent Altarpiece*. This is obviously more than has been 'achieved' by any amphibian or invertebrate, even if *Homo sapiens* is still a relative newcomer, yet to prove itself over a long period.

But (and it's quite a big 'but') we are also the only species of which one in a hundred is insane — and here we are not talking about depression, anxiety or eating disorders. Across the world, regardless of climate, nutrition, ethnic variation and genetic drift, humanity is roughly one per cent psychotic. This figure is accepted by researchers worldwide. What do they mean by this? 'Psychosis' is a form of delusional illness, most often characterised by hearing loud voices that are not heard by others; by seeing phenomena — often animals or other creatures — that are not seen by anyone else in the room; by sustained and uncontrollable extremes of emotion, be it elation or despair; or by unshakeable belief systems, usually involving persecution or conspiracy, that have no basis in the reality observed by others. Most of these psychoses are diagnosed as either 'schizophrenia' or 'bipolar disorder'.

Something is going on here. One per cent of cows are

not deafened by the sound of other cows that no one else can see. You'll never find a zebra that thinks it's being pursued by a group of other, invisible, zebras. These species are not driven in their extremes of anguish to take their own lives or, in mercifully rare cases, instructed by commanding voices to attack others. A lamb that suffers oxygen deprivation during birth will be brain-damaged; a dog that's been abused as a puppy may be prone to bite you when it's grown up. But that's not the same thing as psychosis, which so far as we know remains a human-only ailment.

While the fully functioning human, with memory and reason, altruism and dexterity, is certainly the 'paragon of animals', the species as a whole is too flawed to pass a consumer standards test. One in a hundred of us doesn't work properly. If *Homo sapiens* had been manufactured and put on cosmic sale, there would by now have been a product recall.

In addition to Matthew, there was a boy we knew as children who was a good friend of Edward's. His name was Ben. He came from an ordinary family who lived on a modern estate in the next village. He was a bright lad who behaved in a normal way. After he had left school, he trained to be an accountant. He still lived with his parents, I think, but while Edward and I went on through further academic years, Ben acquired a car and money and frequently went over to Paris, where, he told us, he had a regular table at Maxim's restaurant. We thought he was exaggerating a bit, to make himself sound important. Being away at university, I saw less of him at this time, though I gathered that his galivanting had attracted the interest of MI5, who set a tail on him. At the age of twenty-three, unable to deal with the strain of surveillance, he killed himself.

This happened in my second year at university, when I had just discovered alcohol and thought it might make up for the shortcomings of my personality. To begin with, I used it in addition to marijuana, nicotine and quantities of powerful cough medicine procured from the college nurse. It was a way of getting through the evenings, though it was expensive; so I took to brewing my own beer. You could buy a kit from Boots the chemist and if you doubled the amount of sugar recommended on the side of the pack, you could get fairly drunk for about fifteen pence. A few more pints in the college bar or in the town pubs would do the trick. By the summer term I had given up work altogether to devote myself to drinking. My college friends remonstrated a little, but not much. There was no 'pastoral' care and we were all experimenting with life as it came blundering towards us.

I awoke one morning after a day-long binge and got up unsteadily from the bed. I was halfway through dressing when I woke up again. It seemed I had only dreamed my first awakening. I had finished dressing and was leaving the shared sitting room when I woke up again, still in bed. I climbed out once more, determined that I was now awake, dressed and crossed the room to brush my teeth in the small scullery. I got as far as the stairs when I awoke again to find myself still in the single bed of my college room. On my next attempt I got almost as far as the dining hall, in time for the still-warm fried eggs with the hard little caps on the yolk, when I awoke once more. Each time it took an effort of will to force myself up, but each time I found I was still in bed. It took everything I had to get myself at last, physically, into the sitting room and cling to the table, praying that I was finally and truly awake. If I could get out of the college, maybe, or meet someone I knew and talk to them, I might snap back into the reality that for twenty years I had so foolishly taken for granted. Sweet reality . . . How I would treasure it now — if only I could find it.

The next two years were challenging. I could barely hold the pen in Part One exams. In August, I had to come home from Greece when I awoke on a beach to find the sea dragging shingle through my veins. There were meetings with doctors, pills and a visit from a peripatetic consultant called Arkle, like the racehorse, who seemed to be the only psychiatrist in the south of England. There were panic attacks, agoraphobia, white nights of insomnia; every light seemed to be blinking in a dashboard of dismay. I took a train to London to visit a faith healer in North Kensington; there was an afternoon trip to the Park Prewett hospital, the old county asylum in Hampshire.

It was a bad time for my parents, who had nothing to offer but baffled sympathy. I remember standing with my mother in the kitchen listening to *Desert Island Discs* one day and telling her I didn't think I could go on. 'You will,' she said. 'I promise you will.'

The music was Ravel's First Piano Concerto, where the melody runs like a clear stream in the Auvergne. Thirty years later I chose the same music when I was interviewed on the programme, though I couldn't bring myself to say why. My mother said she would think of me each day at five o'clock and send me strength.

I went back for my third year and steadied up a little, using prescribed tranquillisers in place of marijuana, but still drinking to oblivion in the evening. I thought I sensed my mother's willpower at the agreed time, but perhaps I imagined it. In addition to Ravel, I listened to Mahler and Sibelius and to another intriguing record by Procol Harum, this one called *Grand Hotel*. My favourite track was 'Fires (Which Burnt Brightly)', where Keith Reid's lament for the loss of youthful idealism was set to a wistful minor-key melody by Gary Brooker. Rather than sit the full hand of final exams, I wrote two long essays, as you were allowed to do, and managed a respectable degree.

Then I went to live in Bristol, where my old friend David was in his last year. I slept in a cupboard on his landing to begin with, then on a shelf above a door in another student flat. I was writing a novel. (Typing one, anyway: it was pretty poor.) I'd registered with a G P, and one day, after a panic attack had left me in despair, I telephoned him. I was worried that, in my attempt to recover from the episode, I had taken too many pills. He came to the flat and drove me to a hospital outside Bristol, a place called Barrow Gurney, where I was put into a dormitory and slept heavily. I was able to discharge myself the next day, while agreeing that I would be treated as an out-patient, going in three times a week for group and individual psychotherapy.

My problem was that the world and everything in it appeared unreal. The table, the cup, the book, the window were like unconvincing replicas of the actual things. I felt that I had severed my link with the life I'd known and was now lost in a shadowland. The most urgent project was to believe that the material world existed.

'If I could just rewind and get back to where I was. If I could just not go out on a bender that fateful day . . .' 'Why do you want to go back?' asked the therapist, Dr Lawson, a young man with hair and a beard like Charles II. 'You were so unhappy there. Look what happened.'

Good question. He recommended me books of mystical writing, including the works of Carlos Castaneda, and urged me to think less logically. One day I said, 'I think I have to accept where I am, in this new reality, and learn to live with it. I can't go back.' He smiled. On his recommendation, I read a book by a Romanian pastor called Richard Wurmbrand, who had been imprisoned and tortured by the Communist regime. One day in his solitary

confinement Wurmbrand remembered God's instruction
to be happy and to dance. So, in his cell, while his torturers
looked through the spyhole, he danced. I tried to follow
his example. I prayed hard to a childhood god I had forsaken. I tried to become a better person.

In the unit where I went there was an old woman
called Marjorie who stood all day in front of a window
with her arm raised, as though waving to someone. There
was no one there, just a car park and a few chestnut
trees and other hospital buildings – garages and depos-
itories, wards with locked doors where the psychotic
patients lived. I have often thought of Marjorie over the
years. Perhaps she wasn't waving to an imaginary lover,
or a lost child. Maybe she was just easing a stiff shoulder.
She never spoke, though. And to me she seemed like a
piece of driftwood, someone whose life was literally too
sad for words.

I had something called 'abreaction', in which you're
supposed to remember important things while sedated; it
didn't do much good. There was talk of ECT, which I
didn't like the sound of. Slowly, very slowly, by accept-
ing that I had no choice but to embrace what I still saw
as an unreal world, I started to become better. It was, in
retrospect, a mixture of the philosophical, the religious,
the physiological and the inevitable. At the time, it felt
like spring in the Arctic, when huge frozen blocks begin
to thaw and move. Richard Lawson was a subtle therapist, and I was lucky to have found him: he was simply the

doctor on the NHS roster at the city overspill hospital.*
Sleep returned, patchily, and fear began to ebb. I slowly
came to manage agoraphobia by walking ten yards further
every day. 'You know you can get to the second pillar box
because you reached it yesterday,' I told myself; 'so every
step after that is a new victory.' It seemed that after two
years of holding me at unnatural panic stations, day and
night, my nervous system was beginning to grow tired
and slacken its grip.

In the summer, I left Bristol and applied for a job
teaching at a school in London. I was worried they'd see
through me, so I bought a suit from Take 6 and found
some old reading glasses that I thought might make me
look respectable. Before the interview, I had two pints
of Guinness in an Irish pub on Camden High Street, and
some Extra Strong Mints. A week later, to my surprise,
I was offered a job as the junior teacher in the English
department.

My adult life began. The Dwight Franklin International School was only three years old, and working
there was an education in itself. I didn't want to think
about what I'd been through in the past two years. I had
had some post-adolescent adjustment difficulties, that
was all — a minor 'breakdown'. It had perhaps had a

---

* Barrow closed in 2005, when it was said to be the dirtiest hospital in
Britain. It lay derelict for ten years, its ruins a subject for many ama-
teur photographers and some paranormal investigations.

biological element in the process of neurodevelopment that was coming to its conclusion; it certainly had a drink and drugs component. Yet if the experience had been that excruciating, what must it be like to be really ill, I wondered — to be Matthew, Ben or Marjorie?

That was not something I was ready to think about, I decided — or at least not until I had put a stretch of ordinary life behind me.

About twenty-five years later, I felt the time had come. I planned to show at last how the question that had been asked of poor Matthew — 'Is it real or is it all in the mind?' — was nonsensical. It was first necessary to do some background reading.

What a sad yet fascinating history it was. Madness has apparently been with us for ever. If you watch or read *King Lear*, you can see a depiction of senile dementia that is almost clinical. Presumably young people's dementia, since it seems so ingrained, was also around in 1600; there were Bens and Matthews in Tudor England, pursued by commands from nowhere. The Old Testament is full of wild-haired prophets hearing disembodied voices; Homer's heroes will do nothing until instructed by the words of an absent being. The New Testament description of John the Baptist is that of a casebook schizophrenic — of the kind you can see, sadly, on the streets of New York or London any day, arguing with the air. One of the reasons *Don Quixote* is so hard to read is that it tries to make a comedy of the delusional illness of its hero; Mr Dick in *David Copperfield* might today be offered some sort of drug treatment to keep King Charles's head under control. And every medieval village had its 'idiot', perhaps brought on by birth trauma or by inbreeding. For thousands of years, it seems fair to conclude, human societies must have dealt with their oddballs as best they could — caring, shunning, stoning, loving or ignoring. The one thing they couldn't do was understand.

It was not until after the scientific advances of the Enlightenment that ambitious Europeans felt ready to confront this enormous issue; and from about 1800, initially in Italy and France, the work began. The first challenge was to figure out which symptoms belonged with which, and to give them a name that distinguished them from other groups. This woman thinks she's Joan of Arc; this man thinks his thoughts are controlled by the Home Secretary. But are they suffering from the same illness? Or is the apparent similarity merely a small overlap in a Venn diagram where the circle entities have different underlying causes? For its first active century, the medicine of the mind was largely taken up with this kind of grouping and description, or 'nosology'. There were no cures; and, with no knowledge of genetics or brain function and no electronic scanners, the laboratory offered little hope of finding any.

Victorian Britain was late to join the European endeavour, but set about it with its own vigour and optimism.

On the instruction of the government, each county built a large brick asylum with a water tower, a kitchen garden, a brewery and workshops for the 'lunatics'. Local councils were required to foot the bills. Patients were brought in from the towns and villages in their hundreds, then their thousands. Here were people we would now recognise as suffering from senile dementia, bipolar disorder, depression, epilepsy, schizophrenia, congenital defects, alcohol or drug addiction, learning difficulties, severe phobias, psychological distress and a variety of neurological complaints. Some distinctions were made. 'Dementia', 'mania' and 'melancholy', for instance, were viewed as separate categories that corresponded with later, more scientific diagnoses. For the majority of patients, however, the move to place them in an institution, while well intentioned, was premature. The staff weren't ready for them; they could only herd them together and observe. Often they didn't even have time for that, so the people were just locked away, noisily protesting. It was Bedlam.

The new asylums were overseen by superintendents, some of whom were medical men and some not; psychiatry was not yet a speciality with its own training. 'Mad-doctoring' was badly paid and looked down on because it had so few good outcomes; it was a branch of the profession for those not qualified to be physicians. Classification of new patients was based largely on whether they were docile or 'refractory' — on how easy, in other words, they would be to control. And on the basis of a quick once-over, it was decided whether you would be locked in a basement or put in a room off a long corridor with a daily hour of exercise in the 'airing court'. The main corridor at Colney Hatch asylum in north London (later Friern Barnet hospital) was one third of a mile long. By the time I visited in 2001, it was in the process of being converted into 'luxury flats' with fitness rooms and saunas. I collected a brochure from the developer's site office; it boasted that the building had won two design awards, though it didn't mention that the first, in 1851, had been as the Second Middlesex County Lunatic Asylum.

Then, on the outside of the building, I walked the length of that corridor: almost six hundred yards. It was longer than the entire street on which we then lived — five times longer, as a matter of fact. Five entire streets, off which opened room after locked room, crowded with individuals — with brains whirring, manic or demented; of trillions of synapses wrestling with the fires of human consciousness.

Some unscrupulous families used the asylums as a dumping ground for people they found difficult to deal with — unmarried mothers or their offspring, the over-promiscuous, the deaf, the mute and the blind. With no reliable diagnoses, anyone might be termed a lunatic. And if they were not behaving irrationally when they went in, they quite soon did. Who if locked up in a room with demented people for twenty-three hours a day would not start to exhibit signs of distress?

The asylum system was set up in good faith; the boards of governors and visitors were often kind or pious people. But the weight of numbers and the lack of medical understanding were a dead-end combination. At the start of the nineteenth century there were about a thousand people in hospitals for mental illness in Britain; by the end of the century there were a hundred thousand. The word that was often used to describe their management was 'warehousing'.

The greatest breakthrough in psychiatry concerned patients who developed GPI, 'general paresis [or paralysis] of the insane', which might begin with simple things like headaches, dizziness or insomnia, leading on to tics and convulsions. In the late stages, these were accompanied by delusions, often of grandeur, so that patients might believe themselves to be Don Juan or Cleopatra. For a long time, their condition was put down to weakness of character, bad breeding or 'feebleness' of mind. In the mid-century, however, a tentative connection was made with syphilis, for the early manifestations of which many of these patients had been treated, some as long as thirty years before. So the careful observation of patients and their symptoms – good detective work – began to pay off. A French dermatologist called Jean Alfred Fournier established the connection in the 1880s and in 1913 the syphilis bacterium was found at post-mortem in GPI patients. In the 1940s, in the shape of penicillin, there was a cure.

The passage of about a hundred years from first ink-
ling to workable remedy is not a long time in the history
of medicine, and in psychiatry it is almost supersonically
fast. GPI patients had made up between 10 and 25 per cent
of the population of psychiatric hospitals in 1900. And the
greatest advance in the history of psychiatry lay in the discovery that up to a quarter of its patients were not 'mad',
but suffering from venereal disease.

Meanwhile, some patterns in the baffling symptoms
of what is now known as schizophrenia were also being
observed by doctors throughout Europe. Outstanding
among these observers was the German Emil Kraepelin,
who believed that many severe 'mental' illnesses had
a neurological base: in other words, that the patients'
bizarre behaviour and beliefs were not a response to the
events of their lives but to a problem in the brain tissue.
His belief became established in about 1900 at one end
of the psychiatric spectrum, known as the 'medical' or
'biological' model. Most doctors could see the logic. It
would explain, for a start, why psychosis was limited to
humans — because our nervous system has evolved in a
different and more complex way than that of other creatures. The medical model also debunked the medieval
idea of 'lunacy': just as GPI patients were not 'mad' but
had venereal disease, so schizophrenic patients weren't
'crazy' either, but had a neurological condition. Its pecu-
liarity was that instead of affecting the nerves in the brain
responsible for movement (like motor neurone disease),

it affected those to do with perception (hearing, seeing) and thought (including belief systems). Kraepelin's medical model would also explain something else that puzzled 'mad doctors': why did individuals with such different lives present such similar symptom clusters? The answer was: because their voices were not a response to their particular experiences but to the same defect (or 'biomarker') in the brain.

The difficulty lay in proving it. With some other neurological illnesses, doctors had located the lesion that was responsible for the symptoms. So, for instance, in Paris in the 1880s, the neurologist Jean-Martin Charcot had found a lesion in the brains of dead multiple sclerosis patients, which he showed had led directly to their 'motor' issues of balance and tremor. Unfortunately for Kraepelin and the medical model, no such lesion – or any other underlying material cause – for schizophrenia could be found.

Restricted as he was by the limits of contemporary science, Kraepelin continued with his descriptive work. He made an important division of the major psychoses. He called the first one *dementia praecox*, or 'young people's madness', because he had noted that it usually strikes soon after the age of twenty. This is what came later to be called 'schizophrenia' and is what Matthew and Ben suffered from: that harsh reality in which loud voices come from speakers unseen. The second psychosis Kraepelin called 'manic depression', an unfortunate term because to the layman it implies that patients are 'madly' depressed, when in fact they veer from mania (high) to depression (low). Symptoms were not exclusive to one psychosis, Kraepelin believed, but patterns were; and it was on this skilful pattern-watching that he built his reputation and a legacy.

A prominent Swiss psychiatrist called Eugen Bleuler decided in the 1920s that he didn't like the sense (which he believed implicit in the word 'dementia') that the disease was degenerative and therefore resistant to therapy. He proposed that it should henceforward be known as 'schizophrenia'. Bleuler was by all accounts a thoughtful doctor, good with patients, but he was no wordsmith; and his choice of a Greek-based neologism meaning 'split mind' achieved the near-impossible feat of making the suffering of those with it even more intense, because it made their problem so widely misunderstood. Schizophrenics do not have a 'split personality'; on the contrary their experience of the world is powerfully coherent. They are not 'in two minds' about anything; they believe in their own reality with a strength that would make a religious fundamentalist look half-hearted. A healthy person who describes their life as 'schizophrenic' because they have a second house or a part-time job is as ignorant and offensive as someone who calls their unreliable car 'spastic'.

In the continuing absence of any observable neural basis for psychosis, researchers in the twentieth century began to wonder if they had been going about it the wrong way. It was a question of returning to first principles. What do we really know about this terrible experience that affects one in a hundred of us?

Well, it appeared to run in families, that was the first thing to say; though the early researchers were hampered by the fact that they didn't know how heredity worked. Darwin, after all, had believed that parents' characteristics were 'blended' in their offspring by means of 'gemmules' — tiny particles invisible to the microscope. Mendel's foundational theory of dominant and recessive alternatives (later christened 'genes') was not fully established until the 1920s and not married to mainstream biology before the 1950s, at which point psychiatric researchers could look at the question of inheritance with a little more certainty.

Family studies of schizophrenia in the 1960s showed that you were much more likely to suffer from it if a close relation had it, too. Yet it was a complex, not a simple inheritance. Just how complex began to emerge when they studied identical twins. They found that it was possible that one twin might develop the disease and the other, genetically identical, might not. The hope had been that it might prove to be a 'single gene' disease, like sickle cell anaemia, the gene for which also gave its possessors immunity to malaria, which, in the simplest Darwinian terms, explained its 'success' in parts of Africa. You hadn't died of malaria, so of course your genome was passed on.

The only logical conclusion from the identical-twin studies was that there must be more than just genetic agents at work; and these were termed 'environmental' factors. This was nothing to do with climate or rainfall; it meant, essentially, life experience. This could include the emotional trajectory of a life, its stress and grief and joy, but more often it came down to drink and drugs. So if one twin smoked skunk, emigrated, drank alcohol, got sacked from her job and lived in bad housing she would find that the stress caused by these events played into a genetic pre-disposition and, as it were, lit the blue touchpaper; and the next thing you knew she was hearing voices. The other twin, who'd lived a purer, happier life, was able to escape the potential downside of her genes because the catalyst of bodily response to emotional dismay never made the final electrical connection in her brain.

This was obviously a setback for the medical model. But the good news was that it suggested the disease might be treatable. If life events could, to some extent, precipitate schizophrenia, then psychotherapy might, to the same extent, assuage or cure it. This optimistic belief was supported by the success of the brand of treatment that lay at the opposite end of the spectrum to the medical model: the talking cures.

Beginning in France and Germany, but finding its most famous exponent in Vienna, the idea that you could deracinate the cause of your distress (and any accompanying bodily symptoms) by talking to a skilled therapist had been growing in popularity throughout the nineteenth century. Freudian psychoanalysis made large claims for its ability to help people with all sorts of psychosomatic* illnesses and to lay bare the bones of human nature; other, less grandiose, schools of psychotherapy followed after it and achieved measurable results with unhappy, bereaved or conflicted people. So it was argued that psychotherapy, wisely used, could help not just the emotionally over-wrought, but psychotic patients, too. Nonsense, said the medical model: that's like saying you can cure Parkinson's by just talking to the patient. And in any case, all those twin studies were flawed, because at the time they were done, in the 1960s, researchers lacked the genetic tools to establish that the twins in the test were truly identi-cal, the fruit of a single sperm/egg embryo that had split. Most were in fact fraternal twins, the result of two simul-taneous conceptions with different parental genes. Forget 'environmental factors': one fraternal twin had inherited the genes for psychosis; one hadn't.

What most people could agree was that schizophrenia

---

* Another misunderstood word. It doesn't mean fanciful or invented. It means originating in the mind (psyche) but expressing itself in the body (soma). A tear is an example. The mind, which is a function of the brain, has a sad thought, which the brain registers; the brain sends messages down neural pathways to various glands, including the tear ducts. They produce fluid from the eyes. A thought made water. This duality makes psychosomatic events arguably more 'real' than purely physical or purely mental ones because they involve more systems: a greater part of your whole being is committed.

was a 'neurodevelopmental' illness, which meant that it kicked in at the moment that the wiring of the human brain becomes complete. The dispute was whether the moment the last connection was made inevitably triggered the faulty inheritance, like turning the switch on the Christmas tree lights, or if it needed something more: a life event or 'stressor'. Or perhaps both: the same combination of genes could express itself in different degrees of susceptibility — sometimes needing an outside agent, sometimes self-fulfilling. It has been argued that senile dementia is essentially late-onset schizophrenia, affecting those who have avoided it at the age of twenty-one by having a less hard-wired predisposition or by not experiencing an environmental stressor that would otherwise have completed the circuit.

Most of this genetic argument was rejected by the psychological model, whose continuing attraction lay in the fact that it didn't make its patients sound condemned by their inheritance. By contrast, it treated them as individuals, listening to their voices and their stories; it honoured the content of their delusions, believing it to be significant, whereas to the hard medical model it was little more than electrical interference. And in the 1960s and 1970s the psychological movement was encouraged by the countercultural mood of the times. An 'anti-psychiatry' movement in the United States and Europe claimed that all ideas of 'madness' were, at heart, means by which the state controlled its more unruly citizens. Writers such as Michel

Foucault in France, R. D. Laing in Britain and Thomas Szasz in America argued the case in their own ways; but it helped that they were all gifted polemicists. Writing talent counted for a lot, as it had for Freud. Here is a line from Thomas Szasz: 'If you talk to God, you are praying. If God talks to you, you have schizophrenia.' I wasn't sure how much scrutiny such statements could really bear, but as a way of dismissing medical orthodoxy they were bracing and effective. Ken Loach made a moving film called *Family Life* based on Laing's beliefs that 'schizophrenia' was little more than a restraining label; Ken Kesey's novel *One Flew Over the Cuckoo's Nest* and Miloš Forman's film of it drew on similar beliefs.

As a riposte to the fact that a schizophrenic parent was much more likely than a well parent to have a schizophrenic child, the psychological model argued that the reasons could as easily be cultural and economic. The child of a mentally suffering and erratically behaving person is already at a strong disadvantage. The illness is overrepresented in poorer families with housing and financial difficulties; the life-changing challenges of migration seemed to have an impact, too. Later writers in the field, such as the English psychologist Richard Bentall, have usefully muddied the genetic water (already cloudy enough) and made the case for greater attention to the experience of the individual.

It was only recently (in *Control*, a 2022 book about eugenics by the British geneticist Adam Rutherford) that I read the most convincing argument for the environmental factor. In Germany, from 1933, Nazi doctors sterilised or killed roughly 250,000 people they believed to suffer from schizophrenia. This accounted for between 75 and 100 per cent of all such patients. In 1945, therefore, the people with the genetic predisposition left alive or fertile should have been close to zero. Yet within thirty years, the incidence of schizophrenia in the German population had not only rebounded but had exceeded pre-Nazi levels. The only logical conclusion is that it was the poverty, hardship and malnutrition of postwar Germany that were responsible for activating potential psychosis. The implication for the human genome is frightening, however. It seems that it is not just one in a hundred of us who is incorrectly wired, but many, many more. We are a very young species and it may take more millennia for our complicated software to bed in. One thinks of the new electronic warning systems in sophisticated and reliable motor cars, which are always the first things to go wrong.

Back in 2001, I found the idea of this 'mixed model' confusing, but it became easier to live with once I had understood another medical and philosophical consensus: that there is no such thing as 'dualism' — of mind and body being separate. Mind is no more than a function of brain, just as movement is a function of muscle. The fact that you can't see or touch either thought or movement doesn't make them less dependent on tissue. There is no separation; it is not a question of *cogito ergo sum* ('I think, therefore I am'), as Descartes had suggested, but *sum: ergo, inter alia, cogitare possum* ('I exist: therefore, among other things, I can think').

This is an axiom of all modern thought on the issue. It is supported by the evidence of powerful new scanners, which have shown that mental activity or lack of it can change brain tissue as much as vice versa. Some areas of the cortex, including those that process speech, which are unused for a long period may show visible alterations and deficits. People suffering from PTSD also show interesting brain tissue changes. Some abnormalities in the frontal lobes have been observed in those diagnosed with antisocial personality disorder (people previously known as psychopaths); though whether tissue change precedes life events or the other way round is hard to establish.

So in the case of psychosis, the idea that response to an experience can cause an electro-chemical network to join up and become active is not fanciful. I have actually seen it happen, when a work colleague, who was bipolar, entered an acute phase of his illness. The key moment came when we were checking in some heavy bags at La Guardia airport. The check-in clerk was so helpful that my friend felt a sadness that he might never meet this man again. He must have been in a vulnerable state, in which almost any emotion might have tipped him over, but this was the one, he believed, that completed the wiring, filling him with a cosmic despair that a few days later, back in London,

caused a neural short-circuit to express itself in hallucinated animals climbing the walls of his hospital room. He
showed me where on the paintwork.

And that is roughly where I found the consensus — less
a consensus, more an uneasy ceasefire, perhaps — about
twenty years ago. The next step was to meet some patients.

I'd spent some time with Billy, our next-door neighbour,
a schizophrenic young man in his late twenties, who often
used to come to our house, where he would sit in the kitchen, smoking, while my wife stopped what she was doing
to listen and try to comfort him. Billy's mother described
his life to me one day. It took her only four words: 'He
lives in hell.' Billy had smoked a lot of genetically modi-
fied skunk in his teens and it was believed that this had
'brought on' his schizophrenia. This was not quite medic-
ally possible, according to my understanding of things,
unless he already had the genetic predisposition; but it
seemed pedantic to argue — and skunk certainly qualified
as an 'environmental' agent. The reluctance of the medical profession to warn young people about the dangers
of recreational drugs, particularly the toxic new strains of
cannabis, was frustrating to Billy's parents.

A retired NHS psychiatrist lent me hours of video
tapes he'd made of interviews with schizophrenic patients
in the 1970s; he showed me what signs a diagnosing doctor
would look out for. Another psychiatrist described to me
what he called 'that *praecox* moment' when a patient said

something that made a pattern in the previously random narrative. For instance, the puzzle of what a patient had been told by someone might be solved when it became clear that the 'someone', while real and overbearing, had no physical existence.

And then I met Mary. She was a woman in her thirties who suffered from a classic and acute form of schizophrenia, in which several voices spoke to her. However, she was unusual in that she responded well to some of the drug treatments on offer in hospital. Most of these chemicals, developed in the 1950s, were blunt instruments. The most famous had originally been developed for use in the dyeing industry and its psychiatric use had been stumbled on by chance. They could dampen the more florid symptoms, but offered no cure and often made the patients sleepy, apathetic and fat. Mary, however, enjoyed interludes when her symptoms were tolerable. She could leave hospital and go home. At such times, she volunteered to help educate the police in how to recognise symptoms of possible psychosis when they had been called to a disturbance.

I drove to her terrace house in north London one morning in 2002. I was aware of being in the presence of someone polite and reasonable. She showed no signs of distress and listened carefully while I outlined why I had come to see her. There was coffee and biscuits and a radio that she turned off so that we could both concentrate. 'So, if my book is to deal with all these difficult questions,' I said, 'then I have to understand the experience itself.'

Mary smiled. 'You want to know what it's like?'

'Yes.'

She described what the voices were like. Insistent, repetitive, sometimes bullying.

'And are you hearing them now, as we speak?'

'Yes.'

'How many?'

She put her head to one side and listened. 'Actually, do you mind if I don't count?'

'Why?'

'Because I'll get lost.'

'Why?'

'Please don't take this the wrong way, but what they're saying is more urgent than what you're saying. And louder.'

I was taken aback. Then Mary said, 'Would you like to do an exercise? This is something I do when I'm training the police.'

She handed me an old Sony Walkman. 'We're going to do a role play,' she said. 'I want you to imagine that I'm interviewing you for a job.'

'OK.'

'But you must press the Play button on the Walkman when we start.'

'Fine.'

We began. Mary asked me how I had come to the interview and I told her I'd driven. There was a voice in my headphones, but I was able to ignore it and give a humorous answer about the traffic. She asked about my strong points and what my previous boss had made of me. A second voice began in the headphones. As I went through my CV and my possible weaknesses, a third voice started up, and all three became louder.

We moved off my previous job and on to more general matters of politics and current affairs. By now the voices in my head were louder than Mary's voice in the room and it was hard to follow what she was saying. Eventually, I began to find the volume and aggression of the voices not just distracting but upsetting. I pulled off the headphones.

Mary smiled. 'You lasted longer than most.'

'That was horrible.'

She stopped smiling. 'Tell me,' she said, 'who was the Prime Minister before Tony Blair.'

'John Major.'

'But you didn't know that when I asked you just now.'

'Yes, but I couldn't concentrate! Those voices. I do actually know who—'

She looked at me tolerantly. 'That's what it's like.'

I nodded.

'And,' she said, 'do you realise that for the last minute or so you were lip-reading me?'

'Because I couldn't hear you over the voices in my headphones.'

Mary leaned forward in her chair. *'That's what it's like.'*

This was the moment at which I began to understand. Schizophrenics don't think they hear voices; they do hear voices. The absence of a speaker's lips or larynx is beside the point.

I visited some Victorian asylums — Haywards Heath, Springfield, Friern Barnet — but I was too late. In the 1990s, a few years earlier, the government had decided to close down the old asylums and offer the patients instead something called 'care in the community'. As it turned out, there was little care and no 'community'. There was only the world at large, which hardly cared at all, while a community, however ramshackle, was exactly what the patients were leaving behind. But the 'c-word' had been snapped up by politicians as a replacement for 'society' because it implied pre-existing concern and mutual help — which excused them from having to provide any.

But before I came over all Foucault about it, I had to admit that closing these huge institutions was the right thing to do. They had never worked as they had been intended and had become the twentieth-century equivalent of the workhouse: a place where people could be left and forgotten. I talked to a psychiatrist who had worked at Friern Barnet in its final days and he told me that more than half his patients had been *born* there. As a comment on the hopeful Victorian adventure, that seemed to be the final word.

However, I still needed to see inside a functioning nineteenth-century asylum, because one of the main characters in *Human Traces* would be employed there as a young man. The last working Victorian asylum seemed to be Broadmoor, well known to the public as the home of Britain's most deranged murderers. I made an arrangement with Gwen Adshead, the senior resident psychiatrist, that in return for her guided tour, I would give a poetry class and a talk to some patients.

A feeling of dread came over me as I drove up through the residential estates and saw the high walls with the barbed wire on top. How crazed were the patients? Hadn't Peter Sutcliffe been stabbed in the eye with a sharpened biro? In any case, I wasn't interested in crime, only in atmosphere. Security was tight. Not only your keys and mobile phone, but pens and mints had to be handed over before you went into some sort of compression chamber, where I think a body scan took place. Eventually I was through another set of locked doors and out into the open air.

The institutional redbrick and cast-iron drainpipes were at once familiar. It reminded me of my old school, which by chance was in the same village. With Dr Adshead, I walked down to the famous 'terrace', from which the patients for a hundred and fifty years had eased their minds by looking out over the flat lands of East Berkshire.

We went into one of the redbrick buildings, to a ward that was assessing new female patients. It was surprisingly rowdy, with young women in tracksuits shouting and gesticulating.

The most common diagnosis was schizophrenia, Dr Adshead told me. Most of those who suffer from it are meek and gentle, but in very rare instances their voices issue violent and irresistible commands. And because it's such a common illness, those instances do mount up. Many patients had become unwell in custody elsewhere and had been transferred to hospital on the basis of a diagnosis by a prison board some months or years after their trial. The second most prevalent diagnosis was 'personality disorder', which included 'antisocial personality disorder'. This cluster of symptoms had been described by Kraepelin a century before as a condition in which the patient was devoid of empathy and unresponsive to social norms or the feelings of others. However, it was still in 2002 highly controversial (its critics point out that there were no non-criminal psychopaths receiving treatment in regular hospitals and that it was therefore just a fancy term for 'evil').

In a modern block, I then went into a day room, escorted by a nurse, to give my class. In Broadmoor, for safety's sake, the patient sits on the far side of the desk, next to the window, and the therapist sits on the near or 'visitor' side, closer to the door. I perched on the desk itself, with the open door beside me. I had chosen to talk about a poem called 'Considering the Snail' by Thom Gunn, which I had come across in the first-year sixth form, in the valley below. My volunteer students were all men, about twelve in number. Most seemed quite organised and calm. I tried not to think why they were in this hospital, what they had done. I talked about the poem, and how it was not about feeling sorry for animals. It was, I tried to explain, about how very snaily a snail is; it was about the fierceness of being – about ipseity, selfhood. Two men in the front began to question me about my own books. 'That bit in *Charlotte Gray*, where you . . .' This was from a youngish patient in a smart sports jacket. It was the type of thing I'd been asked in Waterstone's, Kensington, and he looked just the sort of person who might have been in the audience.

Afterwards, I told the nurse that a certain curiosity had threatened to make me lose my concentration. I said I knew that patient confidentiality was paramount, but wondered what exactly . . .

'Well,' he said, 'you're not likely to be here unless you've killed someone.'

'And that man who asked me . . . The one with the . . .'

He stopped in the corridor. 'Oh yes. More than one.'

We continued our tour of the institution, which brought us to the chapel, a neo-Gothic building with painted tiles. I thought of all the men and women who had come here and confessed their sins. And I thought of all those who had been made to suffer for their madness — those innocents who had been despatched by them. Gwen Adshead had found a way of balancing her concern for patient and victim: 'I've come to think of my patients as survivors of a disaster, where they are the disaster — and my colleagues and I are the first responders.'

In another Victorian corridor we went past a room with three pairs of shoes outside. 'That's our mosque,' said Dr Adshead.

'I see. And do you have a synagogue?'

'No.'

'Why not?'

'Jewish people don't seem to commit murder.'

I was already at the edge of what I could comprehend, and now this . . . It was time to take a deep breath. I thanked Dr Adshead and said goodbye. I went back through the numerous locked doors, reclaimed my mobile phone and Polo mints, then drove down the hill. On a whim, I stopped in the lower part of the village, outside a sweets-and-fag shop where David and I used to go most afternoons as teenagers.

The rain was falling softly. It was eerie to feel the different ages of my life rub against each other, as parallel but separate existences; and it was comforting to think how much happier I was at the age of forty-nine than I had been at fifteen. Middle age suited me, I couldn't help thinking. Experience when you're young is pungent and hard to evaluate. But when, for instance, you swim in the sea as a middle-aged man all your younger selves — from Bexhill, Costa Brava, the Aegean — are available to you in the taste of salt water and the pull of the tide.

I checked my watch and thought I should ring home. But I wanted to linger for a time in Lower Crowthorne, standing in the darkness, in the rain, trying to make out a pattern in all the extraordinary things I'd seen.

I'd heard a voice once myself — on 11 September 1992. Veronica went into labour at about seven-thirty in the evening. We had organised a home birth, so I rang the number we'd been given. After an hour of contractions, however, the midwife still hadn't turned up. I rang again. She was stuck in traffic and the notes were on the other side of town. I consulted a sheet of photocopied paper from an illustrated book of childbirth that she'd left on a previous visit and offered a silent prayer.

The process moved on swiftly; there were no complications, and I was able to present the baby to her mother on the bathroom floor, then set about cleaning up. About ten minutes later, the midwife arrived and cut the cord. Twenty minutes after that, another midwife came. And then my wife's parents. I began running up- and downstairs with their tea and coffee orders, pausing only to pour myself a Famous Grouse. William, aged nearly two, came in to see his new sister, Holly. Then, as we were all sitting at the bedside, there was a knock on the door and a Spanish girl put her head round. It was the babysitter.

I had forgotten that we were meant to be going out and hadn't given her a thought. Her mouth fell open, her eyes widened, then filled with tears. I'm not sure she had even known that Veronica was pregnant. We gave her the baby to hold. By eleven, the visitors had all gone home. I left mother and baby together, finished cleaning up and settled William in his bed. I thought it would be a good idea if I spent the night in the spare room and within minutes had fallen deeply asleep.

I was awoken about three hours later by Veronica screaming my name from the top floor. 'I'm coming, I'm coming,' I shouted back. Assuming cot death or worse, I ran up and burst into the bedroom. Mother and baby were both peacefully asleep. My heart still pounding, I demanded to know why she had been yelling for me. She hadn't. They had both fallen asleep and had not stirred till I blundered in. But I had heard her voice.

There is an event in the Bible when the infant Samuel is called repeatedly in the night by the ageing priest Eli and runs to his room only to find the old man asleep. In 1976, a psychologist at Princeton, Julian Jaynes, published a book about voice-hearing.* His theory was that the ability to hear voices had once been widespread and was in itself no cause for alarm, let alone a medical diagnosis; it had been an intermediary stage in our brains' development. We were wrong, Jaynes thought, to think of the voices heard

* *The Origin of Consciousness in the Breakdown of the Bicameral Mind.*

by people in the Bible and Homer as literary metaphors constructed by sophisticated authors. They were in fact literal descriptions of how ancient people knew what to do: they hallucinated heard instruction from their absent leaders. As modern consciousness, with its memory and metaphor and writing culture, developed, voice-hearing was selected against. By the later books in the Old Testament it has become a rare yet valued asset, belonging only to select prophets or to the witch at Endor; by the time of the New Testament, cousins John the Baptist and Jesus Christ are almost the last two with this gift. However (big conjunction), the faculty did not disappear.

The question of why the phenomenon of voice-hearing has survived remains intriguing. People with psychosis have fewer children than average; many take their own lives prematurely. By the logic of genetics, as I understood it, this could mean only one thing: that in order to persist, the combination of genes that gives rise to psychosis must be related in some way to genes which confer considerable advantages. To put it in very simple terms, the malfunction of one per cent must be the price we pay for some indispensable characteristic in the ninety-nine.

And what is that priceless gift? Was it speech that was so important? Maybe, but we now think our cousin *Homo neanderthalensis* had the wherewithal to talk. Creativity, then? No Mozart without schizophrenia? It sounds fanciful unless you broaden the idea of 'creativity' to include all forms of ingenuity, including the manual. Was it handedness — the way that having one dominant hand (more so than other apes) is so much more effective than being ambidextrous? Was it the freak of consciousness itself?

While we recognise how weird that faculty is in evolutionary terms — not the standard slight advantage at the feeding trough but a quite unnecessary superpower — we don't know how it works. The search for the 'neural substrates' of consciousness remains the grail of many neuroscientists at work today. I proposed a fanciful explanation in a book called *A Possible Life* in 2014, but it was not until later that I came across the so-called 'spandrel theory'. This supposes that consciousness itself is not being selected for. It's just that the genes that underwrite it sit next on the genome to others that *are* selected, possibly those coding for something as mundane yet critical as disease resistance. (It's quite feasible for genes to hitch-hike anywhere in the genome, grabbing a lift where they can find it: a memory-refiner can sit next to an ankle-builder.) So consciousness may be like the flashy logo on a pair of trainers: it sets the price and gets all the attention, but it's the shoe that counts.

The short answer to all these genetic questions turned out to be: we don't know. The mapping of the human genome was celebrated as a triumph of scientific ingenuity; but it also revealed just how complicated was the miracle of life that it had rendered legible. In 2018, research using the new evidence in a genome-wide association study (GWAS) located 145 genetic variables that seem to contribute to a predisposition to schizophrenia — though we do not yet know how, and still more variations are likely to be discovered with time.

Pharmaceutical companies have spent millions of dollars on trying to find drug treatments that can alleviate the symptoms more subtly than the so-called 'chemical cosh' that is all we have now. Sadly, the research has not always been undertaken in good faith; it has often resulted in findings that suggest a drug made by the sponsoring company is the best answer. 'Big pharma' companies, including GlaxoSmithKline, Johnson & Johnson and Pfizer, have been fined billions in both civil and criminal cases.

There is despair in the profession at how unhelpful the categories of diagnosis appear to be, and in the United States there is widespread contempt for the government handbook doctors are supposed to use. The latest edition is viewed as so compromised by warring factions as to be functionally useless. Future psychiatry may well abandon all diagnostic labels and grade people only on a scale of distress, from the happy individual who's never had a sleepless night at one end, through to the poor person who barely functions at the other. We are all on there somewhere.

After my novel *Human Traces* came out in 2005, I was invited to talk to an international conference on schizophrenia in Venice. This is not quite the honour it may

sound, as such symposia often invite a lay speaker (preferably a comic, I gathered) to lighten the tone. I remember
proposing that the misleading term 'schizophrenia' be
dropped and that it be renamed delusional psychotic illness, or DPI for short. I was told that moves were already
afoot to rename it general psychotic something-or-other,
but my protests that calling anything 'general' was unhelpful were dismissed. A distinguished psychiatrist told me
later that these conferences are often a way of spending
(he may have said 'laundering') the vast sums of international money being pumped into research. That would
certainly explain why we were all moved to a swankier
hotel on the Lido as soon as we arrived. Soon afterwards,
the Tavistock Clinic in London offered me an honorary
doctorate for my efforts to get to grips with psychiatry,
which was generous of them when you consider how much
they revere the legacy of Freud and what short shrift his
early work, lightly fictionalised, was given in the novel.

You can't expect to change things with a book. The
sales, the prizes, the acclaim (if any) seem ultimately to
amount to very little. The process – the work itself – must
be its own reward. I still feel a mixture of sadness and
indignation when I think of how much human beings have
had to suffer in return for the unrequested and unnecessary gift of consciousness. It is a 'gift' that has separated
us from the rest of nature and made us, in the words of
the Spanish philosopher Miguel de Unamuno, lower than
the jackass or the crab. My main reward has been in letters

that have reached me, including one from a young man who chose to make psychiatry his career on hearing me speak at the Cheltenham Science Festival, and one from a retired psychiatrist in Canada who told me he reads the last exchange between Thomas, the English doctor, and his former patient, Daisy, every night before he goes to bed, to reassure himself that his life in medicine has not been in vain.

Before the book came out, I sent a proof to Mary, who had done so much to enlighten me. She wrote back, 'I had to put the book down, because there were times I couldn't tell where he [Olivier, the schizophrenic character] ended and I began. To be honest, I envy him that he's out of it.' I fear that in the end she took the same way out herself. Poor Mary. And Ben. And Matthew. And Billy.

The outcome of most endeavours is probably best described as qualified failure. My 'qualification' to the failure of this project, *Human Traces*, was that after nearly five years in the back wards of the mind, I felt that I had at least come up with an answer to the question that had first intrigued me as a child: 'Is it real, or is it all in the mind?' The answer was: It's real — as real as anything on earth. And it's all in the body.

6.

Truth to Tell

In my mid-twenties, I was still failing to write a worthwhile novel. I was also not certain I was much good as a teacher. We were a young staff at the International School of London (as the Dwight Franklin had renamed itself) and to a large extent were making it up as we went along. This was fun, and I had befriended many staff and pupils. But I felt reluctant to commit to the expansion that the school had undertaken, pioneering the International Baccalaureate and later moving to bigger premises in west London (where it still flourishes).

It occurred to me that I might try journalism. I had graduated from the cupboard in David's Bristol hallway to my own room in a garage near Paddington station. This draughty space took up half the ground floor of a small mews house. Edward, my brother, had the top floor with its bedroom and bathroom and there was a sitting room on the first, with bits of cast-off furniture and sagging bookshelves installed by an odd-job man. It was a good base.

At the old civil service desk I'd picked up for a fiver, I wrote to every magazine and newspaper I could find on the shelves of the corner shop. Editors, literary editors, features editors . . . Few remained un-pestered. I had never actually met a journalist, but a teacher friend remembered he had once played trumpet in a jazz band with Miles Kington, who worked for *Punch*. So I wrote to Miles and we met for a drink in Fleet Street. He was friendly, but had nothing to offer.

Most of my begging letters went unanswered. I tried unsuccessfully to get on to a *Daily Mirror* training scheme in Plymouth. I was granted ten minutes in the offices of *The Economist*, but again nothing materialised. A letter I had written to the *Sunday Times*, about a Christopher Ricks book review, led to a reply from the literary and arts editor, J. W. Lambert, and I first limped into print on his pages with a short notice of a collection of essays by Kenneth Tynan. This was followed a few months later by one of a baffling book by Roland Barthes (*The Pleasure of the Text*). To my dismay, Jack Lambert then retired. His successor, John Whitley, wrote me a flattering letter about a review I did for him (of Virginia Woolf's letters), but seemed to have little else to offer: too many reviewers under contract, I gathered.

So I resumed the letter barrage. To do something for the dire sales of 'literary fiction', the Arts Council had instructed a body called the National Book League to start a book club — the New Fiction Society — through which you could buy a monthly choice of new hardback novels at a discount. It had a quarterly magazine, whose editor, David Hughes, was on the receiving end of one of my letters. It was fifty years on from an interesting year in publishing history, 1928, and David commissioned me to write a 'review of the year', which included *The Well of Loneliness* and *Orlando*. I couldn't resist what I thought were some neat 1928 touches in the prose and David seemed to like it. At some point soon afterwards, he and I met for a drink and rather fell for one another. David was a man for whom the word 'raffish' might have been invented. Kind, talented and immensely humorous, he had been married to the film actor and director Mai Zetterling and was an old-fashioned man of letters, living off a mixture of fiction, journalism and charm.

My letter-writing had meanwhile also taken in *Encounter* (no reply), the *New Statesman* (no reply), the *Times Literary Supplement* (discouragement) and the *Spectator*, where the young literary editor, Peter Ackroyd, invited me to the office and, later, to his flat in Chelsea, where I met his dancer boyfriend. I arrived on a Honda 125 (a true 'wanker's bike', I'd been assured by my friend David Tucker), wearing an army surplus jacket I'd borrowed from someone, with a newspaper stuffed up inside to keep the wind out. I'd no idea what to expect or why I was there. I told Peter I was shortly going to New York and he recommended I look up his friend John Ashbery, the poet, whose recent collection *Self-Portrait in a Convex*

Mirror had made him famous beyond the dreams of the avant-garde. 'I think you'd really get on,' said Peter, with a twinkle.

At any rate, Peter gave me some work to do for the *Spectator* before annoyingly doing a Jack Lambert and retiring from the literary editor's chair. But if I cobbled together everything I'd now written, including a few things for the *Telegraph* weekend magazine, it was beginning to look like a portfolio – or a scrapbook, anyway. With this tucked beneath my arm, I managed to get through the door of 135 Fleet Street, the monumental art deco offices of the *Daily Telegraph*, where I had a conversation with the managing editor. The paper was printed in the basement by unionised labour, he explained, which understood its power to stop the presses. The journalists were paid less than the printers, but had their own closed shop, the National Union of Journalists, of which I was not a member; neither could I become one unless I was on the staff. Check.

However, the fact that my grandfather's name (P. H. Lawless) was on a memorial tablet in the *Telegraph* reception area counted for something. He had been a sports journalist, but volunteered when the paper was short-staffed to go as a war reporter with American troops in 1945. He was killed by German shrapnel as they crossed the Rhine. It was this family connection, I am almost certain, that got me into the office of Bill Deedes, the editor, and which led eventually to the offer of some shifts as summer holiday cover on the paper's diary column, 'London Day By Day', better known by its sign-off as 'Peterborough'.

But first I had to be vetted by the column's editor, Michael Hogg, a red-faced man in his fifties with a fruity voice, said to be an opera lover, who took me to the famous El Vino wine bar. As more of a Stevie Wonder man, I steered off opera and asked him instead what a typical day was like. 'We get in about ten, and read the papers,' he said. 'About twelve I tend to go to the Cheshire Cheese for a drink, come back, see if there are any messages, then go off to lunch. We reconvene after three, make a few phone calls, then round about five try to put some sort of column together. Other days, we just drink.'

I found this reassuring. There was a tailor next door to the *Telegraph* called Dombey & Son, where I spent my first week's wages on a grey double-breasted suit that I hoped would make me look like a reporter. I arrived at 9.59 on the appointed day to an empty office. The first man in, a few minutes later, was John Coldstream, a tall, thoughtful character of about thirty with large glasses and a polite but friendly manner. He was also the paper's first-ever pop and rock music reviewer, which meant he was viewed with suspicion by the gerontocracy. Naturally, we hit it off at once. There were three further reporters on the column, which only contained about ten short items each day, so the workload was not heavy. In fact, it was used in part as a nursery for young potential; and the paper, selling 1.25 million copies a day, with a huge revenue from classified advertising, could afford it.

Michael Hogg offered me a few press releases to look at and I made some calls; there were quite a few launches and events whose organisers invited us along in the hope of a friendly paragraph. Specialists on the paper also fed in 'amusing' bits and pieces they couldn't use on the news pages. It was a mild-mannered column which preferred a regimental reunion to any mention of 'celebrities'. I was encouraged to cultivate literary connections and take people out to lunch. At the end of my first week, I entered an expenses claim for £17.50, but Michael told me that £80 was what I should be aiming at, so would I be good enough to try again.

Quite early on, I made a factual mistake — a wrong spelling, wrong date or something that I could and should have checked. The paper hated carrying corrections and it was made clear to me that any future slips would bring my career to an early end. Then I made another mistake, by referring to a vicar in the second mention as 'The Rev Smith' rather than 'Mr Smith'. Luckily, Michael caught this one in time, though not before he had called it an 'unforgivable solecism'. The people whose absences I'd been covering returned from holiday and I feared that I would soon be back to the letter-writing; but just in time I was offered a few weeks' holiday cover in the features department.

The *Telegraph*, by common consent, had the best news and sports pages in Fleet Street, but it had never much cared about features — analysis, interviews or background articles that might involve a degree of style as well as substance. The paper's preference was for news. It had made its name on hard facts, in short words.

My new job was to 'mark up copy'. This meant taking typewritten articles from outside contributors — the motoring column, say, or 'Country Diary' — underlining the capital letters, putting a square bracket at the start of each new paragraph, writing 'mf' (more follows) at the bottom of a page and 'ends' when it was (obviously) finished. I didn't point out that this could have been done by a literate ten-year-old. The triumphantly marked-up bits of paper were despatched in small cylinders through a suction system, one copy to the print room downstairs and one to the paper's second plant in Manchester. I imagined our verdict on the new Vauxhall Viva being sucked all the way to Salford.

After a bit, I tried to join up a few of the staccato sentences, introduce the odd semicolon and give the art critic — him at least — a touch of elegance. The features editor put a hand on my shoulder and said, 'We generally just let him run.'

When the articles had been typeset, they would be returned to us from the print room on long, wet galley proofs. Once dry, these had to be corrected. The management, held to ransom one night by printers threatening to stop the presses, had agreed that the compositors could be paid *pro rata* to correct mistakes in their own typesetting. It was about this time that I read *Towards the End of the Morning* by Michael Frayn, a novel that so brilliantly described the world in which I found myself that, for the first and only time in my life, I fell out of bed laughing — on to the garage floor.

There was a problem, however. After a week in Features, I developed an allergic reaction to something. Every side of my fingers, every part of my hands, wrists and forearms was covered in pullulating, weeping, itching blisters. The soles of my feet had come out in sympathy, so I could barely walk. It seemed that my career as a journalist had come to an end before it had started, for the simple reason that I was allergic to ink.

I found a dermatologist who gave me some powerful steroid tablets and a corticosteroid ointment whose deep penetration could be assured only if I went to bed with my hands and feet wrapped in clingfilm. The treatments made me look less like a leper, but I was not allowed to use them for long, for fear of side effects.

Salvation came in the offer of more shifts on the 'Peterborough' column, where I didn't have to touch the wet proofs. I was sitting at my large office typewriter one day, knocking out a paragraph about a (possibly 'poignant') 175th anniversary of a minor livery company, when what I had all along been dreading suddenly materialised.

Looming over my desk was the head of the National Union of Journalists, *Telegraph* branch. His name, spoken always in awed tones, was Norman Hare; his title was Father of the Chapel. And his power was without measure.

'I seem to have seen your face around the place an awful lot, young man,' he said.

'Yes, I've been standing in for various people on holiday.'

I knew that a strike had been started on the paper for no less a reason than a journalist changing the bulb in his own desk lamp — a job that could be done only by a member of the bulb-changers' trade union, NATSOPA.

'And tell me. Are you a member of the National Union of Journalists?'

'No, sir.'

Yet here I was, churning out copy for the next day's edition. How many days would be lost in the strike I was about to cause? Whom could I blame?

Norman Hare shifted on his feet. 'And would you *like* to be a member of the NUJ?'

'God, yes. I certainly would.'

'Well, you'd better come and see me in my office this afternoon.'

I had not considered all the ramifications of a closed shop. It must, of course, work both ways. Something had convinced the NUJ that I was not going to go away, so it was better to have me inside the tent, looking out. Shortly afterwards, I was offered a permanent job on the column at £7,500 a year, which was twice what I had earned as a teacher. And with the protection of the union, it could be a job for life. Meanwhile, David Hughes, who was off on his travels, had offered me his position running the New Fiction Society; and after a number of interviews with Martyn Goff at the National Book League in its mighty Mayfair offices in Albemarle Street, I was offered that, too. By motorbiking back and forth between Fleet Street and the NFS offices in Covent Garden, I reckoned the double life was feasible. I managed to find out (probably from the indiscreet Martyn Goff himself) that Iris Murdoch was going to win the Booker Prize that year for *The Sea, The Sea*. I was amazed by this, as the book seemed shapeless and unedited, but perhaps they felt bad about having overlooked the superior *Black Prince* in its time. Anyway, Michael Hogg ran the prediction as the lead story and when it turned out to be true, he was happy for me to carry on doing both jobs.

Most of the time, I felt like an imposter. I had had no proper training and had little interest in most of the things I was meant to write about. Doggett's Coat and Badge (a sort of chivalric Thames boat race) or the American Chamber of Commerce lunch meant nothing to me. But I knew it was a time I needed to get through, a job to cling on to. When I'd read the papers at home in the morning, I'd put on 'Kid Charlemagne' by Steely Dan ('Is there gas in the car? Yes, there's gas in the car . . . ') and squeeze the last from each guitar note before jumping on my new

Yamaha 650 twin and roaring off to Fleet Street to resume my impersonation of a reporter.

As nurseries go, 'Peterborough' was fertile. Michael was a benign boss and at its best it was an easy-going job. We finished at six o'clock each day, when John Coldstream left the playpen to go off and review Siouxsie and the Banshees while I biked home with time and energy left over to crank up the stereo before venturing out into the night.

Facts were sacred in the *Telegraph* of those days. The paper was respected and famous for the huge extent of its foreign coverage, for its sport and City pages and for the detailed home news reporting, particularly of court cases. Features and comment were few and cranky, but that didn't matter. What the paper was offering was the latest news, factually checked. The division between comment and news was absolute; in fact, we believed it to be the definition of a serious newspaper.

In December 1982, I applied to edit 'Mandrake', the diary column on the *Sunday Telegraph*, bundling up my scrapbook of cuttings and leaving it on the desk of the paper's editor, John Thompson. Another rebuttal followed, but with it a lifeline . . . Something in what I'd written had caught his eye. As a consolation, would I like to join the Sunday paper's feature-writing staff? John, a quietly spoken Yorkshireman, hadn't quite finished outlining the conditions, let alone the salary, before I'd accepted.

The feature-writing department lived in a building a few doors down from the main office. It had started life as an attempt to rival the famous *Sunday Times* 'Insight' team and had been called 'Probe' or 'Focus' or some such thing. My new colleagues included Oliver Pritchett, a great raconteur and a stylish writer, and Peter Taylor, who could smoke a packet of Bensons and chew through three pen tops before taking the cover off his typewriter — to good effect, though, when he finally got down to it. You needed to write only one piece a week, so there was no excuse for getting any of it wrong.

The man in charge of us was Desmond Albrow, a Yorkshireman like John Thompson, also in his sixties — florid, large and altogether delightful. We gathered in his office in the main building on a Tuesday morning while he smoked a Senior Service with a cup of coffee brought by his secretary. 'Stand easy, men,' he would say in Captain Mainwaring tones, before telling us what tasks he was assigning us. We were also meant to think up things of our own to write about, but I was hopeless at this. What I liked best was to be given a really boring task by Desmond, then set about making it interesting. 'It's the 165th anniversary of the Ordnance Survey . . .' 'There's a new junior minister at Work and Pensions . . .'

An ideal week would see me leave London on a Tuesday and return on Friday evening, timing my journey back to coincide with dinner in the restaurant car of the British Rail train with its surprisingly good Malmaison house wine. Before leaving London I'd read all the cuttings in the *Telegraph* archive, but on the train I usually read a relevant book from the nearby public library in Shoe Lane. Books gave a better historical perspective than newspaper reports and even the drabbest had at least one useful anecdote. We were left to find our own accommodation; and since the N U J decreed we must travel everywhere first class, I tried to save the paper money with some B and B's. I didn't like hotels anyway; I just wanted a quiet room with a telephone and a yielding pillow.

Often a feature writer will follow up a news story, not necessarily from his own paper, and one of the things I discovered was how inaccurate most of these original articles were. According to a broadsheet national paper, there was a row in a famous city over a new bypass that would run through the cathedral close and destroy the sacred water meadow: the bishop, they said, was up in arms. But when you got there, you discovered it was a car park, not a bypass, and that the bishop was all in favour. This endemic inaccuracy didn't reflect well on the profession. On the other hand, it made my life easy, because all I had to do was explain what was actually the situation, which was invariably more interesting than the initial report had claimed.

One of the causes of the inaccuracies was a tradition — which flourished in all English newspapers — of what you might call 'reduction to stereotype'. News editors have to think fast and act decisively. Nuance is not their friend.

They prefer to have stories boxed up into a familiar compartment before the reporter is despatched — particularly if they feel that the familiarity will appeal to their readers' prejudices. Anything to do with an island is therefore 'trouble in paradise'; a quarrel at Oxford or Cambridge is 'red-faced dons choking on their port'. The reporter leaves with received ideas buzzing in his ears.

When I went off to interview some struggling politician, Oliver Pritchett would wish me good luck with the words, 'Remember, Seb, it's a back-me-or-sack-me plea.' There seemed almost nothing that couldn't be reduced to 'corridors of power' or 'two cultures'. But while this way of thinking was absurd, it offered a useful starting point. The Conservative Party in Cheltenham has selected a black candidate. Retired colonels exploding in their gin and tonics! But when you got to Cheltenham, you found it wasn't like that at all. The candidate, while technically 'black', was no Marvin Gaye or James Baldwin; he was a real petit-bourgeois hardliner, whose skin tone was irrelevant. Cheltenham was not that Conservative anyway; it was a curious place, dominated by spies, both active (at GCHQ) and retired, and was inclined to the Liberal Democrats. And in any case the town had happily voted for an out gay MP for years, so who could care where the new candidate's parents came from? By the time you'd overturned or corrected the received ideas, half the article had written itself.

*

The paper itself looked a mess. It was typeset on Victorian hot metal presses and when a new part was needed the management had to go to a museum to find it. The pictures were blurred; the ink was often either smeared or sucked in by the absorbent newsprint. More modern technology had been available for years, but would have resulted in job losses and had been successfully fought off by the print unions.

Our deadline on the Sunday paper was generally teatime on Friday, and this meant finding a phone box and asking for the 'copy takers', to whom you would, on a reverse-charge call, dictate your thousand or so words. Often they made you spell out the names of even well-known people and I suppose this was another layer of fact-checking. I think it was enjoyable for them to be first with the story and, from the comfort of their office, to picture you in your draughty coin box on a street corner in Liverpool. Perhaps they also knew their days were numbered, since there was already a little electronic keyboard made by Tandy which could be plugged into a phone socket and would transmit what you'd typed down the line.

Some of the print-room practices were criminal. People were being paid to do shifts for which they were not present; thousands of copies of the paper were carried off in unmarked vans and sold on to wholesalers or shops under the counter. Journalists were not beyond reproach. Expenses were often fiddled or inflated. If there had been four journalists at dinner somewhere, each paid his share but took a copy of the bill to claim the full amount.

But still the papers made money, plenty of it. The reckoning with reality seemed infinitely postponable and the cashiers in the hall continued to reimburse your expenses with enormous wads of cash. If you went abroad, you could take hundreds of pounds in advances and were never chased on your return to fill in the relevant paperwork. I may still owe the *Telegraph* some yellow forms, if not some actual money, from a trip to the US in 1984 to cover the elections.

Of course you're often lonely being a reporter. You have crises of confidence, thinking, How the hell should I know what 'really' happened? Truth is complex and elusive; I've only got two days — and the person who apparently knows all about it won't return my calls. This was particularly true of foreign assignments. Everyone was envious of your luck as you set off for Heathrow, almost as if you had a bucket and spade in your case; but time differences, transfers, hotel registration and so on all brought the deadline rapidly closer. There were no cocktails on the beach; there were only hours sitting on the bed with a phone against your ear, hoping your French would hold up; then desperate taxi dashes to a face-to-face meeting in a place that might give you some 'colour'; and finally a late and solitary dinner, wondering if your half-full notebook would be enough. This was all long before the Internet, so there was no Wiki-source of (fairly) accurate information; often there was not even a radio or a television. You had to ask everyone to spell and re-spell every name they mentioned and hope you would have time to double-check in reference books back in the office.

In 1984, Desmond sent me to his home town, Bradford, following a cry for help from a local headteacher who feared that Muslim children were drifting away from the mainstream. Having lived in London for several years, I was used to streets and shops of many nationalities. Bradford, however, was hardly varied at all. A culture and a people had been lifted wholesale from their roots and dropped entire into another world. The expression on their faces suggested they were not much taken by rain and redbrick, by disused mills with no fields to farm; they shrank from local women with bare legs and drunken youths reeling out of Yates's wine lodges. The previous inhabitants meanwhile looked shell-shocked as they gazed at a new landscape.

You could hardly imagine a more abject failure of politics. When the government had asked for help from the West Indies in the 1950s there were jobs for many of the newcomers – on public transport and in hospitals, doing work that the existing UK citizens had, for whatever reason, decided was not for them; but for the farmers of Kashmir and Bangladesh, transplanted to Yorkshire, there was nothing. The closing of heavy industry had laid waste towns like Bradford that had once been prosperous. Who could have thought it was a good idea to invite tens of thousands of rural people to live in an urban wasteland?

There had been no proper discussion of the realities of large-scale migration. The Right, having met its historic obligations to former colonies, was unwilling to reflect on the human or cultural aspects. The Left was more ready to do so, but was quickly spooked by the R-word, which sterilised debate. People could talk only for a few minutes before the word 'racist' was first used, like a trump smacked down on a card table. No one wants to push on with a debate in these circumstances. Why suggest that a more managed flow might have made the incomers happier if that is going to get you compared to a police officer in apartheid South Africa?

Yet you only had to walk around for a day or so to see how politics had made everyone miserable. The Socialist Workers Party had moved in to exploit the woe of the exiled and the British National Party to stir up the anger of those who felt displaced. The multitudes who had arrived from far away found it easier to stick together. What was the point of learning English when there would be no job at the end of it? Why mingle with the old inhabitants when much of what they did was offensive to your beliefs?

Writing about Muslim Bradford made me see how much I disliked the polarities of British politics. Which is not to say I wasn't interested. Quite a lot of my job involved interviewing MPs, and there was then still a debate between the last of the old Left and the beginnings of a new Right. The latter believed that the free market was an economic miracle rather than a wild bull that needed careful watching. On the other side, the faith of former Communists that the State could decide what was best for its citizens, while diluted by the needs of the Labour Party to win elections, still exerted philosophical force. Politics being a broad-brush business, it was not an intellectually subtle argument, but it could be a lively one. On a BBC *Question Time* with Denis Healey, Michael Heseltine, Neil Kinnock, Shirley Williams or Ken Clarke, you could still see interesting differences debated.

The *Sunday Telegraph* was a Conservative paper in its columns and editorial sections, but John Thompson never seemed to mind when one of us wrote teasing accounts of interviews with Mrs Thatcher's ministers. No criticism or joke was ever toned down and I presumed they just thought a bit of dissidence helped vary the tone. I loved this job, mooching round alone in strange places in my reporter's mac, writing thousand-word articles that needled away at received ideas. Then back to El Vino at Saturday lunchtime with Oliver and Peter to compare notes on the week. What could be more fun?

But just when we had convinced ourselves that the party could last for ever, the lights went out. Rupert Murdoch moved the printing of *The Times* and *Sunday Times* to a new site in the London docks, using modern technology without the old print unions. It was an extraordinary coup and had involved the 'setting up' of a completely imaginary new evening title. So detailed was the subterfuge that even those who were busy hiring staff for the new venture had no idea that it was a mere front, a Potemkin paper. The *Telegraph* papers had meanwhile been bled by union malpractice not quite to death, but to intensive care, where they were bought by a Canadian called Conrad Black. He was said to be an expert on Napoleon – an obvious danger signal.

The happy days of the Thompson–Albrow command were no more. An excited new assistant editor stood over my typewriter and urged me to insert more clichés. 'Call it "Violence: the canker at the heart of our society"!' he told me. No, thanks. I had a talk with the new editor, Peregrine Worsthorne, who offered me the job of European editor, which was nice of him, though neither of us was sure quite what it would entail. Then I heard about a new paper, the *Independent*, that was being started by three *Telegraph* journalists who were looking for finance in the City. This was in the spring of 1986 and there was a mood of optimism abroad. Old restrictive practices were being replaced; 'deregulation' was the new word. The childishly named 'Big Bang' was about to hit the City, opening the door to American investment banks and their practices of short selling, leverage and synthetic bonds that would eventually bring the country, and the world, to its knees in the Financial Crisis twenty years later. We didn't understand that then, in 1986. I didn't even know what 'shorting' was. All we knew was that instead of waiting three weeks for your telephone to be fixed, you could get a line tomorrow; after all these years, we were turning into a 'can-do' kind of place. And for people who had lived through blackouts and the three-day week, there was a lot to like about these developments.

But there had been no new daily newspaper in England since the 1920s, so it still seemed a tall order. And anyway no one had heard of these three guys, apart from Andreas Whittam Smith, the City editor – vaguely. The Chernobyl nuclear reactor was melting down as I took a taxi to City Road to meet the people in question. Andreas, the editor designate, had an episcopal but reassuring presence; Stephen Glover, who was to edit the foreign pages, seemed gravely plausible; while the third *amigo*, Matthew Symonds, had a punchy self-belief that I thought could come in handy. I told them I might be able to do a job as the new paper's literary editor. Andreas asked me to rough out some dummy pages and write a plan for how we might not only rival, but surpass the opposition.

I did as I was asked and my job duly changed from being a travelling guy with a notebook, timing my dash for dinner on the train, to being a computer operative at a desk all day. It took some getting used to. As a deputy I had signed up Robert Winder, a young reporter on

Euromoney magazine whom I'd met playing cricket in Colombo. Robert was ironic, clever and well-read; he was also good with computers, even operating the layout machine — a demarcation-breaker that would have halted production for weeks at the *Telegraph*.

Then, shortly before the launch, I had a call from a friend downstairs in the foreign room. 'Listen, this glamorous girl has turned up looking for a job, but we're fully staffed. She's a friend of Ollie Pritchett. You should really meet her.' A few minutes later, a tall, dark-haired young woman of twenty-two came into the office. She was modest about her abilities, but she could type at a hundred miles an hour, speak Italian, had a gracious manner and a sympathetic contralto voice. She'd only just left university, but had temped at Condé Nast magazines in her vacations and knew how print journalism worked. Her shy and obliging demeanour couldn't conceal a humorous and idiosyncratic streak, which was something I thought she'd need on a daily newspaper. Her name was Veronica Youlten and we offered her a job as secretary/assistant. Robert and I didn't know that she would also turn out to be the fiercest subeditor imaginable.

The paper had signed a lot of well-known journalists, some of whom lived up to their reputations, though the speed of the hiring process had swept in a fair number of shits and charlatans as well. There was one who seemed to control production and made it difficult to get anything done. He had a superb mid-argument tactic of saying 'as we agreed', referring to a conversation that had never taken place. Another department head was universally avoided as he floated round like a small toxic cloud, issuing invitations to dodgy weekends near Ipswich.

Next door to our small office was the Arts department, which was run by Tom Sutcliffe, who had come from the BBC and never worked in print before. Tom could hardly have been less like my old Fleet Street colleagues. Not for him a table in El Vino to laugh over the gin at his own shortcomings: he was all function and dressed not in a grey suit with ash on the lapels but in chinos and polo shirts. I wished that I had had the confidence to do the same, but felt I might not be taken seriously without a suit (the Dombey & Son prototype having given way by now to a couple of nattier outfits from Paris). I managed to lure Tom only once into the local pub, where he asked for a 'St Clements'. I hadn't the faintest idea what this was (orange juice and lemonade, it transpired). What mattered was that we were both committed to making the paper work and admired the same journalists, many of whom Tom had persuaded to write for his pages.

On the foreign pages, Stephen Glover had hired the poet and former *Guardian* reporter James Fenton, though he had sent him to the Philippines, where nothing seemed to happen. Journalists tend to over-rate the pull of well-known (to them) names on the public, who, in surveys, repeatedly fail to notice who has written anything at all. But the foreign pages as a whole made the *Independent* look as good as, or better than, its established rivals. The bold use of photographs helped the paper set itself apart, and readers were willing to overlook the growing pains of the less successful parts. Andreas was alert to the public mood and could be decisive; within a few months it became clear that, against considerable odds, the *Independent* was going to work.

The contribution of the books pages was minor, though we liked to think it helped set the tone. One of our rivals, *The Times*, had almost given up covering books, so we could easily set ourselves up as *the* literary paper by carrying a review every day as well as a full weekly page, which soon became a double-page spread as the ads poured in. Robert enlisted Godfrey Hodgson, a former *Sunday Times* 'Insight' reporter and *Observer* man in Washington, as a hard-working ally. We decided to review novels on their own, rather than in the degrading down-page 'round-ups' that were the norm elsewhere. On our first-ever page, the lead review was of John Updike by A. S. Byatt; and odd though it sounds now, no one could remember having seen a novel as the lead review in an English paper before. Byatt required daily encouragement on the phone as she worked through *Roger's Version*. 'Ah, Sebastian, it's Antonia. I've been thinking all afternoon about John Updike's penis.' 'Really?' As time went by, we were able also to publish regular reviews by Claire Tomalin, Anthony Burgess, Jan Morris and the Oxford historian Eric Christiansen, a robust writer who was said to have been the model for the main character in Iris Murdoch's novel *A Word Child*, a book I'd much enjoyed a few years before.

We tried to mix famous names with new kids. That seemed to me the *Independent* way — what the designer Paul Smith, as Tom Sutcliffe reminded us, had called 'classic with a twist'. One of the well-known names I'd hired was Auberon Waugh, who wrote a weekly book review column. He was sharp and often funny, though with too much right-wing baggage for some. To me, 'independent' meant free from interference, cross-party and eclectic; so Bron Waugh's column might appear two days after a double-page spread on gay writing, with all gay reviewers, the first-ever such thing in an English newspaper. But to the old Left, 'independent' just meant 'Left', and it didn't matter how many minority specials you'd run on a Thursday, they still wanted no Tory anarchist on a Saturday.

The removal of *The Times* to Wapping had not pleased everyone. Many journalists disliked the politics of their proprietor and felt the paper had suffered in the move. On a whim, I rang Miles Kington, who had left *Punch*, where we'd met ten years before, to become the resident humorist on *The Times*. I asked him if he fancied joining the *Independent* instead (if he couldn't find me a job, maybe I could offer him one). He came over for lunch, met Andreas and signed up. Miles's column was so popular that, even after he'd died at a horribly young age, the *Independent* continued to run it, drawing on his efforts stored up from years gone by.

All was well, it seemed. The *Independent* was fashionable, and it made money; we stood for accurate reporting and freedom from proprietorial interference. Our book pages had discovered some talented young writers, most notably Anthony Lane, who, still in his early twenties, combined erudition, wit and an easy journalistic style. I could, if necessary, leave Robert and Veronica to run the office while I got out of town to write some features. The paper was drastically short in this department, so the move was welcomed all round and even secured me the use of a little car no longer needed by a salesman in Classified Ads. In the early summer of 1987 I did a run of knockabout pieces on the General Election, whose popularity was two-edged, as it meant I came under pressure to stop being literary editor. I was asked to go to Washington to replace Alexander Chancellor, who had come back to edit the new Saturday magazine.

It was a tempting offer that came at just the wrong time in my growing relationship with Veronica; still, in retrospect, I really should have taken it, rather than the next job I was offered, as Stephen Glover's deputy on a new venture, the *Independent on Sunday*. The first thing we did was to sign up Ian Jack, a lifelong newspaperman who was on a lengthy sabbatical to write a book, but clearly felt the pull of journalism while his complicated literary work (it was about Empire and India and trains and engineering) eluded him. Ian and I bonded over a love of cricket, though I wasn't sure at first if he, as a Scotsman, was teasing me. He wasn't. We worked furiously in the cause, the pair of us arriving in City Road at hours unknown to our colleagues, roughing out page after dummy page. Ian had worked under Harry Evans at the *Sunday Times* in the days of time and money and staff to spare; he was as adept at editing as he was at writing. The only thing on which we differed was when we'd commissioned a long piece from a well-known writer, at some inflated fee, and it came in barely literate. Ian would relish the mechanical challenge of taking the piece apart, sitting down with the contributor and giving him what he called 'a writing kit'. I didn't have that patience, and found the bogus reputation and huge cheque infuriating. Stephen Glover was meant to join us for these meetings at eight-thirty − in fact they had been his idea − but he never managed to make it in before ten, when he would arrive complaining about the traffic.

I approached Robert Harris, the outstanding performer at the time, to leave the *Sunday Times* and become our political columnist. Robert was interested, but Stephen wasn't and asked me to 'stop going on about this man Harris'. He gave the column instead to Alexander Chancellor, a much-loved colleague with little interest in Westminster. Ian Jack and I thought it was important to have women not only in the reporters' room but at the top of the paper, too, and I set off to identify and hire such people. Stephen made it clear, at the time and in a book he wrote shortly afterwards, that he found this project absurd, asking only if the latest candidate was pretty, or if she had been at Oxford. I did get one well-qualified female journalist into his office for a chat, but it didn't go well.

The first dummy was duly produced under live conditions and despatched to advertisers and industry commentators. The 'Review' looked impressive and included contributions from Michael Frayn and Alan Bennett, with a book section under Blake Morrison, who had been a judge with me on the Booker Prize in 1988. The news section, however, was drab-looking and struggled from a lack of good columnists.

Stephen Glover was a Conservative of an old-fashioned, rather melancholy kind and had no interest in popular culture. His Tuesday-morning meetings would consist of many staff journalists offering thoughts, names and suggestions and Stephen sitting with steepled fingers, solemnly shaking his head, 'No . . . I don't think so . . . No . . . I think not . . . No.' His manner was grave and sorrowful. At one point he told me he thought some of the staff viewed us as aloof and, to put this right, suggested that I take them all to lunch in groups of half a dozen. He did not himself attend these lunches.

Stephen and I had a friendly relationship on a personal level, but from a professional point of view it was a washout. So why did I not resign? First, because I don't like to quit on things I have put a big effort into. And, second, because I had admired Stephen's foreign pages on the daily paper and continued to hope that some spark would energise him. We had a game of tennis one Sunday and I thought this could provide a breakthrough, but apparently I hit the ball too hard. Stephen was (perhaps, though I was never sure) grateful for what I had done to help launch the paper and was therefore reluctant to fire me — as he, in his turn, really ought to have done. So we found a solution whereby I was replaced as his deputy and went off to write features. This was an amicable gesture on his part — and a benefit to the paper, too, as I was able to contribute more by interviewing a recently freed member of the Birmingham Six than by watching the life drain out of the staff at an editorial meeting.

The harder everyone worked, however, the more it felt like swimming against an unforgiving tide. An economic recession didn't help, and after less than two years it became clear that the paper was not going to survive. Andreas decided to clear out all the senior staff and absorb the Sunday into the daily. This is a move periodically undertaken by British newspapers in the name of economy, though once the personnel have been changed and some hefty salaries disposed of, the two papers usually de-merge.

So my time in journalism ended: from junior holiday cover to redundant associate editor in the space of thirteen years. For myself, I felt I'd had a lucky and largely enjoyable ride, but I was uneasy about the young journalists we'd hired whose livelihoods were now under threat. I arrived home with a redundancy cheque in my back pocket and decided to give myself a year of writing fiction before looking for another job.

So far, I have not had to return to work, though I still have anxiety dreams about it. Sometimes I'm back at the 'Peterborough' column, now run by people younger than my children, where it's noted that I haven't produced a 'story' since 1982 . . . Or I return to the *Independent* books page to discover that Robert hasn't commissioned anything for next weekend and I run around the office frantically looking for a phone on which to call Anthony Burgess.

It was customary in London to mock American papers and their relentless 'fact-checkers'; and on the handful of occasions I wrote for US publications these people could certainly be annoying. It almost got to the stage of having to provide corroboration for the fact that 'President Clinton' was indeed the President. 'What authorities can you provide for giving him this title?' they almost asked. However, the principle of being scrupulous was one from which British papers could have learned. My problem with writing for US publications was not the need to be accurate but the homogenising effect of an editorial process that tended to make all contributors sound the same. So after you had sent in a final version of your 4,000-word piece you might receive a call from a twenty-two-year-old intern telling you it was a 'good first draft'. Oh, piss off, one managed not to say. I once wrote a piece for *Vanity Fair* in which I didn't recognise a single sentence of my own until the second page. The *New Yorker* gave more latitude, though they required me to send the original tapes of an interview I had done in French with Françoise Sagan in Paris. These were airmailed to an interpreter, who noted that I had sanitised some of my subject's saltier comments, though I'm happy to say that in the end they went with my bowdlerised version.

Almost anyone who has had dealings with the press in this country expresses surprise at what emerges in print. The *Mail on Sunday* once rang me to ask my view of the Amstrad word processor, which was enjoying a retro moment. I told them it had been OK while we waited for Apple to get its act together, but I had ditched it as soon as I could and much preferred my new machine. This was not the story that they wanted to hear, however, so it was not the story they printed. 'It's a marvellous old friend,' said novelist Faulks, forty-three. 'I wouldn't change it for the world.' The reporter had been told what his 'story' was to be before he made a phone call.

When we were living in France in 1996 a reporter came to interview me for a magazine about my new book, *The Fatal Englishman*. He had been sent a copy two weeks earlier and had taken the leisurely route down by train. I picked him up from Cahors station and drove him home, where Veronica had prepared a large dinner and put flowers in his room. When we sat down to do the interview the next morning he began by saying, 'I haven't read the book.' I pretended not to mind. When the piece appeared a few weeks later it was snide in tone and contained some simple factual errors (wrong college and so on). Some friends sympathised with me, though I said he was free to be as rude as he liked (God knows I'd been scathing enough myself about various people in the past). But before you let fly, you have to be accurate and you have to read the book. A few years later I happened to sit next to my interviewer at a dinner and he told me the piece had given him the 'biggest moral dilemma of my career'. Had Veronica been less gracious, he explained, he would have said what he *really* thought. This gave me a dilemma, too, though less a moral than a practical one: whether to upend the soup over his head or pour it straight into his lap.

At the Cheltenham Literature Festival in 2021 I was asked about male novelists depicting women characters. It's a vexed issue, so I kept it very simple. I said that as a one-off experiment in *Snow Country* I had not described the physical appearance of the main female character, Lena, through a man's eyes, but only through her own or that of female friends. 'And you know what?' I said. 'It made no difference at all.' In the morning I was woken by a fusillade of anxious text messages. Two papers, one broadsheet and one tabloid, were reporting, 'Male writer says he will never describe a woman again.' Suddenly I was being discussed on the radio and television, being both vilified and praised — for something I hadn't said.

I think the tabloid got it wrong on purpose to make a

better 'story' and the broadsheet got it wrong by being under-staffed and not having time to check its facts, even though all the events were recorded and available. Tabloid editors want to flatter or inflame the prejudices of their readers, so the truth comes second. Sometimes there is a husk of fact in the article, sometimes there isn't. In the end they will run whatever 'story' they feel will please or irritate their readers most, sell more papers and make the proprietor rich. Even if you despise the ethics and the finished product, you can understand that way of thinking. Profit before truth. The ends (money) justify the means (lying). Simple stuff.

The endemic inaccuracy of some broadsheet reporting, however, was harder to explain. Some of it could be put down to rush and deadlines. I don't imagine the reporter who thought it was a bypass not a car park that was planned for the cathedral close had calculated that the former would engage his readers more; I think he had just half an hour in a phone box talking to the local stringer in the pub. He hadn't had time to ring the bishop, so just *assumed* he would be cross about the plan: not such an unreasonable guess, you might think.

Since the rise of the Internet, newspapers have lost their USP: they are no longer first with the news, accurate or not. Readers have deserted them. Online celebrity gossip can keep tabloids in business, but broadsheets need wealthy proprietors to bear their losses. The era in which the *Sunday Times* could despatch several reporters to work on the thalidomide story for as long as it took now seems like a fantasy — a booze-addled dream from El Vino. I was lucky enough to meet and work with many of the 'Insight' people, and although at the *Sunday Telegraph* we had mocked the macho self-importance of the later teams with their improbable details ('At 7.49, the Vice-President strode into the situation room, unshaven after two hours' sleep, with his college tie at half mast . . .'), they were professionally thorough reporters who kept asking questions until they could put a picture together, making the complex comprehensible and exposing the wicked. You can't do that now. It's out of the question.

When the Grenfell Tower block in west London caught fire in June 2017, I was telephoned the following day by a newspaper, asking if I would do a 'comment' piece on it, because I lived nearby. 'You don't want comment,' I said. 'You need to find out what happened. And how. And who lived there. Where they came from. And how many other blocks are vulnerable. And . . .'

The section editor on the other end of the line just laughed. 'We don't have the resources for that,' he said. Angry 'comment' was all they could afford. The vacuum at Grenfell was filled by prejudice and false accusation: some papers talked of an 'establishment cover-up', others blamed the tenants themselves. Within twenty-four hours of the fire, the Socialist Workers Party was leafleting the area, claiming that the rich had set light to the poor. Right-wing agitators countered that the inhabitants were all illegal immigrants. My local dentist had the job of identifying many bodies from their teeth. It took him a long time and he was surprised by how strong the desire in some quarters was that the death toll should be higher. 'Was seventy-two dead not bad enough?' he asked. But no one had been in touch with the man who identified and counted the bodies. Not a single reporter had rung him.

Many of these stories of my short time in journalism sound ridiculous now, as if not just from another century, but another existence. And it was in many ways an absurd world with its criminal rackets in the print room and its drunken reporters. But it did have the resources to get at the truth, sometimes, however complicated.

The *Telegraph*'s huge art deco building in Fleet Street became the headquarters of the Goldman Sachs investment bank. I was told they had taken down the memorial to all the journalists (including my grandfather) who had been killed while reporting from the battlefields of the world. All things pass and we must be stoical about that. But I doubt whether Goldman's, with a charge sheet listing billions of dollars' worth of fines for fraud and malpractice in numerous civil and criminal cases over the years, has provided a public service comparable to that of the news pages of the old *Telegraph*.

7.

Do you do much research?

Late in 1988 I began to think about writing a novel set in the First World War. I was then working at the *Independent*, where my job was to commission and edit reviews of new books. The office was in a modern block in City Road in central London and I used to gaze out of the metal-framed window over the rectangular Sixties buildings beyond and wonder if I would ever be free to live the life of a real writer — like Jan Morris, to whom I sometimes spoke in her Welsh farmhouse and who, if I asked, would describe her view of hills with sheep and running streams. Then, with a sigh, I would stare back into the ATEX computer screen and start to go through a review that had just come in.

It was seventy years since the Armistice, and publishers like nothing more than an anniversary. Books arrived by the sackful, among them the latest by Lyn Macdonald, who had written a sequence of histories based on interviews with veterans of the Great War. Most of this diminishing band of men were well into their nineties, but this had not stopped Lyn's publisher from gathering half a

dozen of them for a trip to the Western Front. A few journalists were invited to join them.

Among the veterans on the bus was a chirpy old
fellow in a blazer heavy with medals. His name was
Johnny Morris and he claimed to be one of the Old
Contemptibles − neither a volunteer like the patriotic
factory hands of 1915 nor a conscript like the pale teenagers of later years, but a regular soldier in Britain's
surprisingly small standing army of 1914. These men had
provided Britain's entire contribution to the Allied effort
until Kitchener's volunteer army ('Your Country Needs
You') was raised with such impressive speed and able
to occupy the northern ninety-odd miles of the Western Front. There was also a Yorkshire medic, long-since
retired, known as 'Doc' Wilson.

It was a merry bus that made its way to Dover and
then across to Calais on the Sealink ferry. Much of what
I'd read about that war had filled me with doubts, mostly
of an existential kind. What did it tell us about human
beings, that they could be driven to such things − to kill
ten million in a largely static battle in the mud between the
nations who believed themselves to be the world's most
civilised? Even the birds and the rats had turned their
backs on this wretched species, us.

The veterans seemed untroubled by such thoughts and
more concerned with when they were going to have tea.
Our billet was a modern hotel in Béthune, a town with
an ornate main square in the flatlands of Artois, near the

Belgian border. Béthune was a little way behind the line and had been popular with British troops on account of its many bars with white wine, *frites* and friendly women.

We were near the battlefields of Neuve Chapelle and Aubers (pronounced 'Awbers' by the English) Ridge, where in 1915 British troops had mounted their first attacks of the war. These set a pattern that became familiar: high hopes, initial success, stalemate, German counter-attack, withdrawal, heavy loss of life and negligible gains. Some of the enemy concrete defences or 'pillboxes' were still there in the fields we drove to the next morning.

It was then, in a field in the drizzle of a November day, as I chatted to the two old men on either side of me, that an odd thing happened. As I looked down at our feet in the same mud in which they'd stood that morning in 1915, their experience seemed to stop being part of 'history' and to become something present.

'So, where we're standing now,' said Doc Wilson, holding my arm as he spoke, 'that's just where I was that morning when my best friend, Malthouse, was blown up by a shell. Over by that tree there.'

'What did you do?'

'I got a sandbag and went and picked up the pieces. Not one of them was bigger than a leg of mutton. I put them in the bag and buried them. I made a cross with two pieces of wood and hung his tag on it. But they never found him.'

There was something about the physical contact, his hand on my arm. I was thirty-five years old — of an age to have been at Aubers Ridge, too, but for the timing of birth. England in France: these men, or me, in this foreign yet familiar field . . . Perhaps there was no such thing as history; perhaps there was only experience and the way we think of it.

Later that day, in the still-drizzling dusk, a small group of us were walking in the Commonwealth War Graves cemetery nearby, where the names are chiselled with hard serifs into the headstones that form lines stretching to a point on the horizon. Ten million of them. God, what did they do? What on earth *possessed* them?

Doc Wilson had stopped walking and was staring in disbelief at a grave that looked like all the others. But not to him. It bore the name, I saw as I came alongside, of Private Malthouse. So they had found him after all. Someone had dug up the sandbag and the bits inside and buried Malthouse in a proper grave — remembered, with a flowering shrub at the foot of his headstone. 'Oh, I say,' said Dr Wilson softly, reunited after seventy-three years. 'Oh, I say.'

When I got back to the office in London, I put aside some of the new books about the war to read later. I had first done some research into this period when writing a novel called *The Girl at the Lion d'Or*. Set in provincial France in 1936, it concerned a young woman who comes to work as a maid in a run-down Brittany hotel and who has undergone a trauma in childhood, from the effects of which she is still struggling to escape. The main concern was the individual's attempt, by courage or willpower, to break what could become a cycle of suffering. The action of the book, however, concerned a love affair and I wanted it to have taken place at a time when such things might have attracted more censure. A process of elimination brought me to the mid-1930s; so by simple arithmetic, the girl — Anne's — childhood must have included the First World War; and her trauma was likely to have been connected to it.

The war, however, was a box I felt unwilling and unable to open — too messy, too big; and in its mud and gas, its drab khaki, its cap badges and baffling numbers (the 15th/21st Fusiliers), just too off-putting, But I dared to lift the lid by reading Alistair Horne's book about Verdun, *The Price of Glory*. In addition to its gruesome details about the fighting, it explained a great deal about something else — something guarded, like an unresolved trauma, that I'd sensed in French villages, with their closed shutters, war memorials and uncommunicative people. At some point I had also come across the story of the French mutinies of 1917. A large part of the French army, along a line from Soissons to Verdun, had revolted. While not deserting, and still obeying their officers in other respects, they had refused any order to attack. This had led to numerous scandals, showdowns and courts martial, but the books I read were short on detail. The authority most often quoted was a doctoral thesis by a young historian called Guy Pedroncini, who in the 1960s had had access to

French military justice archives; but before the Internet, it was hard to get hold of small-press books in a foreign language. However, my old friend Caroline d'Achon, who lived near Nantes, had tracked down a copy of *Les Mutineries de 1917* to the history faculty library of the local university, and it was there I found myself, temporary reader's pass in hand, one winter afternoon. And some hours later, in a statistical appendix, I found what I wanted. 'Murder of an officer. Instances: 2.' An event of the kind I'd imagined had indeed taken place, twice; and as I gratefully smacked Monsieur Pedroncini's book shut, I felt I had looked Anne's father in the eye.

On a return from two weeks in Provence the following year, 1985, I went with my brother Edward and our friend Tim Saloman to visit the battlefield of Verdun. We saw its giant ossuary, the bones of a generation of Frenchmen, and the forts of Douaumont and Vaux in whose tunnels the slaughter had been hand-to-hand; and the memorial on the wooded summit of Le Mort Homme, a terrifying skeletal form carved in stone in which any sense of propriety − of civilisation at all − had been cast aside, above the words: '*Ils n'ont pas passé.*' They did not pass.

Awful. Too awful for words. At least, for any words I was likely to be able to find. My strange education had coughed me up fluent in Latin verse and English literature but with almost no knowledge of science or history. As one morning in 1985 I sat reading the Cambridge History of Modern France, *The Decline of the Third Republic*

1914–1938, it struck me that it might well be the first real history book I had read right through. It was lucky that its authors had done such a good job.

And then to open Alistair Horne on Verdun, a book with an irresistible narrative force . . . This history thing was pretty interesting, I discovered: perhaps too interesting. I needed to re-focus on character and theme, on the idea of a novel as a created world with its own gravity and weather. Reviews of *The Girl at the Lion d'Or* mentioned how influenced it was by French cinema of the period, but this wasn't really true. Visually, it was for the most part imagined, not borrowed; I hadn't even seen some of the films they mentioned. I had read half a dozen books, including Janet Flanner's despatches from Paris for the *New Yorker*, and one that might have been written with my needs in mind called 'Daily Life in France under the Popular Front', which I'd found in a French bookshop in South Kensington. But my real 'research' consisted of looking at buildings, staying in cheap hotels in the Cotentin peninsula, in Picardy and Normandy, places with peeling wallpaper and failed plumbing; it was a question of sitting in cafés and absorbing atmospheres, details of no obvious importance. One such moment had come in a brasserie where I'd watched a young waitress, bored, waiting for an order. She stood in her black skirt and white blouse by the cashier's desk and brushed her foot back and forth across the floorboard, as if in time to some dance music in her head.

The hotel of the title was an amalgamation of places I had stayed in, with additional rooms invented as the plot required. The house in which Hartmann, the main male character, lives was taken — outlook, furniture, paintwork, bric-a-brac and all — from life. I felt then no compunction about putting real buildings into fictional books, though I ought to have warned Hughes d'Achon that his grandfather's tumbledown manor on the Brittany coast was going to be reproduced in detail, and that the kitchen floor was going to collapse into the cellar below.

Being a journalist had taught me that if you were prepared to pick up the phone and ask politely, people are usually willing to help: most things are researchable. Then there was the art of checking. Again, before the Internet, this was laborious. It meant not only keeping meticulous notes, but using previous cuttings and reference books. With *The Girl at the Lion d'Or* I did as much checking as I could, but I wasn't French and I hadn't been alive in 1936; I felt more was needed. I asked Douglas Johnson, professor of French at University College London, if he would read the manuscript for me. He told me that his Scots Calvinist mother would not have approved of his reading a novel in the mornings, but he would find time in the afternoons. I took a case of wine from different parts of France to his house in Hampstead and we became friends. I finished writing the book in 1986, but for various reasons it didn't come out until 1989. The delay meant that it forfeited a prize (the John Llewellyn Rhys: not a big pay day, to be honest) that it had been provisionally awarded because my thirty-fifth birthday had made me ineligible; but it made no difference otherwise. Late one Saturday night I went with Veronica to buy the early editions of the Sunday papers from a news-stand in Leicester Square. An ecstasy of fumbling. Then relief.

But while the reviews were more generous than I could have hoped, the sales over the coming months remained slow. The world of 'literary fiction' was intense but small; it didn't look capable of supporting a family. I had always understood this to be the case and had no problem with relying on teaching or journalism to pay the rent.

Soon afterwards, I had lunch with Anita Brookner in a fish restaurant in Soho. I had written an admiring review of a novel of hers, *A Friend From England*, and she had said kind things about the *Lion d'Or*. I told her I was worried I had put everything I knew in that book and that I would never find other themes to write about. She put aside her dissected sole and lit a small cigarette. 'Don't worry,' she said, 'you'll write more.' 'How can you be so sure?' She laughed. 'I've read your book. I can tell.'

I gave up full-time journalism in 1991 and completed a novel called *A Fool's Alphabet* that year. It was then I decided that the time had come to write the First World War novel I had hesitated to start before. I had continued to read steadily for three years and one thing always perplexed me. French mutinies apart, why had the men carried on, complicit in this holocaust? When five million

were dead, did they not think that was enough? The average Tommy or *poilu* had little influence, but there were
officers, weren't there — men whose job was to make
decisions? And there were politicians on all sides, sensitive, as politicians must be, to the public mood. What was
their notional upper limit? At what point would they say,
Maybe this is not such a great idea. Eight million corpses?
Ten? Twenty? Last man in Europe?

The first notebook I began had the working title, 'How
Far Can You Go?' I knew that David Lodge had already
taken this title and that it was more suited to a comic novel,
but the question still summed up the idea that most interested me. But how do you 'research' a war? I don't know. I
just wanted to know what it 'felt like', I suppose. How the
day passed. What they ate, what they carried, where they
slept. The smell of gas, the feel of a bullet spinning on the
bone. Leave, women, sex. Weather, fear, latrines. What
happened if you got flu? While I'd need a basic understanding of how an army worked, I would try to avoid
the 15th/21st stuff.

I had read a helpful book called *Death's Men* by Denis
Winter. It gave a lot of everyday detail, gleaned by Winter
from his work in various archives, though with frustratingly scant notes and attribution. But if Winter could
do it, so could I; and the Imperial War Museum, I discovered, had a huge collection of unpublished letters,
diaries and papers, donated by the families of those who'd
fought. Here might be what I needed: nothing of politics

or the causes of the war, but the lowdown on brothels and lice.

The lights in the domed Reading Room were not good and the filing system, though reliable, was old-fashioned. You took a paper docket to the librarian at his desk, writing on it something like 'Trench foot' or 'Mustard gas, effects of', then went back to your seat and waited. A few minutes later a wooden drawer was given to you with perhaps sixty index cards. 'Smith J. Yorkshire Light Infantry. Six letters home, postcards, misc. 1915–17. Details of divisional baths. Pay book.'

There was little to tell you how detailed or helpful the collection was going to be, so I would order half a dozen at a time. Then, ten minutes later, up would come an armful of buff folders tied with pink ribbon, some bulging with scrapbooks, posed sepia photographs and diaries, others containing only two or three sheets of paper.

It is hard to describe the excitement with which I pulled open the ribbon and watched the contents tumble on to the desk. I think that I was (bar the museum indexer) the first person for decades to see some of these documents. The ink of the letters was sometimes smudged by drops of rain that had fallen through the roof of a dugout or a tented groundsheet. The officers wrote with vigour, the men with the clarity of the 1870 Elementary Education Act. No one complained about the conditions, or the dying. Their thoughts were of home, as they begged their families not to worry, thanking them for the parcels of cake or gooseberries, tinned ham or preserves, and reassuring them that they themselves were 'merry and bright' and 'trusting to the best of luck'. The idea of these hapless men sitting in mud, thinking of home, beneath the low sky of a Flanders dusk with the rumble of distant shellfire, was at times so pitiful that I had to stuff a handkerchief in my mouth, though in that murky light I don't think anyone could see. The letter I came to dread was the one that said, 'We're all pleased to see some action at last. We're going to put on a great show,' especially if it was dated June 1916 or it came towards the end of the file, when it was usually followed by a telegram of condolence from the King.

It was becoming slowly clear to me that the main theme of the proposed book needed a counterpart in peacetime. As the death by machine gun and shell of ten million was an extremity of destruction, of the dis-membering of flesh, what was the equivalent in peace — what could be the, as it were, re-membering of flesh? And how far could *they* go? In addition to that question, my fascination with what Proust called 'Place Names: the Place' and 'Place Names: the Name' had not been exhausted by *A Fool's Alphabet*. I had often wondered, for instance, what Hiroshima was like before the name acquired its significance — just a commercial port, apparently. But wasn't there something fated in the name? Surely 'Portsmouth' could never have become a metonym for atrocity. Auschwitz may once have lent its name to a workaday cavalry barracks, but those syllables were surely always destined for something more sinister. And if, during the hundreds of years that the Somme and its tributaries were a place where people went to fish on a Sunday, why did its name already sound like a death knell? With these thoughts in mind, I developed the idea of a peacetime story — or to be accurate, an intensely physical love story — that would be the thematic counterpoint to the war but would take place in the killing grounds before they became notorious as such. Eros and Thanatos; Peace and War; Somme and 'Somme'.

I put the car on the ferry and went over to Calais, then drove down towards Amiens. From the Imperial War Museum shop I had bought a reproduction trench map of June 1916. Using this and a book called *The First Day on the Somme*, by Martin Middlebrook, I had located a bed and breakfast on the Ancre that by my reckoning was at the centre of the events of 1 July. Thousands would have poured through its front yard at dawn, had it been there at the time; a handful would have returned at dusk.

From a research point of view, getting a handle on the geography felt important: fixing in my mind where Beaumont-Hamel stood in relation to Thiepval, or Fricourt to Mametz. Those names . . . For hundreds of years so innocent in rural France, then, through the columns of the death notices and lines of the poets, transformed into the Golgothas of our history. But I knew that if I was to do anything worthwhile the names and the places had to come out of myth and into the continuous present I'd discovered with Doc Wilson. I scraped some earth from a ditch by the side of the Sunken Road into the small plastic cylinder that had held a camera film, intending to put it on my desk at home. Not 'history', I reminded myself: fact, soil.

To an extent, it was a case of demystifying. I narrowed down the area where my protagonists were likely to have started the day and walked for hours to give myself a sense of the terrain. Using Middlebrook and a guidebook I now seem to have lost, I found many small cemeteries in which to sit. My favourite was on Hawthorn Ridge, in the middle of a wheat field, through which the farmer had kindly cut a path. There were few graves there and it was serene. I would sit there for an hour at a time while the larks wheeled overhead. I wasn't aware of 'researching' anything in particular, only of sitting there and feeling . . . Angry, more than anything, sometimes almost choking with rage as I took in the names on the headstones, hoping that the ferocity of my gaze might somehow bring them back to life. And then the peace of the landscape would overtake me again and all that was there was an absence and the sound of birds; and then I sometimes felt weirdly at home.

The next day, I looked into the crater on Hawthorn Ridge that was blown by the miners on the morning of the attack and wondered what they thought of their handiwork, watching from a safe distance as the earth leapt into the sky, then seeing the infantry attack at walking pace.

I went down to the narrow River Ancre, which the men would have to cross at some point in their advance — the water running fast beneath trailing willow branches — then up to Thiepval Ridge, where I saw the Lutyens memorial to the missing. To come across this brick-and-stone monster in the middle of a beet field is upsetting. Then to see that every inch of it is covered with names, on every side, as far as the eye can see and finally to understand that these are not the dead, only the 'missing' — those 72,000 who have no grave because no trace of them was ever found . . . This is hard for a modern mind to take in. There was a Faulks there, of course; there is at least one of almost every name in Britain. I went into the woods behind to compose myself and nearly tripped over a shell casing on the ground.

While everything I saw was urging me to believe that the events were still alive, I had reached a practical impasse: I could think of no reason why a young Englishman would have been in this part of Picardy before the war. Why would he be working on a French farm when there were fields enough in Lincolnshire? And in the days before easy travel, what other reason could there be for him to be there?

I drove into Amiens, a charmless place, I thought, much destroyed and rebuilt after two world wars. Its cathedral, heavily sandbagged in 1914–18 and surviving bombardment miraculously undamaged, was chilly, almost soulless. There were no answers there. I bought a book about the city's history. It had a chapter on the textile industry and its labour relations; then a great deal about the grand families of Amiens. It was like reading one of the lumpier passages of Proust.

My spirits falling, I bought some food from an *épicerie* with a half-bottle of Bordeaux. Then I drove out to Thiepval again and ate a picnic dinner in the car, looking over the battlefield, thinking. By the following day, I had made up my mind. What could I add to the witness of the men who had been there? I had fired a loaded gun once in my life, on a rifle range in the school cadet force. It had been a presumption, a kind of hubris all along. Better to leave the names of Beaucourt and Thiepval to return to their bucolic past and to let their myth endure in the works of those who had lived through the events and were entitled to write about them.

Back in Amiens, there was nothing to do. After the cathedral, the only sight for tourists, according to the guidebooks, were the 'Hortillonnages' or water gardens; so, despairingly, I went there, bought a ticket and sat in a punt with a few others. Eventually, our guide boarded and grasped the pole with which to propel us through the stagnant water. He was originally from Warsaw, he told us. A Pole with a pole, I thought, unsmilingly.

This attraction, of which the city seemed proud, was simply allotments divided by narrow canals, a handy place to grow marrows, perhaps, but not much more.

The waterways, our Pole explained, were formed by the backwaters of the Somme. 'Backwater' summed it up, I thought. Heaps of compost, carrot toppings, uprooted dahlias and old onion sets were piled along the banks. The afternoon had turned hot and there was a smell of rotting vegetation.

A rat ran along the edge of the wood that held up the grassy bank. I looked at the wooden planks again. They formed a sort of revetment or revetting — a word I had come across hundreds of times to describe the way timber was used to shore up the front of a trench. And rats had been a constant companion and menace at the front, eating food from the parcels sent from home, gorging themselves on the livers of dead men.

As I watched the rat, something shifted, and fell into place. The prefiguring of war in the rotting water gardens with their trench revetting . . . a hot Sunday afternoon, her leg resting innocently against his . . . the two worlds joined. And what was he doing there? It has been in front of my eyes. Textiles. Lancashire, London, Paris, Amiens. He was not in a village learning how to farm, he was lodging with a textile manufacturer in town; and his lover was this man's wife.

After the boat trip I walked up the Boulevard du Cange and I saw my factory owner's house: large, detached, creeper-covered, a place of soundless corridors and forgotten spare rooms. I could drop it in complete. I knew also what the lovers would do and the words with which

I would describe it. I hurried back to the car, which was parked near the cathedral, but found I had left my notebook behind. I pulled out the Peugeot owner's manual from the glovebox and scribbled in the margins: 'lambent . . . flickering . . . the split lock of her flesh . . .'

I would need to return to the Somme two or three more times, for further ideas, reassurance and for the checking of details; but for now, after dinner at the bed and breakfast, I felt ready to move on to the next stage. I would call home and tell them I was on my way. I packed my bag, paid the landlady and went to look for a phone box on the Albert–Bapaume road.

It felt less like 'research' than discovery. It was as though the book was there and my task was to unearth it. The most important element was luck. That boat trip; the rat at the right moment; the house on the boulevard . . . Pure luck.

In less excited moments, there was still work to be done. One of the books I had put aside in 1988 was about the war underground – in the tunnels that lay beneath no-man's-land, through which each side tried to undermine the enemy's trenches. I had previously had no idea that such a thing existed, a claustrophobic hell within the larger inferno. Although contemporary writers (Robert Graves, for one) had mentioned them in passing, no one else seemed to know much about the tunnellers either, and this was reassuring. My strong hunch was that the First

World War as a whole — for reasons to do with a second war following so soon, along with the Holocaust and with the way it had been memorialised — had fallen out of the collective consciousness and was ready to be re-imagined. However, there were clearly people who did know all about it; there were, after all, universities, historians and new publications. In order to find an audience, the novel ought therefore to include elements that would surprise even the well-informed. The war in the tunnels could fulfil that role, I thought, as I resumed my seat beneath the dome of the Imperial War Museum. There was not much there beyond the book that had come through the office and a very slim volume called *Memoir of a Tunnelling Company in the Great War*. The Royal Engineers, it seemed, had been practical, not literary, men and had let their saps and shafts speak for them. So it was back to the card index and many more afternoons looking for any reference to the work underground.

It was no great gamble to think most readers would recoil from the claustrophobia of those narrow tunnels in which the sappers were often unable to stand. I had been down a coal mine once, in Yorkshire, and I'd seen how the men were inured to their conditions; the same professional hardness might apply to the ex-miners under no-man's-land, I thought. But for the infantry to be down there, men accustomed to the open sky . . . that might be a scene that would draw the reader in. And then there was the possibility of German tunnellers coming back the other way, of gunfire underground. It was imperative to have a man in your unit with unusually good hearing; he could be helped by sound detection devices, stethoscopes he pressed against the soil or planks of the tunnel wall. But what if the air feed, a mechanical wooden bellows at the foot of the shaft dug down from the trench, was making too much noise? What a choice then had to be made: to risk suffocation in the hope of helping your man locate the enemy; or inhale fresh air and run the danger of being shot at close range as the Germans broke through.

The more I discovered about the life of the tunneller, the more it shaped my character, Jack, and the responses he would have. At this point, 'research' and characterisation were becoming indistinguishable: the fact-finding and the invention were for a time complementary. This situation needs you to push and pull, to be active and passive at the same time; methodically industrious but mentally open. You don't want to look down, or you might fall; you hardly want to breathe, really, because at such moments the book is almost writing itself.

Most writers would, I think, agree that every sentence in a novel worth reading is first shaped by a negative: the avoidance of familiar phrases or received ideas. I would take this a stage further to include the rejection of any element that might let the reader feel comfortable or at ease. Think of the first sentence of *Pride and Prejudice*. The author states as 'a truth' that is 'universally

acknowledged' something that is neither. You are desta-
bilised before you have begun. But you are alert.

The process is similar when you are forming a character. The British archetypes of the First World War are the
young officer-poet and the stoical foot soldier with his old
kitbag. For the first, I had been moved by Vera Brittain's
Testament of Youth and by the writing of Edward Thomas;
it was respect for them that made me want my main character to be far away from theirs. And for the second, I had
read enough of Tommy's letters home to love and admire
him, too; but he was not the man I needed for the novel.
Stephen had to be someone more driven and unreliable;
someone who would form a relationship with Jack, the
tunneller, not because he liked him, but despite himself.
And this would be partly because of his childhood and
partly because of what had happened to him with the factory owner's wife — Isabelle — before the war.

I wrote the book in the course of six months in 1992.
Needing in those days absolute quiet in which to work, I
walked over to my brother's house, about half a mile from
where we lived. I would say hello to my nephew Leo, a
few weeks old, make a thermos of coffee and take it up
to Edward's soundproof study on the top floor, which he
had made available to me while he was out at work. Then
I wound a sheet of paper into my Olympia portable and
began to type. The rattle of the keys on the platen and
the smell of the ink ribbon were as important as the sight

of the pile of A4 pages that began to accumulate beside the typewriter. When a stack is an inch deep it becomes easier to believe in the world you have invented, however unconfident you feel, however bad your typing. Mine was fast but with repeated inaccuracies, such as 'teh' for 'the'; and the main character was almost invariably 'Stehpen'. Sometimes, usually when narrating something I knew to be true, such as the men seeing their own mass grave as they marched to the front at Auchonvillers, I couldn't go on. I made it a rule not to write at such times because I felt my job was not to pound the keys in anger but to find a correlative for my own feeling in the detail of the story, and in that way to evoke a response in the reader.

Occasionally, I would go and talk to Leo in his cot. If I still felt overwrought, I went into the back garden for some air. Some time later, I discovered that a worried neighbour had telephoned my sister-in-law, Catherine, and told her, 'I think you ought to know that Edward doesn't go to work. He must double-back from the Tube a different way. I've seen him in your back garden at midday, unshaven, smoking a cigarette.'

Each night at home I dreamed I was in a trench. But they were not nightmares; a trench was simply where I lived. About three months in, on 11 September, our second child, Holly, was born, so domestic life took me away from the trenches for a time. Then in October I started a new regime: writing a thousand words before taking the Tube (the Central Line at first, the line that Jack in better times had helped to dig) to the Imperial War Museum, so I could re-immerse myself in documents. I wouldn't say this was 'research', because I wasn't looking for anything in particular; it was more like a booster injection of trench life. One letter written home on the night before the Battle of the Somme, however, was so perfect that I broke my own stern Rule of Invention* and put it in the book almost verbatim, changing only names. I wish I had logged and noted which collection it came from, but the apparatus of my notebooks is almost as full of holes as Denis Winter's. Anyway, it is the letter attributed to Byrne. More than thirty years later, I still can't think of it, particularly the PS, with equanimity.

'Do you do a lot of research?' is in the end a difficult question to answer. I think readers want me to say yes, because they would like to think that with *Birdsong* I took the trouble to honour the reality of the men's experience. However, I also think that some want to feel reassured: to believe that if they too had been lucky enough to be unemployed and to have as much time to spare in the archives, they too could have written the book.

So I have experimented with different answers. 'Not really,' I have sometimes said. 'The background, yes, the facts, the dates and so on, of course. And I always have

---

* If you have created a coherent fictional universe, something dropped into it, unchanged, from real life will strike a false note.

it checked by experts afterwards. But most of it, really, I just . . . I made it up.' This went down badly once with a gentleman at a literary festival who exclaimed in horror, 'You *made it up*?' 'Yes,' I said. 'That's what fiction is' — which made him splutter more. The idea of invention can be alarming. Vince Cable, the Liberal Democrat politician, wrote warmly about the novel, but said it was 'based on some letters Faulks found in his grandfather's attic'. Many readers have found it hard to understand how an author can invent within a historical framework; they find the process puzzling — which is why I've tried to explain a little of it here.

However playful I have sometimes been with readers (not very playful, in all honesty, and not very often), I was nothing but earnest about fact-checking when I had finished writing. Who better, I thought, to read the manuscript than Martin Middlebrook, whose outstanding book, inspired by his own visit to the Somme battlefields in 1967, had been so helpful to me? A poultry farmer from Lincolnshire with no previous experience of writing, Middlebrook had overcome indifference from world-weary London publishers to force his story into print. When I contacted him he was resistant to the idea of fiction about the war. I offered to pay him, thinking that a man with a chicken run might be glad of the extra cash (I had no idea at that point that he was in fact a successful businessman). Then I told him he could skip the peacetime sections if he liked. He hesitated. Somehow, in the end, I wore him down.

When the manuscript came back, the early sections were marked 'Not Read'. The marginal comments on the wartime passages began unpromisingly — 'NO. They are corps staff, not divisional staff!' — and I began to worry that my reluctance to engage with the cap-badge side of things might be my undoing. However, as the book went along, the remarks became fewer and less peppery. There were only a couple of things that would take time or ingenuity to fix, and I had already discovered that when your narrative has an improbability or when your protagonist needs to behave in a way that is out of character, the best thing is to draw attention to it. 'Normally so secretive, she was moved on this occasion by an impulse to confide . . .'

'Interesting,' commented Martin Middlebrook at one point towards the end; and I felt I might be winning him round. Finally, on a sentence describing the way New Zealand tunnellers packed explosives, was the comment I'd been hoping for: 'I did not know that.'

The business of research has been changed by the Internet. In 2006, at the invitation of the Fleming family, I wrote a James Bond novel to celebrate the centenary of Ian Fleming's birth. There was a very short scene in a drug-smuggling town on the Iran–Afghan border. I didn't think it worth going there for the sake of half a page, and luckily someone had done it for me: I found a home video on YouTube with commentary as the tourist-cameraman walked the lawless streets of Zabol, complete with sound-track. All that was missing was the smell. A few weeks later, flush with the Bond-sized advance, I employed a young researcher to find out what Cold War customs and border checks would have confronted a small boat leaving Russia and entering neutral Finnish waters in 1967. He spent ages checking with academics all over this country and abroad, but no one seemed to know. Since he was on an hourly rate and was moving into week two of his work, I decided to call off the hunt and fudge it.

Old habits of research are enjoyable, if ridiculous. A few years ago, I was poring over a *Times* Atlas open at the southern Italy pages with a pair of dividers and a ruler, trying to see whether Hendricks in *Where My Heart Used to Beat* could feasibly have had a romantic weekend with Luisa in Pozzuoli and got back to the town on the other side of Naples, where . . . Hang on, I thought. A minute with Google Maps established that the journey by car would have taken him thirty-seven minutes – 'in current traffic'. I was rather sad to put the dividers back in their Helix Oxford Mathematical Instruments tin.

I have tended to do less research as the years have gone by, partly because I have returned to some of the same areas of interest. In *Paris Echo*, my knowledge of how the city had functioned under German occupation was already fairly detailed from the work I had done on the

Vichy years for *Charlotte Gray* about twenty years before. I had, for instance, already visited the awful site of Drancy in the northern suburbs, from which gendarmes on RATP buses had taken Jews, both refugee and French, including children, to the railway station to be transported to Auschwitz. Whenever I think of 'research', I think of Serge Klarsfeld, the French-Romanian lawyer who in the 1970s maintained in the face of official denial that France had exported eighty thousand Jews to the death camps. Ridiculed by the French state and its civil servants, he decided to do the only thing that would prove him right about the number. Working with his German-born wife, Beate Künzel, he named them. From SNCF passenger manifests (the railwaymen, being largely Communist and lukewarm about this enterprise, were likely to keep the evidence), and from scouring German and Polish transport records, the Klarsfelds managed to find the first and second names of more than seventy thousand of them. Now that's research.

It was while I was walking round the site at Drancy, now a run-down housing estate which oddly resembles the deportation centre it was in 1943, that I bumped into a thoughtful-looking woman who was standing next to the cattle truck that had been installed by the Paris authorities fifty years later as a guilty acknowledgement of the human transports. We each wondered what the other was doing there. She pulled back her sleeve to show me a number tattooed on the inside of her forearm. As a child she had been deported to Auschwitz in just such a wagon; the municipal bus to the station at Drancy-Le Bourget had left from the very spot on which we were standing. She had returned for the first time in more than half a century to look at the place from which her journey had begun.

I asked her to tell me about it. From her description of arriving on the ramp at the railhead I borrowed details for the experience of André and Jacob in *Charlotte Gray*. Rightly or wrongly, I felt I had been authorised by this conversation to describe such a scene in a way that I might not have felt from reading written testimony alone.

The idea for *Paris Echo* had come to me in San Francisco, where in a hotel in the Presidio district one morning I told Veronica, 'I think there's something for me in Paris.' 'What? A croissant? A long weekend?' 'I don't know. I'll have to go and live there to find out.' This was self-indulgent of me, and inconvenient for us both. In the early months of 2016, I dossed around from spare room to cheap hotel to a rented flat off the rue des Martyrs, looking for my book. I hired a guide to take me to places no one ever went, including the most iffy Islamist suburbs. It was good that my guide was female, I thought, as this would pose extra problems for the fundamentalists. But in the most notorious café in the dodgiest suburb they could hardly have been more friendly; the only problem was the likely lads outside who kept asking for my guide's phone number. '*T'as un zéro six?*' 'What's your mobile?'

For the rest, it was a question of pounding the streets

alone, much as I had done at the age of seventeen, though this time I was due to have a double partial knee replacement on my return to London and the pounding was restricted to ninety-minute bursts. My awareness of the Paris remembered through the eyes of a seventeen-year-old, now revisited by someone in his sixties, began to chime with a long interest in whether knowing about history actually made you a better or a wiser person. And so the characters of Tariq and Hannah were starting to take shape, as well as what I needed from them: he to ricochet from one experience to the next, like a pinball, without pausing to think; she unable to act at all without being weighed down by awareness of the past and its repercussions. I didn't much want to go to Algiers, Tariq's birthplace, and the Foreign Office website was not encouraging about 'unnecessary' visits; so instead I made Tariq a native of Tangier, which, since the Algerian War would anyway be a constant background presence in the book, was a less clunky choice — as well as being a lot more congenial when I eventually got there in the autumn, on my new knees.

When I was writing *On Green Dolphin Street* in 1999, I found that the plot stalled if I was not in America, where the book was set. This was an expensive discovery, even with the help of a travel agent who showed me I could fly first class to JFK with Kuwait Air for less than economy with British Airways. There was no alcohol in the

Kuwait cabin and a fair bit of Koranic incantation from the cockpit before you took off, but arriving sober had its advantages. Even so, I couldn't afford to go to America every time I wasn't sure what Mary would be expecting Frank to do next.

By chance, I had met a young researcher in London. She lived in New York and had access to office computers that, rather than make a whirring sound for twenty minutes, could actually find information on the Internet. I asked her to check out the toll on a bridge near Chesapeake Bay in 1960. Two days later, she emailed the answer, gleaned from the port authority and other records: two dollars fifty. I smacked this figure into the relevant place, adding a little grumble from Charlie about the price.

The trouble was that neither my London nor my New York publisher would accept the figure. I showed them all the researcher's documents, but while they grudgingly conceded their authenticity they insisted that I alter the charge to something more believable. In the published book, Charlie and Mary therefore cross the bridge for a bargain seventy-five cents. And that is a significant difference between fact and fiction. One of them has to be plausible.

Some subjects become so interesting to you that you continue to 'research' them long after the relevant novel is published. In 1994 or thereabouts, I was having a conversation with Hughes d'Achon about his latest commission as an architect. It turned out to be the transformation of an old monastery in the south-west of France into a hotel and had necessitated many long conversations with the abbot. God, commerce, art and the passage of time . . . I at once began to re-imagine these conversations as being between a young Englishwoman, not an architect, but someone under intense personal pressure, perhaps in danger, and a man who, though devout, was actually not a priest and had once been worldly. So the central scenes of *Charlotte Gray* were spontaneously suggested to me and the book was built outwards from them. The main difficulty was in finding a reason for an English (now Scottish) woman to be there. It was like Stephen in *Birdsong*. It seems absurd, but if I didn't want her to be married to a Frenchman, which I didn't, then dropping her in by parachute was the most feasible way of getting her into France. So the entire SOE side of the story was initially no more than an elaborate type of entry visa to enable Charlotte to have her conversations with Levade.

The authoritative English-language book on the period was still Robert Paxton's *Vichy France: Old Guard and New Order*, an analysis based on first-hand documents, the sort of magisterial history you don't often find. But it had no bibliography, because French writers at the time Paxton wrote (1974) had not dared go near the period. Paxton recommended a couple of novels for 'atmosphere' and that was it.

The dominant character was Marshal Pétain, whom

I'd encountered at Verdun in 1916, where his steadiness and care for his men's lives in the 'meat-grinder' had made him a national hero. Recalled at a time of crisis to be the country's leader in 1940, Pétain made the immediate decision to collaborate with the occupying Germans. 'Collaboration' was not a hole-in-the-corner business, but an official and well-reasoned policy that led to France having a better deal than any other occupied European country. How it went wrong, ending up in Drancy, is a long and fascinating story told elsewhere. After the liberation of France in 1944 by American, Canadian and British forces with the aid of one Free French division, Pétain was arrested, tried for treason and sentenced to death. The sentence was commuted on appeal to life imprisonment.

A senile and deluded old man, he was eventually exiled to the Île d'Yeu, off the west coast of Brittany, where he died in 1951. One summer, Hughes and I and our young families found ourselves on holiday on this very island. Although *Charlotte Gray* was written and published, I was still keen to know more. Hughes and I cycled to the empty garrison where Pétain had been held, and persuaded the caretaker to get us into the very rooms above the gatehouse where the old man had seen out his last days – hallucinating naked women dancing round his bed, while he shouted orders to his subordinate officers on the slopes of Le Mort Homme.

We stood in silence, but bristling slightly, as though

the current of the godforsaken twentieth century itself were somehow trapped inside that room. We looked at one another and grimaced.

Then we rode to the municipal cemetery at Port-Joinville and found Pétain's grave, somewhat larger than the average local fisherman's, but not that grand for a man who had once been the saviour of his country. It was a bright Sunday morning in August and as we were about to go back to our holiday cottage, a motorcycle pulled up on the path beside Pétain's grave. The rider dismounted and laid a wreath on it. When he had ridden off, Hughes and I had a look at the label. It said, '*Maréchal, nous voilà,*' the phrase chanted by loyal schoolchildren under Vichy more than fifty years before. This is how, it seems to me, the passage of time is of no consequence. This is how history lives in the soil scraped from the Sunken Road, the sand taken from the beach at Anzio, in the wreath on a municipal grave.

And as for 'research' . . . I have sometimes felt that I was looking for fiction more than fact. In the year 2000 I was filming for an *Omnibus* programme with BBC television. Our main expedition was to Moscow, which I needed to visit for some scenes in *On Green Dolphin Street*, but the producers also took me back to Amiens, where, without my knowing, they had found the house on the Boulevard du Cange from whose exterior I had imagined the home of the Azaire family in *Birdsong*.

The present-day owner was a man of great respectability, full of a certain French *politesse* that involves hand-shaking, dry biscuits and tiny glasses of wine. He was at great pains to explain to me that my book was not an accurate depiction of the family who had lived in the house in 1910 — a family that had included his grandmother.

I apologised for taking the liberty of having borrowed the outside of the house for fictional purposes and explained that it had never occurred to me that people would actually read the book, or make a connection. In any case, the idea of fiction is that . . .

'And so my grandmother,' the gentleman went on politely, ignoring my explanations, 'was an extremely respectable woman, not at all like the person in your book . . .' As he continued his defence of his grandmother's virtue, I had an awkward picture in my mind of Isabelle in the red room. What was 'lambent' in French? I wondered, as Monsieur led us upstairs.

After a time and having made his point, the owner seemed to enjoy the process of being filmed. He presented me with a picture-book history of Amiens.

'And so you see,' he concluded, throwing open a door on to a small back salon with a parquet floor, 'it is not at all the house in your book.' Yet in wainscot and espagnolette, in the passageway that held the stuffy air, in the atmosphere of thwarted passion, it was (though I managed not to tell him) almost everything I had pictured.

8.

O, America

I am crossing the lobby of the hotel in West Hollywood. Three weeks on the road and I can barely walk. It's the end of the coast-to-coast line. On the far side of the lounge, about a thousand yards away through the open double doors of the dining room, I can see them waiting for me. An earnest dozen, sipping cocktails wrapped in paper napkins. A man with a teacher's beard, a woman in a crocheted poncho . . . I know what they're going to ask, even the words they'll choose. Beside them stands the West Coast publicity chief, whose husband spilled red wine on my last clean shirt at lunch in Santa Monica. The wide expanse of floor is beginning to ripple under my feet; a sweat has broken out on my upper lip. The faster I walk, the further away the group seems to get. The floor is buckling now. I'm not going to make this. 'Bathroom?' I say to the bus boy, who gestures upstairs. Bent over the basin, I retch several times. Nothing comes up. I splash cold water in my face and retch a couple more times. My life depends on this. If I can't make this book succeed here, my children won't be fed or clothed. We'll have to sell the house. And those people, booksellers, waiting there . . .

they need me to perform: their livelihoods depend on it as well. I swill water round my mouth, close my jacket over the wine stain, give myself one more hard look in the mirror ('Just *do* it, dickhead') and head off downstairs.

Later, I'm back in my hotel room. Having been unable to eat or drink at the event, I cast around me. The Chateau Marmont 'minibar' consists of an open wicker basket with a bottle of gin, a bottle of vodka and a bag of potato chips; there's no price list. Okay. Any port. Some storm. Half a pint of gin-and-Poland-Spring-water later, I fall asleep, but only for an hour or so. I wake up and ring home.

Veronica answers. 'I thought you were in San Francisco.'

'No, that was yesterday. I'm in Los Angeles.'

'So, what time is it there?'

'It's . . . twenty past three. In the morning.'

'Well, you've nearly finished, haven't you? Just one more date?'

'Yes. Tomorrow. But do you know where that is? It's in Miami.'

'But that's—'

'Yes, it's on the other side of the country.'

I'm a terrible flyer. Turbulence sets off an atavistic reflex. I am a hominid falling from the tree in which I sleep, not yet bipedal. A therapist explained that, even after a couple of million years of evolution, the panic response still has no gradations in my head. There are no 1–10 settings. I have only 0 or 10. Or, to be precise, 11.

And jet lag loves me. How tenderly it wraps me in its tingling, sweaty arms, leaving me displaced, fogged, with surges of adrenaline at inapt moments. Is this Boston? No, it's Thursday. So am I, let's have some icy chardonnay from a quart balloon. I'm on 10 mg a day of anti-turbulent, washed through on a tide of Russian River pinot noir. This in addition to all the normal stuff — espresso, afternoon naps and Black Label heart-starters.

At three-thirty in the morning at the Chateau Marmont, I'm sitting on the edge of the bed and I'm coming apart. The tiny particles that make a self are leaving in a centrifugal whoosh, out of my head, out of the window, off over Sunset . . . There's an axon gone. And there's another micro-bit of me, wafted away on the Santa Ana winds, carried out to sea.

Of course, I'm not the first person to have unravelled in this hotel. But I am almost certainly the first to have come apart while publicising a novel about the First World War. How did it happen? Like this.

New York. Feet jammed beneath the vertical partition that separates you from the driver, bulletproof, they used to say when I first came to the city of Mayor Ed Koch, when you had to claim 'I heart NY' because no one dared to visit and less than no one 'hearted' it . . . The boxy houses by the Van Wyck Expressway that set you wondering about who lives there, recent immigrants, perhaps — the chance to have a life at all, successive waves from desperate corners of the earth . . . But who starts by the Expressway? Or maybe moves *up* to it from a project in the Bronx? And then the first sight of Manhattan that makes you brace yourself — no modern megalopolis, the buildings far from gleaming, more like the burned-out valves of a giant wireless set, battered, but still pulsing; while to your right the looming posters of lip-glossed TV blondes, Dewar's Whisky, Radio 4071 FM, Storage Units, E–Z Pass, and suddenly you're in the grid.

Click. Closed. Looking for the combination that unlocks the puzzle. Amsterdam and 85th. Third and 53rd. Fifth and 29th. It's like searching for a new prime. And then the defining tastes — of bourbon, and pickle; the crash of a dumpster as it crosses a pothole. The *smell*, that burnt, tarry edge on the thick island air. Summer dusk at the foot of Central Park when the chocolate rocks are sweating and downtown shimmers like a furnace.

I'm staying, to the astonishment of my publisher, at the Wyndham on 57th Street. It's not somewhere a New Yorker would spend the whole night; it even featured briefly as a place of assignation in a Woody Allen film. The rooms are huge, as you'd expect in an old apartment building; most are suites with handsome lounges where Rock Hudson might have courted Doris Day. In the bathrooms, water thunders from the Fifties faucets into the iron tub. But to modern, style-aware New Yorkers, the cracked grouting whispers one word only: 'roach'. Like having 'lint' on your clothes, it's an American thing. A roach is what we call a cockroach, but that first syllable is never spoken in Manhattan.

The Wyndham is not for everyone. But if your experience of a city comes through a lens comprised of all the films you've seen and all the books you've read; if the history of the faded stencil names on a warehouse wall on Canal Street interests you more than the contents of a fashion store on Madison, then the Wyndham could be what you're after. There's an art cinema one street over (Jeremy Irons: *Swann in Love*), a French-themed brasserie on the corner, a stream of vacant yellow cabs, and only three minutes' walk away is the bar of the Warwick Hotel where you get a dry Martini served by a solemn grey-hair who looks like he's worked at the Warwick since William Randolph Hearst commissioned it.

It's time for dinner. My anglophile editor takes me to a French place, maybe worried I'll find American cuisine uncouth. I can't bring myself to tell her that modern New York cooking is better than anything you'd find in Paris. I'm appearing at a big bookstore, Barnes & Noble, Borders, one of those giants that smell of burnt coffee and muffins. I think I'm following Elmore Leonard. I wonder what he and I will talk about, if the author of *Get Shorty* will also be an expert on the Ypres Salient.

When we get there we discover Leonard had been on the day before. Shame. But the 'event' goes well, the audience small but apparently interested. Random House have bought *Birdsong*, hard- and paperback rights, for ten

thousand dollars, the same as I was paid to do a single article for *Vanity Fair* magazine. My agent, Gillon Aitken,
had to go down on his knees and beg even for this much
from Harry Evans, the English former editor of the
Sunday Times, who is president of the company. Harry
is said not to read books, being a newspaper-only kind of
guy, but no one else would touch it. My previous publisher
told me I needed to cut it by a third and 'relocate it in a
more recent conflict'. I told her to piss off. No, of course I
didn't. I said how very interesting and I'd certainly think
about it, and thank you very much . . . And then I stumbled out on to Sixth Avenue.

Next morning, the second day of the Tour, I go into
the office of Katy Barrett, the Random House publicity
director. She explains the rigours that lie ahead, the need
for punctuality and sticking to the schedule.

'No problem,' I say.

'Right,' says Katy, 'let's get those airline tickets in.' She
leans in to an intercom and says, 'Honya? Please could
you bring in some coffee and Sebastian's tickets?'

'Honya' is the American way of saying 'Hanya', and
the owner of the name knocks and enters a few moments
later.

'Sebastian, this is Hanya Yanagihara, my assistant.'

'Hi, Hanya.'

'Hi. These are your tickets,' says Hanya. 'And here's
the itinerary.'

American airline tickets are printed on a single stiff

card. The travel agent has joined them all together, so I can tear them off one by one at the serrated edge. But what Hanya's handed me is something like a book. And not a slim one either — something in the Harold Robbins line, with chapters headed Delta, United, Northwest Airlines . . . I weigh it in my palm. It's a *Moby-Dick* of jet lag, a *Tom Jones* of turbulence.

Hanya smiles politely and withdraws. She looks like she has more important things on her mind. And so it turns out when, some years later, she publishes her own novel, *A Little Life*.

'OK,' says Katy. 'You're all set. Make sure you call and let us know how you're getting on. The last guy gave up in Cincinnati!'

'I won't do that, Katy, I promise.' I have a pharmaco-poeia in my flight bag to make sure.

New York . . . I'll be sorry to leave it behind. I love the Korean convenience stores where you can buy cigarettes late at night and Duane Reade with its furlongs of handy little notebooks and useful drugs, like Tylenol PM. What can this glut of plenty look like to an arrival from Belarus or Bombay? I think they must cry with joy. Or disbelief. When Edward, David and I first came in the cold December of 1979 we were warned that we'd get mugged and beaten up, but the opposite was the case: when we asked for directions, people backed away from three men over six feet tall, as though we were the ones about to pull a knife. We persuaded David to buy a chequered red wool jacket from a barrow on freezing Houston Street, telling him it would make him look more streetwise. Then the Oyster Bar at Grand Central, with its chalked-up list of Californian chardonnays (Frederick P. Furth: thank you) and the chowder pumped as concentrate through pipes, then turned to soup and heated in a tiny metal cauldron at your seat . . . And Christmas Eve on Park Avenue, snow falling on a gridlock of cars trying to escape the city, through whose honking lines wove a giant Harley-Davidson, ridden by a Santa Claus with his white beard flying out behind. Another hard winter, under a different Mayor, outside Van Cleef & Arpels, I came across a man naked except for a black bin bag in which he'd cut leg holes. He was jabbering, shouting at the snowy air, a minute from the Oak Room at the Plaza. He had nowhere to put my dollar.

Back on the Tour. Day Three. It's a 6 a.m. start to get to La Guardia. The Random House people have detailed Anne Messitte, an editor at Vintage, to come with me. Anne is a quietly spoken young woman who some years later will persuade the company to publish *Fifty Shades of Grey*. Today her menial job is to make sure the Limey doesn't go off-piste.

On these East Coast morning shuttles, the commuters know the cabin crew and there's a friendly to-and-fro. The seats are leather, cracked and comfortable, though the belt always needs tightening (the day you have to loosen an American lap-belt is the day you take a good look at yourself). There's a bit of teasing as the attendant tries not to laugh during the safety demonstration.

As we fly south, I tell Anne about previous visits to Washington, about the *Telegraph*'s huge office with not one but three senior correspondents as well as a telex guy with an eye shade and full support staff.

'The whole deal, Anne,' I'm saying, 'was to see if you could get Frank Johnson to buy a drink.' It had never been done. This was the *Times* man who couldn't, for some reason, say 'Hello' and had never paid for anything, even though it was all on expenses.

Anne looks bemused by this reminiscing as we drive into town from the airport. I apologise. I think I'm having one of my adrenaline surges as I unpack my minimal luggage in the room at the Jefferson, with its walnut four-poster.

The evening event is at a shop called Politics and Prose. When I first had to do this kind of thing, appear in public and perform, I was frightened of a crowd. But over the years, things have changed. The more people the better now. Anything less than forty makes me think I've been rumbled as a fraud; more than a hundred and I can relax. The crowd at Politics and Prose has critical mass, and it passes off OK. The next morning, Anne returns to New York, trusting me to fulfil my second evening date in Washington.

I spend a lot of time looking at Hanya's schedule. Every morning seems to have an 8.00 flight, check in 7.00, cab at 6.30. I pack and re-pack the small, wheeled suit-case, which holds one spare pair of shoes, space-savingly stuffed with socks; underwear, a sweater and the bulging spongebag full of help. I also have a suit bag with my 'smart' jacket and trousers and am allowed to carry on both bits of luggage and stow them overhead, so I can run through Arrivals at the other end. At Katy's suggestion I have bought a warm leather jacket at Saks Fifth Avenue (own brand).

In the snowy morning, I run out of the hotel into a cherry-and-white cab. 'National Airport.' Not Dulles: National. Boy, did I learn *that* the hard way . . . 'Where you headed?' 'Boston.' 'You'll be lucky, pal.' The wipers are on double-speed against the churning white flakes. At the desk, they insist I check in my bag. Annoying, what with all it contains, though I extract some emergency sup-plies and pocket them. Then at the departure gate, we're told the flight is cancelled. There's a possibility of later flights and something called 'standby'. Since my fear of being late is almost as great as my fear of flying, standby is not something I've ever dealt with. I call Katy Barrett from a coin box, showering quarters on the floor.

As the day wears on, my determination to get to Boston reaches a strange intensity. My kids' lives, my reputation, Katy's job . . . I ask at the ticket desk every fifteen minutes how far up the standby list my name has got. 'I'll tell you how far, sir,' the clerk says at about 4 p.m. 'This far.' He hands me a boarding pass. I can see my bag on the tarmac outside in a pile of luggage carried off the cancelled morning flight. There's a glass door. I try it and, to my surprise, it yields. I nip outside on to the apron, grab my little black bag and run to Gate 34. I may have broken state and federal laws.

I arrive at the hotel on Boston Common twenty-five minutes before my event is due to start at 7 p.m. I throw the cases on the bed and pull open the minibar. Dewar's. That'll do. I shakily pour it into a glass and down the hatch. It isn't whisky, though. It's . . . God, what is this pale liquid? It's cold tea. The previous occupant has obviously drunk the Scotch but not wanted to pay for it. Jesus. Could have been worse. Could have been any pale yellowish fluid. I run to the elevator and stand jabbing the call button. I arrive at the venue at 6.59. 'Good evening, Mr Faulks. We'd almost given up on you.' 'Sorry. Long story.'

Boston to me means Robert Lowell and his poem 'For the Union Dead'. Strange, bipolar Lowell, who for once found his mania and his gift aligned, so that almost every phrase is lapidary. The statue of Colonel Shaw 'as lean as a compass needle' with his 'angry wrenlike vigilance' . . . And the nobility of the Union cause:

> On a thousand small town New England greens
> the old white churches hold their air
> of sparse, sincere rebellion; frayed flags
> quilt the graveyards of the Grand Army of the Republic.

I mutter the lines to myself as I walk round the Common. The words 'sparse, sincere' send thrills down the skin of my forearms.

And Boston, to be honest, also means my favourite TV comedy, *Cheers*, with its bar-room philosophers, Norm and Cliff, and Norm's *cri de coeur*, 'Women, huh! Can't live *with* 'em . . . [*expectant pause*]. Pass the beer nuts.' And Cliff, the mother's-boy mailman with his white socks and whiny Boston accent: 'Sometimes I'm ashamed God made me a man.' To which the crabby barmaid Carla: 'I don't think God's doing a lot of bragging about it, either.'

This is the America I love. Lowell and *Cheers*. The first so dignified and erudite, recording how a nation discovered itself: a place that speaks in the measured baritone of Morgan Freeman or Gore Vidal. And the other, comic, light of touch and fast on its feet, brimming with swift ironies and cross-currents of affection. To think that some poor plodders back in England maintain that 'Americans don't get irony'. I suppose they've never seen a Woody Allen film or a *New Yorker* cartoon, let alone an episode of *Cheers*. All the Americans I've met in Europe have by definition been passport-owners, educated and informed. And their representation of the working class is dignified as well, in a film like *The Deer Hunter* and in all the great music of the century, in blues and jazz and country. I know there is a more Caliban-like and *un*dignified side to the United States — of obesity and guns and ignorance; of unregulated greed and lobbying and tax dodging. I'm aware of this, but I suppose I try not to think about it. Certainly not now, on the Tour, where I'm going to stick with Lowell and Norm.

While I'm in Boston, I think I will go and see John Updike. I have a commission from a London paper to do so, if I can find the time. I get the number from his English publisher and call.

A solid, distant ring.

'Hello. Is that John Updike?'

'This is he.'

Terrific use of the nominative.

We meet in the waiting room of Massachusetts General Hospital, where he has an appointment to discuss his psoriasis. We talk about his hymning of the texture and fabric of American life. In one of his novels the protagonist is seated on the lavatory and describes the 'miraculous weave' of his own jockey shorts, stretched between his ankles; the narrator confides that what he will mind most about being dead is no longer being an American.

The most highly rated American novelists of that time, Bellow, Roth and Updike himself, have discovered drama in their own milieux. As Updike puts it, 'I gazed through my window at troubled, middling America. I needed to look no further for my subject.' And, despite the occasional spasm of fantasy, the work of all three had been grounded in the actual, the observed; it had been imbued with what Updike called 'the savor of reality, its cautious grind'. Yet Britain, or England at any rate, had no novelist like that, I tell him. No one writes seriously, grandly, about realistically rendered daily life. It seems that Chicago, Newark or Shillington, Pa could be mined for the material of art, but that Leeds, Bromley or Halesowen could not. Updike looks baffled.

The meeting is cut short when a nurse calls him in for his appointment, but he signs my copy of his latest book: 'With warm regards, here in the hospital, sick as we are.' His compulsion to write and to celebrate the country of his birth will survive chemotherapy and the death sentence, as we will one day read in his collection *Endpoint*:

> Be with me, words, a little longer; you
> have given me my quitclaim in the sun,
> sealed shut my adolescent wounds, made light
> of grownup troubles, turned to my advantage
> what in most lives would be pure deficit,
> and formed, of those I loved, more solid ghosts.

I don't believe anyone has put it better than that.

But enough. It's six-thirty in the morning, and the electronic bleep is hauling me out of my dreams. It's Thursday, so it must be Chicago. Yay!

O'Hare is a mad-house, with packed shuttle trains between the terminals. I stagger outside to be met by a local escort/driver, who will take me to the hotel. Normally this is a bookish woman of a certain age, returning to part-time work after years of childcare. These women offer water, snacks and sympathy as we chat about our families; one of them talks euphorically of the benefits of Ziploc bags, which she promises will solve all my food storage issues. On this occasion it's a man, called Bill, who offers a tour of the breweries of Milwaukee.

Chicago first dented my consciousness through the map of its rail system that was reproduced on the cover of an album by Chicago Transit Authority, a 'progressive' band with added horns that emerged from the city in 1969. I am already inclined to like the place. That night, when the cab is taking me from just east of Michigan Avenue, past Goethe (pronounced here 'Go-Eathy') Street, beneath the El tracks, then up a ramp on to the expressway, I let the city lights rattle on my eyes like Danny Seraphine's staccato drum fills. And in the rain-blurred signs to Evanston I hear Robert Lamm singing 'Does Anybody Really Know What Time It Is?'; I find the white-on-green words of the Wilmette sign transport me back to that LP cover and the garret where I lodged at school; at which moment, strangely, I can also taste the sheep-cropped grass of the Lake District that was so present to me from reading Wordsworth on the bed — and all these images of elsewhere close at hand, flowing through me in Terry Kath's growling Stratocaster, merging with the hotel bourbon in my veins, filling me, as the taxi goes on through the rainy, glittering dark, with something that feels very much like . . . Wow. Here we are. The venue.

The passage from *Birdsong* that I tend to read is the part where a soldier called Michael Weir, not long after the Battle of the Somme, goes home on leave to see his parents in Leamington Spa. The scenes of war seem too violent and the passages of love too private for a room full of lone readers who've ventured into the night to hear an Englishman they've never heard of, on the simple say-so of their local store. Weir's home leave, on the other hand, gives some idea of private individuals struggling to deal with overpowering public events.

It's never easy reading prose because, unlike poetry, it's not designed to be spoken or declaimed. In a novel, you aim to build a relationship with the reader over a long period. One of my favourite writers, Henry Green, explained: 'Prose is not to be read aloud but to oneself alone at night, and it is not quick as poetry but rather a gathering web of insinuations . . . Prose should be a long intimacy between strangers with no direct appeal to what both may have known. It should slowly appeal to feelings unexpressed; it should in the end draw tears out of the stone.'

After a preliminary talk, in which I give thanks to the bookshop owners, acknowledge Oak Park as the birthplace of Hemingway, set the scene and attempt to explain what Weir has witnessed on 1 July 1916, I begin to read. After about three minutes, I find my voice thickening with emotion. It's nothing to do with my own writing. It's caused by contemplating once more the facts of what befell real people on that actual day; of how, in the historian John Keegan's words, it marked 'the end of an age of vital optimism in British life that has never been recovered'. I'm used to this thickening, and it adds a certain frisson: I invariably cough and get over it. But not this time. A huge wave of sadness rises up in me and I begin to sob, standing at the lectern, the tears drawn, in embarrassing numbers, out of the stone.

A gasp rises from the audience, some of whom are wiping their eyes. I smile, apologise and pull myself together. Eventually, I complete the passage and we move on to questions. Afterwards, I take the proffered glass of water, then hurry to the waiting cab. I slump down in the back for the return journey. Shit. What would Terry Kath and Danny Seraphine have made of *that*?

I have one more day in Chicago, and the hotel concierge conjures me a ticket to the Chicago Symphony Orchestra, where I see Alfred Brendel play the 'Emperor' concerto. The crowd is dressy, but younger than they'd be in London. In front of me a man loosens his tie and falls asleep on the shoulder of his coiffed, cashmered fiancée, presumably exhausted by a day of shouting out the forward price of wheat on the floor of the Exchange. It doesn't seem to matter, though, as the music takes us far beyond such indignities. I close my eyes for a moment, and the embarrassment of Oak Park begins to recede.

Bleep, bleep. Six a.m. already. As we drive in from the Minneapolis–St Paul airport, my eye is caught as always by the legend printed on the car's wing mirror: 'Objects in mirror are closer than they appear.' Pardon? When seen through jet-lagged eyes, this is a perfect closed loop of meaning, a Zen Möbius strip. Objects appear in the mirror to be further away than they truly are . . . Objects seen in the mirror are not as far away as they may appear . . . Objects are closer at hand than they appear to be, if seen only in the mirror . . . Objects in . . . Oh, stop it.

I've asked my escort if we can go and see where Scott Fitzgerald came from. It's a bit disappointing. I don't have the feeling that he was a real St Paul boy because his family moved around so much, and only rented, never owned. And what are you hoping to find anyway? An undiscovered manuscript? A Blarney stone to kiss, so you can write like him in the final paragraphs of *Gatsby*? And if so, are you quite sure about that word 'orgastic'?

We arrive at the hotel (I'm now the owner of a dozen Ziploc bags). I ask the receptionist where I might find some relaxation: 'Where's the downtown?' 'We don't have a downtown, sir,' he replies. Fair enough. I'll spend the afternoon getting ready for the evening event. My hand-baggage-only regime means I buy books one at a time, then dump them; and at the Hudson News in the last airport the only thing I could imagine enjoying was *Captain Corelli's Mandolin* by Louis de Bernières. I've tried this before and found it hard to get into; but sometimes, as in *A Fringe of Leaves* by Patrick White, you need to just push on.

I'm starting to feel quite tired now. The first wave of jet lag peaked in the National Art Institute of Chicago, when the floor began to sway beneath my feet. I'm over that. But the 6 a.m. alarms, the airports, the time zone changes and the strain of nightly performance are starting to react with the heavy fuel on which I'm running. (I've omitted here a three-city loop into Canada – much as I loved Toronto and glad though I was to make it out of Calgary on the last flight before snow closed the airport for three weeks.)

Also, I'm missing home and the touch of my small children. Nothing prepared me for how tactile an experience fatherhood would be. I suppose it begins when they can't speak and you need to show your love in other ways; you hope that your tight embrace will reassure them and allow them to sleep peacefully. You wonder how this skin, these eyes, the whirring brain as yet wordless, came out of the void. Then you check yourself before you become sentimental. But the expression of parental love does contain sentimentality. I wonder if it evolved that way to make the emotion more bearable. It might be too much otherwise.

The evening reading in Minneapolis is in another independent bookshop, rather brightly lit. Part of the idea of coming to these small places was that publishers used to know which bookshops the compilers of the *New York Times* bestseller lists would ring to check on sales. Even twenty extra copies through the till after a reading would make a difference; and being in the list was the best advertising of all. Why didn't they just ask the publishers how many they had sold? Because they thought they'd lie. And nowadays they have more accurate ways of telling.

After the reading, I'm signing away at a table, wondering if these eighteen copies will constitute the flake that gives the snowball critical mass and sends it rolling into the bestseller list. People stand and push their book across, open at the title page. 'Who shall I make it out to?' 'You can make it out to me, if you like.' But they almost never volunteer their name. 'And would you mind telling me what your name is?' 'It's Holly.'

I feel a gush of love. 'That's amazing! That's my daughter's name.' 'Oh yeah?' It's only when the customer brings the book back later that I see I've written, 'To Holly, with love from Daddy.'

Denver. Gateway to the Wild West. I like Denver. It's at altitude and the air is clear. And, boy, do you have time to breathe its pure serene on the way in from the airport, which is about five hundred miles away from the city. I ask if this was a Tammany Hall compromise between land developers and the Mayor, but my escort says she doesn't know. What she can tell me about is her husband's vasectomy and how they had sex just fine the night after the operation. Right-ho. We drive past a dozen vacant sites that would have made an ideal airport before we arrive in the city and I'm dropped off at the Brown Palace Hotel. The exterior is a triangular flatiron structure; inside, it's built round an atrium. It will appear in a novel I write many years later, *A Possible Life*. The bar is called something like the Mariners' Tavern. The stools have padded armrests and are so well upholstered that even Norm from *Cheers* could comfortably get his butt in. Oysters with lemon and tabasco, clams on the half shell, iced chardonnay . . .

I LOVE AMERICA . . . And it annoys me that hatred of the USA performs an important unifying force in French national life at times of uncertainty — say, for instance, the period from 1789 to 1989. The inside story of how this works is told by a French academic, Philippe Roger, in his 2005 book *The American Enemy*, where he quotes the Parisian critic Jean Baudrillard writing of his 'profound jubilation' on seeing the planes plough into the World Trade Center. Many English friends are a little sneery, too. To them, America is the dropper of atom bombs on Japanese paper houses and prosecutor of paranoid, unwinnable wars in Korea and Vietnam; sponsor of apartheid in its own Southern states and persecutor of liberal ideas through its closeted Senator McCarthy; destroyer of indigenous culture worldwide through its export of infantile film franchises, 'superheroes' and fizzy drinks:

a dimwit that licenses the massacring of its high-school students on the grounds of some imagined 'right' to carry automatic weapons.

But I don't see it that way. I think it's something to do with my grandfather being killed while going with US troops into Germany in 1945. The Yanks loved him and recognised his disdain for danger, as I've seen from the press cuttings in the little scrapbook my mother put together at the age of twenty-two, which is how old she was when he was killed, leaving her alone in the world. 'Peter the Lion' the American troops called him, one officer commenting, 'They don't come much better than that guy.'*

And those young men from Ohio and Illinois getting bogged down in the Saint-Mihiel Salient near Verdun in 1918 . . . What were they even doing there? Some generous, reflexive outreach to an old world they'd never visited and didn't understand. My feeling also has a little to do with Dean Rusk, an otherwise pedestrian secretary of state under Lyndon Johnson. When President de Gaulle withdrew France from NATO military command in 1966 and ordered every American soldier out of France forthwith, Rusk asked him, 'Does your order include the bodies of American soldiers buried under French soil?'

And it has a great deal to do with maps, studying

* Reported in *46 Not Out* by R. C. Robertson-Glasgow (London, Hollis & Carter, 1948).

which you can imagine the making of a country through the names of the pioneers, the surveyors, the engineers and, alas, the peoples they displaced or killed. And the ability to create a myth, to take something new and make it sound eternal. So much of American history is disturbing; but in the music of Miles Davis or Bob Dylan you can hear a country protesting its own past and forging from it something rich. It's the opposite of the wry English self-awareness or what you might call the 'Neasden cringe'. It's the dividend of youth. You *can* call your broad-shouldered band Chicago. You *can* make a modern *Odyssey* from a family of sharecroppers going west from Oklahoma in an old jalopy. And what heroic invention was shown by European immigrants in Los Angeles beneath Mulholland Drive. Was there ever a more banal place, with its perma-sun, its Valley Girls who say 'Woke eye' for 'OK' and 'Think YOW' for 'thank you', and miles of badly surfaced intra-city freeways — anywhere in the world less promising for the re-imagining of history?

At the end of Scott Fitzgerald's 1929 story 'The Swimmers', the main character, disillusioned by American greed and profiteering, emigrates to Europe. But, as he looks back from the deck of his ship at the receding continent, he reflects, 'The best of America was the best of the world . . . it was the graves at Shiloh and the tired, drawn, nervous faces of its great men, and the country boys dying in the Argonne for a phrase that was empty before their bodies withered. It was a willingness of the heart.'

And in 1999, as I go to my Denver hotel room, this is the quality I feel inspired by. I choose to ignore how Fitzgerald despaired of racketeering America, both here and in *Gatsby*, where the Dream and the sleaze are one. I can put out of my mind the way the country has always had a problem with 'race' — a concept of scant scientific validity that it chose to interpret through the cloudy lens of eugenics. I'm going to overlook the fact that some leaders in a country made up of immigrants who murdered most of the original inhabitants have seriously claimed that some of the resulting population were 'more American' than others.

Barack Obama is still unknown in 1999; and it can't yet be argued, as it will be, that presidents like him and FDR are exceptions to a crooked rule. Donald Trump is still just a man with a gold-plated building in New York that everyone laughs at. The case has not yet been made that Trump as President is not an aberration, but is in a straight line of American populism and that his catchphrase 'America First' was the battle cry of successive generations of home-grown fascists, including Charles Lindbergh and the Ku Klux Klan.

No. It's still all right. I turn over and fall asleep thinking only of a sparse, sincere rebellion and the willingness of the American heart.

Beep, beep. Six-thirty! Shaved and bathed and checked out the night before. Now just: zip up the bags, coffee on a tray, tip the bellhop from huge roll of dollars kept ever-handy for the purpose, check passport, tube of Life Savers, Hanya schedule. Brush teeth, water in face. Tip concierge, tip doorman, tip driver, tip porter, tip check-in guy. Let's go. Seattle, here we come.

On the flight I pick up *Captain Corelli*. It suddenly breaks open, like an oyster shell revealing not just glistening fish, but pearls. The sun shines through the Perspex window of the plane, but it could almost be the light of Cephalonia. It's the best novel by an English writer that I've read for a long time and I'm pleased to see on the jacket that Joseph Heller thinks highly of it too. I finish damp-eyed with exhilaration and salute the author from afar.

It's raining in Seattle. I'm driven to some out-of-town district which is still in the course of being built. It's all half-finished condos and conference centres. In the hotel, I team up with a fellow writer, John Burnham Schwartz.

'Tonight's going to be tough,' says John. 'It's a trade fair. The Northwestern Booksellers annual something.'

We're taken to a recently finished convention centre about half a mile away. It's a desolate area. Grey construction. Girders, concrete. The thronged highways of Seattle's restless traffic.

'Hi, I'm Sally, I'll be helping you sign your stock.'

We go into a grey windowless room with moveable walls and strip lights. It's by Ikea out of Kafka. I sit next to a woman signing 'puzzle packs'. In the middle of the room are three tables with paper cloths, slices of shop pie, undressed salad and plastic glasses of water.

'This is the authors' dinner,' says Sally. 'You have a ticket for a single glass of wine when you go in to join the booksellers next door at seven.'

'A single glass? But I'm speaking for fifteen minutes at five different tables.'

'I'm sorry. I think there may have been some issues last year.'

I take Schwartz to one side. 'Listen, John. Let's find a bar.'

We slink out of the Kafka room, go down the escalator and head for the street.

'Where's the nearest bar?' we ask the doorman.

'Bar? It's not that kind of neighbourhood. But there's a Marriott hotel about two blocks that way. I don't know if they—'

But we're already gone, barrelling along beside the highway.

'Christ,' says Schwartz. 'We're like John Cheever and Ray Carver at Iowa. They used to meet outside the liquor store at eleven each morning. Cheever was still in his pyjamas.'

The Marriott, the Marriott . . . Never has the name sounded so sweet. We run up the steps and the first thing we see is . . . A bar. A real bar, with beer on tap and a ball game on TV.

'I'll have a Scotch and a glass of beer.'

'Would you like an extra shot of Scotch for three bucks?'

'Do bears live in the woods?'

Schwartz also takes a beer. The beer is good. It is cold, the way Schwartz likes it.

'*Dos cervezas*,' he calls out to the barman.

The spirit of Hemingway is on him.

'Tell me, John,' I say, looking at the screen, 'why is it that in baseball the man with the bat so seldom hits the ball?'

'I'll explain another time,' says John. He looks at his watch. We're fifteen minutes late for dinner. The spirit of Hemingway leaves us.

There's enough time back in the Kafka pod for the piece of rubber chicken and the plastic glass of iced water before the moveable doors roll back to reveal an immoveable feast of . . . of booksellers in their hundreds at circular tables with paper cloths and dry salad.

'Here's your drink ticket,' says Sally. 'Now might be a good time to get it from the bar in the corner.'

'How do I get another drink after this one?'

'I don't know, though I guess . . . I guess you could always, like, *buy* one. But you won't have time, because when the bell rings you have to move table at once.'

'Here's twenty bucks. Stick close to me.'

I sit down, where indicated. Ten booksellers look at me sceptically. 'Well,' says one, a woman with grey hair and narrow glasses. 'You'd better give us your pitch.'

The bell rings and I move to another table. I begin the spiel again. These people don't look up from their plates. One has a badge which says 'Hometown Mysteries'. Throughout my sales pitch an old man reads a catalogue, licking his fingers and thumbing noisily through the pages.

My throat's getting raw. '. . . and you just *have* to know how it ends,' I conclude, all bonhomie and forceful charm.

There's a long silence, as in an old folks' home when Matron comes into the day room to tell them someone's died in the night.

The catalogue guy looks up. 'Shame about Terry's review of your book in the *Times*,' he says.

'Oh well. Never mind. Perhaps he preferred *The Girl at the—*'

'No, he hated that, too.'

At the final table, my voice begins to waver. I feel the long lacerations in my throat, like fingernails scratched down flesh.

We're back at the hotel.

'Shall we get a drink in the bar?' says John.

'Good idea.'

An hour later, I let himself into my room with a plastic card, pull the nylon blind against the Seattle traffic and set the alarm for five-thirty.

San Francisco, oh, balm to my soul! City of music and old Spanish mission and cable cars and bursting vineyards and gay rights and Thom Gunn and Boz Scaggs and majestic bridges and summer of love and Chinatown and admittedly quite dodgy weather . . . But Burt Bacharach is playing in my head through Dionne Warwick's girl's voice as she says a little prayer and I challenge anyone to drive in from the airport, going past the signs to San Jose (sure I do, you make a right just there . . .) without their spirits lifting.

At the hotel, I ask the concierge if she can find me a Harley-Davidson. My aim is to get into the Napa valley for some R and R before the evening event. She conjures one from a rental place in the Mission District; I taxi downtown, say yes to the optional helmet and set off. Have you ever ridden a Harley over the Golden Gate Bridge? The crosswinds are terrible and that bridge is a monster. You end up with forearms rigid from just clinging on. I haven't map-read the distances properly and were I actually to ride all the way to Napa I'd not be home before midnight. However, I get plenty of the *Easy Rider* vibe and try to take a picture of myself beside the dusty road on a disposable camera to send to Katy Barrett to show her that, despite Seattle, I'm having a good time. My arm isn't long enough to get a good snap, so instead I call her on my return to the hotel.

'You did *what?*'

Katy had set up a meeting with a literary biographer and had hoped that I would pass the afternoon discussing the poems of Anne Sexton over a cup of Earl Grey. But

I can do that tomorrow, I assure her. And I have at least made it back in one piece.

The evening event, in a bookshop, is not great. As I near the climax of the reading, a man in the middle of a row of seats stands up and leaves with a lot of chair scraping and shuffling among the people he has to squeeze past. Before the second reading, I ask if anyone who is bored would mind leaving now. It's like the time when a journalist I know tried to disrupt an event I did in Putney by theatrically yawning, pointing at his watch and noisily exiting when I was in mid-stream, banging the street doors as he went.

It's not possible to feel put out for long in San Francisco, however. A seat at the bar, a goblet of chardonnay from Sonoma, then a stroll through the Tenderloin and Chinatown . . . I have a long talk with a chatty panhandler, who wants to pose for a photograph. In other faces you do see what Jack Kerouac called that 'end-of-continent sadness' — the sense that for Americans in hard times the dock of the bay was as far as you could go, after which it was back to Georgia, or worse. But while the junction of Haight-Ashbury may look squalid now, to English people of my generation, schoolchildren in the Sixties, San Francisco represented one thing only: the existence of a brighter world.

For a late lunch in my room I order the sashimi plate. When it arrives twenty minutes later I can see that in the tension between Japanese minimalism and American generosity there has been only one winner. A shoal of fish that a few hours earlier were idling in the bay now lie sliced beside a mound of miso and a quart of soy. I spend the afternoon sprawled on the bed, burping like an old sea lion.

In the evening we drive to Santa Cruz, which turns out to be a hell of a long way down the coast. If the dream of '67 is still alive, perhaps it's here, where the radio station is a dusty kind of shack and the engineers wear beat-up boots and David Crosby moustaches. Marijuana has been made legal for medical reasons, so maybe everyone here is sick and that's why a sweet cloud hangs over the place. On the streets, you can't help noticing the homeless war veterans who sleep rough, nursing their PTSD beneath warm skies. The writhing metal tracks of the big ride at the Beach Boardwalk loop back on themselves beneath the etiolated palm trees. It all looks rusty and unsafe, a Coney Island for those past caring. Recent history is quite gaudily apparent: the fallout of Woodstock and Vietnam, the good, the bad and the broken.

But how different it must have looked and felt back then, as young Americans resisted the material advances of the postwar years, when a California paradise of sun and palm and sea took on a sense of purpose, fired up first by *Pet Sounds*, then by flower power and the jamming of the Grateful Dead. As children, the hippies had all benefited from the 'little boxes' that comprised the houses of Levittown and its kind across the country; they'd grown up with cheap cars and cheaper gas and almost full employment. You can understand how a weary dad, smoking his Chesterfield and drinking an Old Fashioned, must have wondered whether it had been worth the sweat of corporate life, let alone the hell of Iwo Jima, to hear Junior, six months into freshman psych and with his hair down to his ass, tell him he'd got it all wrong.

The Vietnam War, we've been told, gave the defining push to the counterculture — much more than the equally dubious Korean War, for the simple reason that Vietnam required a draft of civilians, a disproportionate number of them black, to prosecute its unclear aims. The military stuck its long arm into the project, pulled you out and dropped you in the Mekong delta. Something about these wars brought out the worst in America, most notably its reluctance to learn about other countries. For a nation of immigrants to show such inwardness seemed a poignant failing — as if, once safe through Ellis Island, millions of people had never cast a backward thought. At the time America first went into Vietnam, in 1965, less than three per cent of its population owned a passport. The jungle was their first experience of abroad.

At the Santa Anita racetrack a burger stall run by a pair of brothers produced the best burgers you could find in California, everyone agreed: grain-fed beef, loose-textured, and a mayo tasting somewhere between hot and sweet. The brothers were loaned enough to start a drive-thru place in San Bernardino, sold an interest to a franchise agent called Ray Kroc and the rest is golden arches and ballooning greed. Decades later European governments would be passing emergency laws against the stuff. That's the trouble with capitalism. It just can't stop. And if some politician tries to introduce an element of moderation for the common good, the corporations will hire lobbyists on Capitol Hill to buy him back. The triumph of American business, especially its banks, was to persuade the legislators that regulation was a dirty word: not a flexible and intelligent check, but a denial of the essential freedom to make billions and not pay tax on it.

Back in spaced-out Santa Cruz, it's hard not to feel sad about the way things turned out. They were right, the hippies, about big business and its power to trample decency. They were wrong, though, about personal excess. Sleeping guilt-free with anyone brought a toll of emotional stress and disease, as if the hidden, underlying rules of life had been rigged by a maiden aunt. And while the little high of wayside California grass was better for you than hard liquor, the secure wards of the psychiatric hospitals were later filled with those for whom more powerful drugs were a gateway to a lifelong hell. 'The road of excess leads to the palace of wisdom,' wrote William Blake, a hippy oracle; but even by his homespun standards, this proved to be spectacularly untrue.

It's very late by the time I get back to my hotel on Powell Street, with these thoughts still swilling through my mind. In the night, I have hot visions of America . . .

Driving through snowy woods in Vermont one morning, seeing a lonely road sign that, bafflingly, said, 'Indian Head Viewing' . . . And Mobile, Alabama, the terrible heat that made me think of cotton fields and hell on earth and Emmett Till . . . and then, when the booksellers' rodeo is over, the scramble for the last plane out, people pushing one another on the tarmac to get on, and the hysterical relief as the plane went down the runway . . . The line for a ride at Disneyland, Anaheim, where the obese can't fit through the turnstile so have to go sideways and lift their bellies over the bar with both hands . . . And all those shuttles up and down the East Coast with John Coltrane and Miles Davis through the Walkman in my ears; and whisky, ice cubes and ginger ale in the plastic glass, 'A Love Supreme', 'Stella By Starlight', gazing down on the lights of Manhattan, the intact towers, this extraordinary self-invented country that I'm so lucky to be part of for a day and—

Wake up, dumbass! I check out of my hilltop hotel, peeling off the dollar bills to tip the willing hands that load me into the cab for SFO.

The plane flies down the coast, the Pacific lying flat against the shore. On the surface of the water, there is no foam, no wave, but a mere stippling, like the grain of a synthetic car upholstery. I breathe in deeply, try to brace myself for one last push. I'm just trying to hold on now. Driving under LA palm trees, wondering if that's Dennis Hopper's house — like a crack den on the outside, apparently, to deter thieves, but once you step through the door . . . When I left London, I told myself that that which does not kill us makes us stronger . . . Who said that? Nietzsche, I remember now. Unfortunately. I don't want to be relying on the wisdom of someone Jeeves regarded as 'fundamentally unsound'. I wish it had been Kant. Or even Go-Eathy . . .

Now I'm losing it. Too tired to concentrate at lunch in Santa Monica, where the red wine goes over my shirt. And then a long drive to the Chateau Marmont. I have driven down this road before, always with Steely Dan playing on the car stereo: 'Drive west on Sunset to the sea. Turn that jungle music down . . .' Trouble is, we're driving *east* on Sunset, *from* the sea . . . This is ALL WRONG . . . and I'm starting to feel unwell. Seriously unwell. And I don't know if I can hold on. The drive goes on for ever through the thickening atmosphere. I think I might vomit.

Arrived at last, I have an hour to 'rest up' in the room. I know the Chateau Marmont has airy spaces where the film stars play, but I'm ground-floor front, on the road, and Sunset is a noisy thoroughfare. Call home. No answer. Shower and try to get ready. Bedside phone rings. 'Your driver's here.'

Getting in the car now. 'How far is it?'

'The hotel's in West Hollywood.'

I crack another Poland Spring from the basket on the back seat. Though is water really going to help? God only knows. As the Beach Boys once sang. And wouldn't it be nice if we were *older* . . . Perhaps the best line in pop lyric history . . .

I click the seat belt. 'All right. Let's go.'

9.

Three Strikes

When you're in the process of writing a book, anything less than a thousand words a day is a poor return. Allowing for a five-day week, that means you ought to produce a quarter of a million words a year. So I should by now have a backlist of eighty titles.

The truth is that most of the time writers are not writing. You're looking for your next book, or putting yourself in a place where it can find you.

And what do you actually do during these off days? You can't hibernate. Your brain is working, your fingers itch for the keys. You feel like Stevie Wonder with no piano. Well. You read, of course; you go to other places, think, watch films, ask questions, listen and read some more. You try not to let your next book know you've got an eye on it, in case it hides its head.

You also try to find other projects, because by focusing on small tasks you can free up areas of the brain where bigger ideas may form: by indirections find directions out. That's the theory. In practice, alas, I think I have only ever found three satisfactory sidelines.

The first was a Radio 4 programme called *The Write*

Stuff. This was a light-hearted literary quiz dreamed up by James Walton, a young journalist from Merseyside who had always wanted to be a quizmaster and had studied the form closely. In order to differentiate itself from any radio predecessor, Jim decided that the programme should have an Author of the Week. The first round would be questions about this writer's life and work and the show would end with a parody of their style. Hilarity, he felt, was almost certain to ensue.

Jim asked me if I would like to be involved and I said a tentative yes. This became a commitment when my opposite number was confirmed as John Walsh, the fast-talking son of an Irish doctor from Battersea. John was known as a lively journalist and literary partygoer; he had done a PhD on Samuel Beckett and had a rapid-repeater knowledge of literary trivia. He had also been a friend of mine since we'd bonded over pints of Young's Special in Wandsworth pubs in the late 1970s, as we compared our windy ambitions. I hadn't always been able to accept John's invitations to go for 'drinks with the new young publicist at Michael Joseph and her flatmate' because on the evening in question I was researching some aspect of trench foot. But I'd felt a kinship with him because we were not part of any magazine clique, but loners making it up as we went along.

Thanks largely to Jim Walton's inventive questions, the show lasted seventeen years. John and I had a guest each on our side, and their calibre determined the shape of the evening; among the best were Lynne Truss, Sue Limb and Miles Kington. It was often recorded in the radio theatre at Broadcasting House, though I preferred the top floor of Waterstones Piccadilly because I could nip out on to a balcony with Miles or Jim for a cigarette between recordings. We used to do two at a time and this could confuse one's preparation. I was once asked the name of Philip Roth's first wife and buzzed in confidently to say that it was Jean Armour. Unfortunately, my mind was already on the next programme and I had married off Philip Roth to Rabbie Burns's Highland sweetheart. I explained under my breath to Harry Ritchie, my quizzing partner, what I'd done, after which we were both laughing too much to answer anything else.

All the questions were blind, though you knew in advance who the author of the week was to be, so you could prepare if you wanted. This was a bit of a sweat, so I used to do the prep on one, but not so much on the other. It didn't always work out. George Orwell's writing had made an impact on me when I was younger and I wanted to show my admiration on air, so I spent a whole day reminding myself; for Agatha Christie, the subject of the other recording, I merely glanced at the back of some Hercule Poirots in Waterstones on my way to the lift. Every Christie question was answered by my five-minute browse; but with Orwell we were easily out-buzzed. So much for prep.

One of the oddest things about the BBC (something

its free-market critics don't understand because they have never worked for it) is how inconsistent its political attitudes are. Some producers were keen on quotas and diversity, others looked at you blankly if you raised the question. I always wanted female voices, for sonic harmony at the very least, but this request met with a mixed reception. One producer did insist on a guest of Afro-Caribbean background, and great was the disappointment when neither name nor voice indicated this heritage. Some guests would try to impose their own views mid-recording. I still remember Jim Walton's face when one exploded, 'That's the first time that a woman's been the answer this evening!' The objection might have carried more weight if the author of the week had not been Sylvia Plath.

On one thing we all agreed: that we should cover a range of authors; so that after we'd done Sophocles, we had to do Jilly Cooper. The trouble with many popular writers, especially the better ones, is that they don't have a distinctive prose style, and this makes them hard to parody. So after struggling with one such, there was always an urge to revisit the imitable Dickens or Jane Austen. It was almost a relief when in 2014 the incoming head of comedy said she found the programme unfunny. I managed to publish some of my end-of-show parodies in a book called *Pistache*, but I missed the thrill of the buzzer and the beery evenings afterwards in various repulsive West End pubs. The fee was negligible, but as Veronica pointed out, 'Since there's no money, that makes it an easy choice. You just do it if you like it.' And I did.

Various people had been kind enough to say I had a pleasant voice and for a moment it seemed that this might provide a way of filling the non-writing days. I did the voiceover for a television series about Nazi doctors and afterwards was offered the same job on several hours of recently discovered colour footage of the First World War. Unfortunately, I was not free to do this and the gig went to Kenneth Branagh; the project, to my almost-sincere delight, was a huge success. I had one more go in the sound booth, which was to read the audio book of *On Green Dolphin Street*. There was no director as such, though the studio manager, a former merchant seaman, would occasionally cut in from behind a glass screen: 'No. Mary's much more passionate in this scene. From the top again, please.' I'm not sure he had read the book. So as a day-filler and next-book-stimulant, this was a definite Miss, though I still nurture small hopes that I will be invited back behind the microphone one day.

From audio, it's a short swerve into television, where in 1999 I presented a series for Channel 4 about Special Operations Executive, Churchill's secret army in the Second World War. The producer, Martin Smith, who had worked on the famous *World at War*, had managed to set up interviews with many of the saboteurs and resistance fighters who had taken part; for most of them it was the first and last time they spoke about their activities. The archive of these interviews, which I hope has survived somewhere, is both poignant and valuable. My presentation was appalling, however. Can a block of wood look alarmed? Apparently so.

In view of this, I was surprised to be offered another television job by BBC2 in 2010, to write and present a series about memorable characters in the English novel. These were to be divided into Heroes, Villains, Snobs and Lovers.

Well, I'm between books, I thought: so let's give it a go.

Soon I find myself sitting alone on a veranda in the jungle in Puerto Rico, where a beach is to stand in as Robinson Crusoe's island. Everyone else is sick in bed. The cameraman had to keep leaving the check-in line at La Guardia to run to the bathroom; the sound guy and the assistant producer have a different virus. The director will be in hospital soon after our return to London. The series appears to be cursed. The director of *Villains* has had his engagement terminated with only half the programme done; the *Lovers* director has already pulled out. Nobody at the BBC seems to know where the whole thing is heading. They feel they owe it to the public to do 'something about books', but they are unsure how to do it.

There was a show years ago on BBC2 with Melvyn Bragg called *Read All About It*, a paperback review panel on which I appeared once, at the age of about twenty-five, greatly nervous in a green corduroy suit. Since then, nothing's really worked. Everyone agrees that the idea of talking about characters rather than books is a good one. But there is a scent of fear: a dread of seeming 'elite' or too literary. It's decided that we can only talk about characters from novels that have been filmed or televised, so that the programme can be illustrated with dramatic extracts. This seems fair enough, but when I'm shown a first attempt at splicing together some of the material from the *Snobs* programme, it's obvious that fear has turned to panic. Between Ronnie Barker sketches and clips from TV films there's almost nothing about books or writing at all.

There are also money issues. In London, quite a bit of filming has to be done in Mayfair, which serves as the background for Becky Sharp and other social climbers. It's midwinter freezing and the camera guys have been up since six to travel into town. Their lunch allowance after several hours' work at a temperature of minus one degree is £5. But you can't get lunch in Mayfair for £5. For some reason, however, the powers above decide that we can afford to go big on Merrick, the villain of Paul Scott's *Raj Quartet*. So five of us set off for the old hill stations of India.

In Shimla, we film in dying light in a tumbledown graveyard where monkeys are roaming over the leaning headstones. Here lie nuns and missionaries, box wallahs and governesses; the air is thick with their ghosts. The director has visual flair, but he is not a words man. 'Stand over there and say something about Merrick. Is he gay or what?'

It's all worth it, I think, for the great creation that is Ronald Merrick. A sadomasochistic imperial policeman, he has the main Indian character (whom he covertly lusts after) wrongly imprisoned; but over the years the net closes in on him. He goes cruising at night disguised as a Pathan tribesman and is finally murdered in bed by a rent boy who has been infiltrated into his household — but only after he has enjoyed the first real sex of his life, dolled up in ceremonial robes.

Then, back in London, when all is looking good, especially the graveyard shots, I receive a call from the series editor. Would I mind rewriting the entire Merrick section without mentioning the fact that he is gay? I look down disbelievingly at the receiver in my hand, like someone in a West End matinée. I can't change history. I mean, would he like me to rewrite the Fagin section so that he is no longer Jewish? No, that was different, that was fine . . . But this . . . There are people who may not like it . . . that someone so . . . er, odious . . . is also . . . er.

But by then I have resigned.

Some months later, I literally bump into Mark Bell, a BBC2 commissioner. I am on foot, he on a bike. When I've helped him up, we recognise each other and reopen negotiations. If Merrick will be allowed to remain as Paul

Scott created him, would I be prepared to reconsider other aspects of the programmes? Sure. The game is on again, though after such a long lay-off, continuity is a problem. We had been halfway through a character from Monica Ali's *Brick Lane* in the heat of summer and I was dressed accordingly. It is now January, and as I pick up the threads and do my piece to camera in shirtsleeves on a windy East End housing estate, it begins to snow. 'One more time, please, Sebastian, but this time without your teeth chattering.'

The remaining bits and pieces are thrown together in a rush. We have no money left, but luckily the producer, Mary Sackville-West, comes from a family with a stately home. So bits of Knole's house and garden in Sevenoaks are the backdrop for Heathcliff and Darcy. That just leaves the question of the book of the series. The BBC don't know when they will transmit the finished programmes, but it could be in as little as three months. To enable the publishers to rush the book out at the same time, I have six weeks to write it. The only way I can think of doing it is to write a long review of the twenty-four books in question, as if I were a first reader. It takes me forty-one days straight through. I hand it in. It turns out that the series is, after all, not broadcast for another six months.

The accompanying book receives some bad reviews. One is from an academic who takes me to task over factual details. The amusing part is that he chides me for errors in some 'facts' that he has himself got wrong. But the day is saved when John Carey, the Merton Professor of English at Oxford, reviews it warmly in the *Sunday Times*. Overall, however, and despite the book's baffling popularity in Simplified Chinese, the whole thing must go down as a Miss.

So much for TV. But, I thought: suppose that while waiting for a novel to form in my mind, I still wrote — but in a different medium . . . Film, for instance. After all, I had read plenty of film scripts, most of them adaptations of my own novels. I had also read some more or less useless guides to the art of screenwriting. I have formulated three rules. First: try to tell the story in pictures. Every time a character is about to say something, put a sock in it. Second, enter the scene as late as you dare. An example of this is when Omar Sharif as Doctor Zhivago goes to finish his affair with Julie Christie's Lara. In Robert Bolt's script, the first heartbreaking line we are privy to comes after he has already told her that it's over. The third 'rule' is to have the characters in conflict, each wanting, as far as possible, different outcomes from the exchange in any scene.

The attempted adaptations of my books have struggled. The first draft of a screenplay of *Birdsong* was so terrible that the then producers wouldn't let me see it. The best of the scripts I saw was by a young English director called Rupert Wyatt. He flew from LA to New York, where I met him in an Upper West Side apartment. It went well. After an hour or so, we shook hands and agreed that we two alone would be in charge of the script and that we would allow no last-minute Hollywood interference or 'polish'. His screenplay was admirably well constructed: he had all the pictures in his head, even if his ear for speech was not the best. Back in London I got to work on the dialogue, correcting some linguistic errors and re-wording in particular the contribution of Isabelle, which was something all adapters had struggled with. A few weeks later, Rupert called me from a car in Los Angeles to say he couldn't accept any input of mine after all, since he needed to feel he personally owned the film.

In March 2009, the *Independent* devoted four pages of its review section to anatomising the protracted failure of the producers, Working Title, to get the film made. They did try hard, but the planets (money, director, cast, availability, script) would never align. Many years later they finally got it away as a two-part television show for the BBC, with the excellent Eddie Redmayne as Stephen. Unfortunately, they had not been able to cast a French actress of the right age, so Isabelle was played by the youthful Clémence Poésy. Although she was good in the role, it was no longer the story of a very young man and an older woman; it had become a Romeo and Juliet affair. The actor who played Stephen's English friend, Michael Weir, couldn't do an English accent, they discovered on set, so had to be Glaswegian. It meant that Colonel Gray, the Scottish commanding officer, then had to become

English. They couldn't afford to film in France, and the interior of the Azaires' bourgeois home in Amiens was therefore shot in some sort of Belgian warehouse. Even though Eddie Redmayne conjured some moving and effective scenes, there was an air of cleanliness about the whole thing. The big, noisy, dirty, epic feature was still unmade.

There was a feature film of *Charlotte Gray*, produced by Ecosse Films and starring Cate Blanchett, who was outstanding in the main part, all repressed idealism and impulsive moral stands. Unfortunately, the script went off at a tangent at an early stage of development and never found its centre, despite numerous and increasingly frantic drafts by the director-designate John Madden and the screenwriter Jeremy Brock. One of the main characters, Levade, was no longer a reformed libertine painter who had found God; he had been rewritten as a sort of handyman, played by a clearly baffled Michael Gambon. Just before it was due to start shooting, John Madden jumped ship to direct something else. You can do this in Filmworld, apparently. At the very last moment, thanks to Ecosse's enterprising boss Douglas Rae, a new director was found in the shape of Gillian Armstrong. She hadn't read the book, however, and had to work with the script she'd been left. It was decided to shoot in a David Lean Technicolor style, even though the wide-angle epic scenes in the book had all been left out.

But no one wants to hear a writer complain about his

adaptations. You don't *have* to sell the film rights, after all. And that was what I eventually decided: that I would sell no more options to film producers unless I wrote the screenplay. I enlisted the help of a young playwright called Rachel Wagstaff, who had adapted *The Girl at the Lion d'Or* for radio and had written a stage adaptation of *Birdsong*. Together we wrote screenplays for *On Green Dolphin Street* and *The Girl at the Lion d'Or*. These have been through the usual sequence of option, momentary excitement, year-long silences, renewed hope, let-downs and as you were. This is the norm, and I no longer expect anything else.

All this made me appreciate even more the professionalism of publishing. I stayed with the same hardback and paperback publisher for decades. Everyone at Hutchinson and Vintage did what they were meant to do, on time, with flair and the odd party thrown in, which left me free to concentrate on my part of the deal. This included doing interviews around the time of publication, going on the radio or television if invited, doing festivals and 'events' and generally trying to help the publicity department. I was never much good at this, being unable to create some glamorous persona that would make it fun for the journalist and give them a few good lines to quote. As both a bad actor and a former reporter myself, I could only be down-to-earth, frank and consultative.

This got me into trouble when I gave an interview to a magazine to publicise my novel *A Week in December* in

2009. This was a contemporary story of sub-prime financial fraud, Islamic extremism, the Internet and other alternative realities. It became clear that the interviewer knew nothing of credit default swaps, voice-hearing or the roots of Islam and in my eagerness to show how all these things were thematically connected in the book, I over-explained, in regrettably colourful language. I had believed that this would be off the record, though I had not in fact asked the reporter to turn off her tape recorder; I had just naively assumed goodwill and collaboration.

One Saturday afternoon some weeks later I was watching the Oval Test match on television when I had a call from the *Sunday Times* news desk, asking me for a comment on a story they were running the next day. 'Well, you're in a bit of trouble, aren't you, mate?' was how the reporter began, before reading to me some lines they had pulled from the magazine interview, of which they had an advance copy. He was calling on various Islamic hardliners for their comments, he told me. Right.

By speaking to a friend on another paper, I managed to place a soothing piece about my respect for all kinds of religious belief. The original magazine interviewer then got in touch to say she hoped I wasn't suggesting that she had misrepresented me. No, I said, it was my own fault for not making her turn off the tape: she had been unkind, certainly, but within her rights; and as a former journalist, I of all people should have known better. Then the *PM* programme on Radio 4 asked if I would like to go on and explain myself, but I thought it better to deny the wretched thing such air time.

Some days later, I was sitting at a sushi conveyor belt in a shopping mall, having just been to the cinema, when my mobile phone rang. It was Emma Mitchell, the publicist at Hutchinson, to say I had received my first online death threat. The police had rung my publisher and said they would compel the extremist site to take it down if I insisted. Gail Rebuck, the head of Random House, called to say she had been in touch with Special Branch and they had the team who had looked after Salman Rushdie on hand and ready to do the same for me. Fuck! I explained the situation to Veronica. 'I may have to go into hiding,' I said.

In the next forty-eight hours, I tried to see the issue from all angles. Eventually I decided to let the threat stand. This was for two reasons. First, the whole book was about the treacherous nature of virtual realities, whether financial, narcotic or extremist. So why should I take some vile website seriously? It was run by a repulsive demagogue (later imprisoned for life); I should not be cowed by such a man. The second reason was that my journalistic experience told me that attention spans are short: there would be other stories along in the morning. But if I went ahead and asked the police to act, that truly would be a story: Author Seeks Police Protection. Every paper would follow that one up, and not unreasonably so.

So I let it stand. And I'm happy to say that after a few

anxious weeks, it faded away. I wasn't murdered and a year or so later *A Week in December* reached number one in the bestseller list. Whether this was due to the death threat, I couldn't say. But if so, it was not a price worth paying.

All these failures . . . But, as I said, there were three projects away from the keyboard that have actually been worthwhile. The second came in 2016.

Three years earlier, I'd been asked to join the government Advisory Group for the Commemoration of the First World War set up by the Department of Culture, Media and for some reason Sport. The committee included former heads of the armed forces, defence ministers and historians, notably Sir Hew Strachan, to whom everyone deferred on matters of fact. Secretaries of state came and went every few months, almost as if the government didn't take culture that seriously; but the officials at the DCMS kept things on track. I was keen to do something other than nod sagely at the quarterly meetings and finally got my chance with the Somme commemorations.

We had all been disappointed with David Cameron's speech at the first big ceremony, at Mons in August 2014. He was capable, we knew, of speaking well, most notably in his powerful words about Bloody Sunday, which even hard-line Republicans had welcomed. But putting on a suit and a long face and talking of 'sacrifice' didn't seem enough, so we thought we should try to help. The DCMS officials were up for it. Working principally with Clare Pillman, one of the best, I wrote the narrative for the main service on 1 July and a speech for Mr Cameron to give at the vigil on the night before. It was a combined Anglo-French commemoration that involved three London and three Paris ministries (defence, foreign and culture) as well as the regional and local councils in Picardy, which had a slight *Clochemerle* or *Vicar of Dibley* tendency, especially after lunch.

The times allotted in the commentary varied. I might, for instance, be given forty-eight seconds to say something about the Royal Army Medical Corps. I would read it and time it and cut it until it was spot on, only to find a week later that the slot had gone down to forty-two seconds. I wrote much of it in Paris, where I had gone to research a novel, but was back in London by April. In late May, the final wording was agreed and sent to the printer, so I was surprised to receive a call from the DCMS when I was on holiday in Cephalonia a few days later asking if I could change one word in the vigil speech because Clarence House didn't like it. 'What's it got to do with Clarence House?' I spluttered. 'Oh, didn't they tell you? Prince William is now giving the speech.'

A few days before the ceremony, I went into the Foreign Office in London, where I had been invited to give a talk to the staff about the significance of the Battle of the Somme. Unfortunately, it was the day after the Brexit referendum and the building was in a state of shock. The staff were pale and shaken. So was I, and made a mess of the lecture when John Keegan's verdict on the day caused me to break down in tears towards the end.

Things were worse when we got to Arras on 29 June. President Hollande, who had been billed to read, said that as a result of Brexit he would no longer be coming. One of the senior British politicians present was the most recent culture secretary, John Whittingdale, a big Brexit fan, who walked around looking both smug and embarrassed. Other politicians helped lower the tone. The Scottish nationalist Nicola Sturgeon paraded in a personal meet-and-greet in front of the memorial to the missing; Seumas Milne, the then Labour leader's *porte-parole*, lurked around muttering into the phone clamped to his ear.

It didn't matter. The vigil began at sundown on 30 June. It was preceded by a short service, attended by Prince William and Prince Harry and their father, then still Prince of Wales. Also present were the British Prime Minister and representatives of French and German governments. There were only a handful of other guests, seated at the base of the Lutyens memorial. I sat next to Veronica, who had persuaded me to go to France with Lyn Macdonald all those years ago. Prince William read the words I'd written. A lone piper played as the dusk fell.

I thought of the tens of thousands of young men gathered in their trenches on the hill opposite a hundred years ago that night, believing that the Big Push would end the war after a seven-day bombardment:

nineteen-year-olds from Belfast and Accrington, from Newport and Stepney, from Shropshire and Dundee, about to walk into a storm of steel that would lead to sixty thousand casualties in a single day. I thought of their trusting faces and how much and for how many years I had longed for the captains and the kings to bow the knee in acknowledgement of their cruel, gigantic folly. And as they, or their heirs, most graciously did so — the young Princes reeling from the Cross of Sacrifice with a stricken look on their faces — I felt that these dead men had been honoured at last. Leaving aside private family events, it was the best moment of my life.

The main service on 1 July was a triumph that no politician could spoil. In fact, they helped to make it. President Hollande relented, turned up and read superbly, as did David Cameron. Brexit was forgotten as the French and British flags fluttered together on top of the memorial. The huge congregation, most of them descended from the men who had fought or died, sang 'Abide With Me'. It was magnificent.

In about 2012, I mentioned my desire for a side hustle in a *Spectator* diary. I hoped to get offers from colleges and publishers and magazines, but only two messages materialised. One was from a solicitors' asking if I would like to rewrite their website content. The other was from a crime writer who wondered if I'd do some dog-sitting for her. I had to explain this was not quite the re-engagement with the world that I'd envisaged — regardless of the dog's collegiate qualities.

My agent, Gillon Aitken, remained an amused bystander. By this time, Gillon and I had become close friends, though like most of the important relationships in my life, it had come about by chance. At a party in London, when I was about twenty-eight, I'd met a publisher called James Michie. He was older than the other guests in the room — bald and cigar-smoking, but with a roguish eye and a Donovan cap. He had discovered Sylvia Plath in a Cambridge student magazine and had published Anthony Burgess and Graham Greene. I told him I was writing a novel; and instead of rolling his eyes he told me to send it to him when (or if) I finished it.

By this time I was a connoisseur of the rejection. I'd submitted my first attempt, aged twenty-two, unsolicited to publishers whose addresses I'd found in the London telephone directory.* The bulky parcel came whistling back within the week, wherever I sent it. A few years later, I showed my next effort to Giles Gordon, a literary agent I'd heard was sympathetic. Giles was tactful, as billed, but didn't think it worth submitting (even under the cunning nom de plume of J. J. Smith).

After aborting two other books at a depressing midpoint, I finished the fifth and sent it off to James

---

* A set of four huge printed books with the name, address and phone number of everyone in Greater London. All four were distributed free to every flat or house.

Michie — as a final gamble before admitting this novel-writing business was beyond me. After a long and irksome wait, he called to say he had persuaded the board of Bodley Head to publish it. 'It was a damn close-run thing,' he told me, as I stood trembling with emotion in a phone box on Holborn viaduct. The book was (incredibly) entitled *Like Ulysses*, after the opening words of a medieval poem by Joachim du Bellay, '*Heureux qui comme Ulysse a fait un beau voyage*'; and it was a condition of the contract, James said, that I find something less off-putting. I plumped for *A Trick of the Light* and the Bodley Head offered £1,500, which I at once accepted before they could change their minds.

James didn't like to splash money about, his or anyone else's, so lunch on the day of publication in July 1984 was a Chinese takeaway in his flat near the drug-dealing hub of All Saints Road. I didn't care. James had done what publishers are meant to do: encourage promise. Being a published writer was thrilling to someone who had pushed on against what had seemed daunting obstacles. I had often wondered if these included lack of talent as well as not knowing the right people. But being in print at last — the proofs, the jacket, the Finished Copy! — gave me the confidence to write the novel I had wanted to write all along, and which had lain concealed inside the first book, dimly discernible, like the foetus in an ultrasound scan.

It was called *The Girl at the Lion d'Or* and I finished it two years later, working in the evenings, at weekends and on holiday from my job in Fleet Street. I handed in the typescript and was taken aback when, a few weeks later, James Michie rang to say he couldn't offer to publish it. The reason he gave was that the Bodley Head was cutting back on fiction. I began to wonder if he was making an excuse and whether my own belief in the book was misplaced. However, James told me he thought I could still have a future and that I should get myself an agent. I don't know any agents, I told him (I didn't mention the Giles Gordon incident). James said he could introduce me to one of the best, Gillon Aitken, with whom he had been on walking holidays. A date was made.

Gillon had been born in 1938 into a Scottish family in Calcutta, where his father was a tea merchant. He had been sent to a boarding school near Darjeeling at the age of four, after which he was shipped off to schools in England, not seeing his parents for years on end. 'I thought they were dead,' he told me. He studied Russian on the interpreters' course during National Service, but skipped university to begin work in publishing. His first job was with Chapman & Hall, where he was soon despatched to take some proofs by train to Evelyn Waugh in Somerset. Within about ten years, he was managing director of Hamish Hamilton.

My agent-to-be was forty-eight when I met him. He was six foot seven inches tall, with a languid voice and a haughty manner, which he enjoyed using to intimidate publishers. He was aloof, without being cold, though some people found him awkward company; his reserve could lead to periods of silence at lunch — something that seemed not to bother him at all. By the time I met him and became a client, he had been running his agency for about fifteen years and had the most impressive client list of any agent in London. His favourite author was Pushkin, of whose prose stories he had written a published translation; but he later also took on Helen Fielding's Bridget Jones books. He liked literature and money in roughly equal proportions; he was a bridge player and a *Times* crossword devotee and he brought a ludic glee to his contract negotiations. For the first ten years, our relationship was coolly professional. We met perhaps twice a year over lunch at La Famiglia in Chelsea, where a negroni kicked things off until a doctor told Gillon to confine his alcohol intake to the evenings.

In the absence of the Bodley Head, Gillon placed *The Girl at the Lion d'Or* with a different publisher: Hutchinson. The fiction editor was Richard Cohen, a dynamic young man who had fenced for Britain in the Olympic Games and drank orange juice with lunch. He offered £3,000 for UK rights in *The Girl at the Lion d'Or*, and we accepted. I liked Richard and admired him as an editor. He gave me advice on sticking to a single point of view within a scene and urged me to revisit characters of whom the reader had been shown only one side.

Unfortunately, Richard left Hutchinson. He was succeeded by Sue Freestone, a heavy-smoking Canadian from Thunder Bay with a beguiling drawl and the cheekbones of her compatriot Joni Mitchell. I met Sue for the first time at a wine bar, a few yards from where Veronica and I were living with our two small children, and told her I was working on a novel set in the First World War. She went very pale. My version of the story says that she then lowered her head into her hands, though Sue always denied this. What is beyond doubt is that she rallied. 'Well,' she said, 'we'll do the best we can.'

In January 1993, I delivered a 650-page manuscript of a novel whose working title had been 'Flesh and Blood', but which at the last minute I'd decided to call *Birdsong*. I was anxious about what Sue would make of the closely described scenes of sexual intercourse and mass slaughter. I needn't have worried. She focused her editorial queries on the modern passages. I hardly dared to ask what she thought of the 1910–18 sections and I'm not sure I ever did. At any rate, I came to love Sue and was fascinated by her basset hound, who accompanied her to work in Vauxhall Bridge Road, where his head and shoulders would suddenly appear in Sue's little glassed-in office while the rest of him was still in the publicity department, turning in a moment afterwards like the trailer of an articulated lorry.

Sue and Gillon could hardly have been more different in style. A characteristic cry of Sue's was that her brain was not working that day, while a glance at Gillon told you that his was already waiting, two moves ahead. But to my delight they became friends not only in the hours they negotiated increasingly Byzantine deals on my behalf, but socially, away from work, as well. Sue was a mighty defender of her authors and the best person to have on your side in the corporate world of Random House, which swallowed more and more imprints before itself being bought by the German conglomerate, Bertelsmann. She was impatient of HR directives and training courses, but she was proud of her books.

By now, Gillon and I were meeting often. He had divorced his Swedish wife, Cari, and sold their house before moving into a flat in the Boltons, in South Kensington. Their only child, a delightful but fragile girl called Charlotte, had chosen to live with her father. She was only a little older than my own children, so Gillon and I swapped paternal anxieties, though he had more to worry about than I did. Charlotte took recreational drugs, under-performed at school and had been known to harm herself by cutting her forearms. This was outside my experience (or Gillon's) and I had little to offer other than sympathy. It was meanwhile an oddly touching ménage, the enormously tall and forbidding father, with the vulnerable teenage girl. Gillon was protective of Charlotte and proud that she had chosen to live with him; she was loving and dependent, but hard to pin down.

While I was writing *Human Traces*, between 2000 and 2005, I sometimes sent Gillon five-page essays on hypnosis, or hysteria or Freud. These were not for publication but merely to clarify my thoughts as I pushed on through the research process. He read them dutifully before asking how I was getting on with 'the real business of the day', by which he meant the *Times* crossword. I had taught myself to do this, partly as a too-late homage to my father and partly to keep up with Gillon. It took me almost two years to crack it, but when I finally completed one I sent an email telling him, 'The help line is open, should you need it.' He replied, 'That's very kind, but I completed it before leaving the house. A rather limp Monday effort, I thought.' It became a competition and a bond. In the days before online subscriptions, Gillon arranged to have the empty grid photocopied and faxed to me if I was abroad. A knock on the door and a breathless bellhop: 'I have an urgent message from London.' 'Ah, yes. Thank you. Just leave it over there.' I worried that this copying and faxing was not the best use of his assistant's time, especially when the assistant in question was Lesley Thorne. However, I guess it didn't derail Lesley too much since she is now the managing director of the agency.

After *Human Traces*, I wrote *Engleby*, a book so different that I suggested we publish it under a nom de plume. But Sue Freestone and Gail Rebuck, her boss, were adamant that it should stay under my name. I dedicated *Engleby* to Gillon, then had a sudden panic. 'You do understand, Gillon, don't you, that the main character is basically a . . . er, serial killer?' 'My dear, I thought he was a most amusing fellow.'

At about this time, we began to invite Gillon to join us on summer holidays in Italy or France and he was easy company, reading in a panama hat by the pool and making appreciative comments about the food at lunch. Charlotte came with him once, and I talked to her long into the Provençal night about the world and how she might find her place in it. 'I don't know what I'm for,' she said, pouring herself a stronger drink than seemed wise for her slight frame.

Veronica and I were in Italy in August 2011 when I had a call from Clare Alexander, Gillon's business partner, to tell me that Charlotte had died at the age of twenty-seven. She had been staying with her mother in Tangier, successfully rebuilding bridges. Cari had died suddenly of heart failure related to her drinking, and in her distress, as she made arrangements for the funeral, Charlotte had misjudged her own intake of alcohol and prescribed medicines. A more physically robust person could have slept it off, and there was no sense that it was deliberate; indeed, I saw the cheery emails she'd written only twenty-four hours earlier to friends in London. It was an awful accident, no more, no less.

It took me a day to pluck up the courage to telephone Gillon. At the sound of my voice, he broke down, but I think it was a relief for him to talk, when eventually he could. I felt frustratingly unable to help. But in the months and years that followed, he came round to our house in London almost every week for dinner. Sometimes we invited other people to cheer him up, but more often it was just the three of us, plus Hector, our dignified blue whippet, and any of our children who might be there. Sometimes we talked about Charlotte and sometimes her name was left unsaid. In her guileless but persistent way, Veronica questioned Gillon about his childhood and his family and his feelings. I set out a bottle of whisky on the table, a glass, a jug of water and some ice and told him to make free. Our friendship became very deep because the emotions we were dealing with were so unspeakable; yet I would never claim to have seen the innermost parts of this proud and solitary man. Some things were beyond reach, and I had no desire to push.

About four years after Charlotte died, Gillon discovered he had cancer in the mouth. It had almost certainly been brought on by his devotion to Senior Service cigarettes, a packet of which sat open on his desk at all times. After the usual treatments, remissions and false hopes, it became clear in 2016 that an end was in sight.

Gillon stopped taking the medicines because they made him feel unwell. But they had also been keeping the cancer in check, and without them it advanced rapidly. He was taken into hospital at UCLH, a tall building near the Euston Road. Hearing of his fast decline, Veronica and I went to see him. He was unconscious, lying alone in a bare room many floors up, with only the occasional nurse passing by. We urged the staff to give him all the pain relief they could. Veronica sat by the bed and held his hand, talking to him quietly, telling him he was not alone, on the off chance that he might still be able to register her words. And if he was, then hers was the last voice he heard.

Gillon, it transpired, had left all his money to be used to set up a literary charity. The speed of his decline meant that his will was not as clear or helpful as it might have been, but his executors asked me if I would like to be involved. After some years of legal grind, the Charlotte Aitken Trust was born and registered with the Charity Commission in 2019. I was asked to chair the board. The next trustee was Clare Alexander, with whom I had formed a close professional and personal friendship over many years. Rachel Cugnoni, publisher of Vintage books and a long-standing friend of Gillon's, was an obvious appointment. Simon Murray, Gillon's accountant and executor, completed the board. In 2021 we became sole sponsors of the *Sunday Times* Young Writer of the Year, a prize with a dazzling list of previous winners. The same year, we sponsored a new production at the Young Vic, *Best of Enemies* by James Graham. We have since formed partnerships with, among others, the Almeida Theatre, the Arvon Foundation and the Women's Prize for Non-Fiction.

So from beyond the grave, Gillon had provided me with my side hustle at last, my third and most valuable non-writing project. It offered meetings, colleagues, glimpses into other lives, the opportunity to feel engaged from time to time with a world outside my study. It was a chance to keep alive one of the great friendships of my life. And a way to remember the towering father and his vulnerable child.

10.

Au Revoir

Sometimes at literary festivals people ask what I would have done if I'd not been a writer. Heaven knows. As a twenty-one-year-old graduate, you were in those days (the 1970s) expected to make a career choice, and stick with it for forty-odd years. At Christmas parties, Edward and I would be cornered by men blowing smoke and gin breath at us while they extolled the benefits of a 'professional qualification'. But I was in no fit state to become a dentist or an accountant; it was all I could manage to read some French poets to see which ones we should invite to the Cambridge Poetry Festival.

I did briefly think of a law conversion course, but with my father, brother, uncle and both his sons already in the law, I thought the Faulkses had that world pretty much covered. If I had become a barrister, I would also have been in competition with Edward; and that didn't seem a good idea. Doubtless we could have found different areas in which to practise, but people do like to measure one sibling against another; and such comparisons are always irritating. A lifetime of it would have been intolerable.

Edward's legal career was, as things turned out, not

something anyone would want to have theirs measured against. After a slowish start, in the course of which he left the Bar for a couple of years, he found a niche in civil work, specialising in clinical negligence, insurance and local authority liability. He was instructed to represent the families of those who had died in the 1987 King's Cross fire; there were also numerous affecting cases that involved people suing hospitals and other organisations responsible (or not) for the infliction of life-changing injuries. He went on to have an extraordinary run in the Appeal Court and House of Lords (later the Supreme Court); he became head of his chambers, took silk in 1995, and was appointed to the House of Lords by the Conservative Party, in which capacity he worked as a minister in the Department of Justice. When he finally said he was going to retire from the Bar in 2023 he had appeared in the Supreme Court more often than any other barrister bar one (Jonathan Sumption). His modesty about his own abilities was not really borne out by the facts — or by the other appointments that came his way quite late in life. These included the chair of IPSO, the voluntary press regulation body.

One day I went to watch him in the Court of Appeal. Some of the same tactics he had used on me when we used to argue over the free racing car from the Sugar Puffs packet as children were still in evidence — albeit honed to a rather higher forensic level. Among these was an ability to switch the argument to the ground of his choosing if he felt his foothold slipping; and a subtle way of implying that the infliction of any further damage on his position would be in some way unsporting. No case at appeal level is clear-cut, by definition: any barrister is going to take some punishment from the bench and from the other side as they focus on the weaker aspects of his argument. However, Edward had a way of bringing the assaults to an end with various phrases that suggested that enough was enough and there were higher interests at stake than merely scoring points. It was not all about timing, sleight of hand or picking the right words: he had clearly been down the mines and made himself familiar with where the crucial point was to be found among the ziggurat of box files that had been wheeled into court.

He often used to arrive at work before anyone else at his chambers in Chancery Lane and take breakfast, bought from the local sandwich bar, at his desk. I used to tease him that while he was hammering on the door of the Fleet Street Pret A Manger, ordering them to open up, I was still in silk pyjamas taking a first glance at the *Times* crossword over a cup of Lapsang. Unlike me, he was a lifelong early riser, so starting at dawn was not a problem. He had always relished an argument and was not afraid to stand up for what he thought, even if it was unfashionable. It would be silly to try to guess where this characteristic 'came from' since only the most simple-minded believe that every facet of a person is 'shaped' by the response to a childhood event. However, I do sometimes think that his success as an advocate was due to more than hard work and rhetorical skill. My sense is that, knowingly or otherwise, he could give the court the impression that, while he was competing hard for his client, he was also interested in justice. And this sense of fairness is something that may have been influenced by the example of our father, one of the most fair-minded men you could hope to meet. Obviously, I can't prove this, but I do believe there's something in it; and I like to think so.

Growing up as the younger brother of such a strong character was a challenge. Our parents had wanted a gap of two years between their planned two children (they 'couldn't afford' more) and Mum had lost one in between Edward and me. (I sometimes wonder what s/he might have been like. Suppose it had been a girl . . .) Had I been born even four months later, with a gap of three years, I'm not sure Edward would have had the patience to hang around and explain things. But as it was, he was ready to share his enthusiasm for sport and films and music and dressing up and confronting pirates and outlaws; and such things are more fun with a Tonto or a Dr Watson trotting alongside. Also, someone had to bowl at him on the lawn, putting in twelve-over stints unchanged as Fazal Mahmood and others of the Pakistani touring team. His decision to involve me in all this was a formative piece of good luck in my life, forcing me to grow up fast or miss out altogether.

I like to think that I gave good value as a playmate; but I imagine there were times when Edward wondered what he had unleashed in this wheezy little sidekick, from whom his rear-view mirror would never again be clear. We had plenty of arguments, some of them quite bitter, but my enduring memory is of how exciting Edward made things sound. The St Leger. Apaches. A stowaway on board. The Saturday of the Lord's Test . . .

People have remarked on how close we have remained, but to me the odd thing is how distant many sisters and brothers seem to be. When you have such a shared stock of memories from the most formative years, a library of in-jokes and shortcuts, why would you not feel close? Who else would laugh when you said, 'He's done a bit of an Uncle Reggie there,' in reference to an incident, alcohol-influenced, at Grandpa's ninetieth, when his brother, a mere boy of eighty-five, repeatedly inserted his arm between the lining and the sleeve of his overcoat as he tried to make a dignified exit? I was once talking about a friend of our parents who as a younger man was chronically over-sexed, visiting strange clubs in Paris with glass-topped tables, but who became in old age worried about going out to the shops, let alone to London, in case he found nowhere to park the car. 'Yes,' I concluded, 'parking and shagging, those were his great obsessions.' 'And what a shame it was,' said Edward, 'that he died before they'd invented dogging.'

In the year 2000, Veronica and I bought the house next door to Edward and his wife, Catherine. This was not out of a desire to be physically close, fond though we were of both of them and their sons, Leo and Archie; it was from a need to find a bigger house, and it was a coincidence that this one came on to the market. I asked Edward if he thought the proximity might be too much of a good thing. He went off to consult and, a week or so later, came back with the verdict (by a majority vote, I suggested) that they thought it would be all right. And so it was, especially for the cousins, who were able to hop over the garden wall and play with one another.

As from the age of about fifty-five, my sporting abilities began to wane, so Edward's began weirdly to improve. I had once given him a shot a hole at golf, but gradually he wore me down, his adapted on-drive bounding eagerly down the fairway while my cultivated fade became an incurable push into the woods. I'd once had to show him the principles of the forehand volley before a tennis doubles match; but as back pain took its toll on me, Edward's time with a personal trainer upped his serve and speed about the court. He must be one of the few players in history to perform significantly better in his seventies than in his forties.

Our father died in 1998, of cancer, a few weeks after his eightieth birthday, and it hit us both very hard. It took me seven years before I could accept it, when in a dream one night I had to break it to Dad, as he was packing up the car to drive us down to the Isle of Wight, that he had, in fact, died. Somehow with Mum it was easier. She had made it clear that life without her husband was not really worth living and that we should not strive officiously to keep her alive, should the occasion arise. It did, in March 2003, when she was a couple of weeks short of her eightieth; and her express wishes helped us to deal with the consultant that dark day in Queen's Square, in the silent stroke ward. When Edward and I went in the next morning, we found she had taken the matter out of our hands by dying in the night. She had left a note in her flat, thanking Veronica and Catherine, as well as her sons, for all we had done, but saying not to worry where we buried her — because she was convinced she would be with Dad in the hereafter. And I dearly hope she is.

I have known Edward for as long as I have been alive and there may be other things I owe him that I'm not aware of. I remind myself that when we were children, he wrote the Christmas plays and thought up most of the story lines of our various fantasy worlds. Some of this was due to his being older and knowing more, but even so . . . James Bagge told me that in their dormitory at Elstree Edward used to make up James Bond stories to entertain the younger boys after lights out. He seemed to be implying that Edward might have made a better job of the centenary novel than I did. And, who knows, he could be right.

One day there will be only one survivor of that tight little band of four from the Victorian brick house at the crossroads in Donnington. I hope for my sake that the last man standing is Edward, because it will be a lonely day; but I hope for his sake that the lot falls on me.

I don't often have such thoughts, because I have another family, all in good health, and they are my main concern. In a first draft of this essay, I gave character sketches of all three children, William, Holly and Arthur, but I changed my mind. I don't think they would want readers to wade through my assessments of them, affectionate though they were. They have a right to privacy and they have their own paths to discover. Our children, I suppose, are 'privileged' in the recent, disparaging, sense of the word and it may be that their strife and their difficulties will always, like my own, be seen, in the widest and truest perspective, as negligible. But we've tried to give them a sense of the world and their place in it; they take little for granted. And we haven't made the same mistakes our parents did with us. Oh no. We've made different ones. I'd be disappointed, though, if any of the three said they'd ever felt unloved.

In an actual memoir I'd have to give more weight to the friendship of women, from pals to love affairs. But this is not the story of a life, and maybe that's just as well because I'm not sure that there's a documentary way of writing about such things. A novel's the best place for emotional truths: it's made for them.

Only once when writing about love did I knowingly take something from my own life and drop it into

a novel. It's early in *Where My Heart Used to Beat*, where
the main character, Hendricks, is remembering an evening soon after he had met his lover, Luisa, in Naples in
1944. 'As I stood there, I had the impression that the
chest of drawers, the dull eiderdown on the bed and the
walls of the room had become iridescent. Even the thin
blind seemed to be glowing. I glanced about to see if
there was an overturned lamp; then I looked at her, leaning towards a mirror as she completed her preparations
for the evening, dabbing at the corners of her mouth
with a white handkerchief. She stopped, turned round,
looked at me and smiled. I took a pace back. All evening
she carried that light in every room we seemed to shim-
mer through.'

This optical illusion befell me in a mansion block near
Olympia in December 1976, with my Scottish painter (of
canvases, not houses). In 2014, the passage earned a tick in
the margin from my then editor, but on reflection it seems
a bit improbable, and perhaps better left to real life.

After we got married I urged Veronica to keep her own
work going, in the belief that she could have a reward-
ing career as a magazine or book editor; but she wanted
to devote herself to bringing up the children. And while
I kept urging, I was also pleased to think that our children were spending each day not with a childminder but
with the woman I most loved and admired. What more
can I say about her? I could write quite a few chapters
about Veronica, and my debt to her, but I don't like it

when couples give long public tributes to one another. They tend to sound dutiful or insincere. When I mentioned that I was writing something about our family and was not sure what to say about her, she said, 'Oh, I like it best when you simply build up an impression of someone from the way they're referred to over the course of a book.'

Veronica is the most altruistic person I have met. For most people, compassion is optional and time-limited: you only need to dwell for a moment on your irritation to be able to turn away from the second homeless person asking for money. But this is a switch Veronica sometimes can't find; so her empathy remains stuck on open. I'm not sure there is a 'reason' or an explanation for this; I think it's just the way she is. She was brought up in an observant − if not very spiritual − Catholic family, but says she has no real faith herself. She seems Christian in all but fact. And while her horror of hurting anyone's feelings and her concern for others can make her seem almost saintly, she has an acidic wit. She is, for instance, a mistress of the dramatic pause. 'Thanks so much for visiting Mum in her care home. Although she's got dementia, I think she's still rather proud of you . . . [*beat*] . . . Or perhaps *because* she's demented.' She was once wrapping up to leave the house on a very cold day when I heard her mutter, 'This sheepskin thing seems to have shrunk. Is that even possible? [*beat*] I feel like mutton dressed as lamb.'

So it's sometimes been like living with a cross between Sainte Thérèse and Dorothy Parker — with plenty of other characteristics of her own. These include a need to look regularly at paintings (and, related to this, a fascination with the chiaroscuro of indoor light, with particular regard to candles); a conviction that a tap, whether on a gas hob or a basin, has only two positions (closed or locked open on max); and a belief that 'move' and 'budge' are synonymous. Like the rest of her family, she says 'catch on fire' and thinks 'bother' is like 'dare', as in 'I didn't bother go.' Two slices of bread with something in between makes for most people what they call a 'sanwidge', but for her is always a 'sand witch', like a desert sorceress. Exactly fourteen minutes into any film, she will turn to me and ask urgently, 'Is it a comedy?' And, as with all the best people in fiction or in life, some of her distinctive traits are contradictory. How could someone who worries so intensely about the feelings and convenience of others be so carefree about punctuality? One evening, after a typical fifteen minutes' standing in the hall, checking my watch and jingling the car keys, I said, ' "Waiting for Veronica". Hmm. That'll be the title of the second volume of my memoirs.' 'No, darling,' she said, sweeping past me towards the front door. 'That'll be the title of the *first* volume.'

At the age of seventy, I think about my parents every day, though not in a morbid way. I'm simply aware of their affectionate if slightly teasing commentary on things I'm doing not as well as they themselves would do them — gardening and cooking, in particular. They always speak in the characteristic way they had, using phrases that brought them reliable pleasure.

My childhood was full of these words and I was surprised when I discovered not all families spoke the same way. 'Of course, by that time I was pretty *browned off*;' 'We met John's brother at the party, I must say, *looks are against him*;' 'I'd be grateful if you could pick up Fangio's Ferrari from the hall floor; I almost *measured my length* on it just now;' 'I took the liberty of throwing away your plimsolls. Though I must say they've *done yeoman service*.' The most damning was the one they used when they had been introduced to a new couple who had arrived with some fanfare in the neighbourhood: 'I'm afraid we thought they *just missed*.' My suspicion is that most of these phrases had been picked up by Uncle Neville from the tea rooms of the Beckenham Lawn Tennis Club in the early 1930s and handed on to my father for use as he saw fit. Uncle Neville, who was left-handed, had once won the Gentlemen's Singles at the club with his cunning little dinks and lobs; Dad found it hard to keep a straight face in the mixed doubles when a Sydenham lady told him as they changed ends, 'Oh, Mr Faulks, your balls do swerve so.'

To my delight, Veronica became fluent in this idiolect and brought some pungent phrases of her own. These include some Larry-isms named after her beloved

doctor-father, Lawrence, a unique golfing stylist, raconteur and dedicatee of my book *A Possible Life*; some of
her mother, Felicity's, more bizarre euphemisms for body
parts; and plenty from Tina Coyle, the candid Glaswegian
who was their long-time lodger and occasional domestic
help. (Tina had a rescue dog that bit me in the buttock
while I was putting up a picture, though this was apparently my fault because I had 'made a sudden movement',
which had frightened 'puir wee Penny'.)

My mother, in the last few years of her life, after Dad
had died, clung to old family phrases — for comfort or
reassurance, I suppose. I was happy to use plenty of them
during my weekly visits to her cottage, over lunch or
when doing the general knowledge crossword with her.
A year after Mum herself had died in 2003, I paid a call on
Mrs Sexton, my old village school teacher, who was still
living in the same small house near Newbury. I asked her
what she remembered of Mum. 'I can picture her sitting in
her little car,' said Mrs Sexton, 'waiting to take you home.
She was always early and was always reading a book while
she waited.'

I liked this snapshot rescued from the past. Mum was,
in a modest way, one of the most determined people I
have ever met. Her father, Philip Lawless, was a charming rogue — a spendthrift, boozing, sports reporter, who
had survived the Somme, played rugby for England and
had a golf handicap of plus two. Mum's mother, Brenda
Tuke, was an actress, in theory, though I don't know

that she ever did much beyond the odd part in repertory. The marriage was short-lived. They were divorced on the grounds of the mother's proven adultery. The judge awarded custody of the infant child to the father, but this didn't fit in with his life as roving correspondent; and the mother made no offer to step in, custody or not. So the little girl, Pamela (Mum), was left to the care of her paternal grandparents in a cottage on Barnes Common, then in a small house at the end of a terrace in Roehampton. Money was in erratic supply, generally short. At one point she was sent to a fierce boarding school to be 'taught some discipline'.

Mum's father remarried, but unwisely. His second wife was an alcoholic who treated her young stepdaughter, Mum, with appalling cruelty. Even so, Mum remained loyal to her father. 'I wish you'd met him,' she used to say wistfully to Edward and me. 'I think you would have liked him.' We rather wished that she'd met him more herself.

Mum left school at sixteen and looked for a job. She trained as a nurse and worked in St George's hospital at Hyde Park Corner, living in digs somewhere. The endless scrubbing with detergent brought out severe eczema on her hands. At some point in the War, she joined the WAAF and was stationed in Berwick, where a kind family called Wood looked after her. She made friends with a fellow WAAF called Pat Lester. In the evenings, she read books, finding in Dickens the troubled childhoods and big-hearted redemptions that resonated with her. Her favourite film stars were Gary Cooper and Clark Gable. She was vulnerable and persevering in equal measure. She was in touch with her father during the War, and was devoted to him. But she seldom saw him. In 1945, he volunteered to leave the sports pages of the *Telegraph and Morning Post* and go as a war reporter with the Americans into Germany. He nearly made it, but was killed by German shrapnel on a bridge over the Rhine at Remagen.

After demobilisation, Mum found work with the cosmetics company Elizabeth Arden, first in Belfast, then in Reading, where she did demonstrations of their products in the local John Lewis. One day in 1947, a law student called Peter Faulks asked her out for a drink. He was almost thirty, but had yet to sit his final exams, having lost his twenties to the War. Both lived in digs with landladies, but after some months of courting (buses, parks, halves of bitter), he said, 'If I pass my exams, will you marry me?' Mercifully, he did pass.

To Edward and me, she was a loving presence. If you had a problem or a wound of some kind, her radiant sympathy could make it hurt less. She was loyal, burningly so, to her husband and sons. It was only later that we saw how much she struggled with the lack of self-belief that was the legacy of her childhood. If friends were not as dutiful or as warm to her as she was to them, she took it to heart. The universal struggle to get builders to turn up, plumbers to plumb and machines to work seemed to distress her more than it did other people. There was an underlying feeling that the world was against her; and any setback could be seen as proof that this was so. She could be fragile, and you needed to know when to tease, when to ask favours and when to steer clear.

On the other hand, she knew that Dad was her saviour and that she was lucky to have found him; she worked long hours to provide the settled life she thought they both deserved. She liked parties and music and dancing and she had a ready sense of humour that became drier and saltier as the years went by. It was difficult for her to sit at lunch every day with three males discussing the latest county batting averages, but she saw that gentle mockery was her best protection: 'I can't tell you how pleased I am,' she said one day, 'that Ken Shuttleworth is likely to get some extra bounce in Australia.' She was always loving and striving, but later in life, before Dad died, she became hilariously good company as well.

When not gardening, cleaning, cooking and redecorating, she volunteered at the local hospital as an unpaid orderly. Whenever she could, she went to the theatre in Oxford and occasionally in London; at home she read constantly to make good the deficiencies of her schooling and listened to classical music on vinyl. In any moments left over, she read books aloud to blind people, worked for the Citizens Advice Bureau and raised huge sums for the British Legion. As you can probably tell, I admired her very much and it drove me mad when this brave and modest woman with all Dickens and Puccini in her

head felt intimidated by some braying Berkshire house-
wife who'd read nothing but Dick Francis. It was a big
moment when in 2021 I was asked by the Dickens family
to say a few words at the author's tomb in Poets' Corner
to mark his birthday. While paying tribute to his genius, I
said I had been introduced to his books as a child by 'my
mother, Pamela Faulks, a great Dickensian'. It felt won-
derful to send those words on their way up to the roof of
Westminster Abbey.

The Lawless family were without doubt a bit racy.
Mum's father had been cashiered from the army for debt,
and his brother, Uncle Arthur, had gone to prison for
fraud, though Mum said it was not his fault and he had
been ensnared by his wicked German wife. Uncle Arthur
certainly seemed hungry when, not long after his release,
he came for Christmas. Mum's cousin Jill, daughter of
her father's sister, boldly went to art school in Boston in
about 1960. There she met and fell in love with a fellow
artist called John Sanders; a few years later they were
married and set up an artists' colony in Medinaceli in
southern Spain. John was African-American with some
Cherokee (the same mix, so it was said, as Jimi Hendrix).
Edward and I thought he sounded the coolest guy ever
and couldn't wait to hang out with him when they came
to visit. Mum was aware that John was the first black man
ever to have walked down the village street in Donnington and worried about the neighbours. Neither Dad's
teasing nor our enthusiasm could put her mind at ease.

For herself, she liked John well enough and had loved Jill as a child; but the insecure person's fear of what others think is an illogical horror. I'm not sure she ever learned the lesson I took when I ran away from school, viz, that other people are simply not that interested.

During the Coronavirus lockdown, I discovered, by dint of some internet searches, that Mum's mother's family was Irish. In fact, her grandfather, Benjamin Tuke, played rugby at half-back for Ireland, appearing in all three matches of their first Triple Crown season in 1894. Mum never mentioned him or the Irish connection, they being associated in her mind, I think, with her mother's abandonment of her. Her mother did eventually marry again, a man called Bill Bennett, who had been badly gassed in the First World War. He managed the Grand hotel in Frinton-on-Sea and later the White Hart in Chelmsford. I met him once and still have a little wooden collar-stud box that belonged to him, but I never met his wife, my grandmother.

Late in life, when she was widowed and in great distress, Mum recalled in a letter to me her father's advice to her in hard times, which was to repeat 'I won't be beaten' again and again. Still heeding his words in her grief, she was able to write, 'Thank heaven for so many years of harmony and happiness in a life that began rather unpromisingly.' Edward and I felt frustrated that we were unable to help her in the five years of her widowhood, but she knew how hard we had tried, and told us so. I think it's important that such things are said and registered, for the long-term peace of mind of the survivors.

When my father was dying, I wrote him a few letters, for this reason, and he wrote back. There were admissions of possible shortcomings or failures; and there was forgiveness. I think he was baffled by the difficulties I'd had and by the attitudes I'd taken. Surely the point of everything his generation had done was to make life better for their children: they'd fought and died so we'd have it easy. I have tried to explain my feelings a little in these pages, though in fact I have come to share his sense of puzzlement. As a parent you do everything you can to help your children, to protect and even shape them, but in the end they slip through your embrace. They remain what they appeared at the instant of their birth: a mystery.

Dad died in 1998, and it was a great pity he didn't live to see Edward become a life peer or to enjoy some more highlights of his legal career; he did live long enough to see me achieve something as a writer and, when we were living in France, wrote movingly to express his pleasure. It was only then, when I was forty-three, that he thought I was settled enough to become an executor of his will.

When I think of my father, I always see him smiling, in a slightly conspiratorial way. His temperament was naturally a happy one, and much of his enjoyment day by day came from pointing out the absurdities of the world, of his friends, his family and himself. He was often half a step ahead of the conversation and some of our teenage friends may have found this intimidating, though he never used his wit to discomfort anyone. He was a modest man, who hated show or boasting; we used to beg him to run faster in the dads' sprint on sports day and to hit more sixes in the fathers' cricket match, but he would hit only a couple, not wishing to show off. His lack of ego perhaps made him unambitious professionally; Edward and I would sometimes try to urge him on. Only after he had stopped working did he say, 'God, I really ought to have made some more money.' He had become a judge at the age of sixty-two, sitting first in London then in Reading. It gave an uplift to the end of his working life and I'm not sure how they would have survived without the pension that came with it.

I have spent a lot of time thinking about twentieth-century wars and their effects on the civilians who fought them, and naturally I've wondered how much Dad was shaped by his experiences. The answer is that I don't know and I think it would be wrong to speculate. He wouldn't want me to. The facts are that he joined a Yorkshire infantry regiment, the Duke of Wellington's, in September 1939, when he was twenty-one, having just graduated from Cambridge. He fought in what he always called 'the Low Countries' and was at Dunkirk, marching three days and nights to get his company to the beach while German planes strafed the lines of refugees. He fell asleep on the troop ship and had no recollection of crossing the Channel or of anything much until he found himself at a party in Dorset dancing with the recently crowned Miss

Swanage. There followed a great deal of training in Britain until the battalion embarked for North Africa. Dad was in Tunisia in 1943 and was awarded an immediate MC after his battalion's action against the Hermann Goering Parachute Division at Banana Ridge, west of Tunis. A few days later he was wounded for the first time, in the arm.

His battalion helped take the Italian island of Pantelleria, a tiny place between Tunisia and Sicily famous for its caper crop. The tide turned the landing craft back to front, so the first Allied soldiers to set foot again in Nazi-occupied Europe were not the shock troops but the cooks and drivers. This turned out not to matter much as, after a battering from the RAF, the Germans had left and the Italians were keen to help.

The battalion returned briefly to North Africa before sailing for Italy in December 1943. The Italians had capitulated, but the Germans were there in force. The mountain landscape and broad rivers were easy for them to defend and difficult for the Allies to attack. A plan was hatched to make a surprise landing at Anzio, a seaside town south of Rome. The regimental history says, 'The Duke's were destined to play a great and glorious part in the operations in the Anzio beach-head.' Dad's annotation reads, 'Being there was neither great nor glorious.'

The operation, in January 1944, was initially a success, catching the Germans unprepared; but instead of pushing on and cutting the road to Rome, the Allied units were ordered to dig in. It was a combined Anglo-American operation cock-up, though exactly where the blame lies is still disputed by historians. The Germans moved fast to bring in reinforcements, which included armaments heavier than those available to an amphibious landing force. The Allied forward units, including Dad's 'D' Company, had little cover or support because they were in a salient pushed four miles out of the main beachhead line, the furthest forward of any Allied forces. A 'salient', by the way, is a bit that sticks out, like a sore finger, exposed and painful. After about ten days of being under fire, Dad was told by a runner from battalion HQ that he was to return to rest at base, or 'B Echelon' as it was known. The 1st Battalion commanding officer, a popular and admired regular called Brian Webb-Carter, was absent on a short rest period and the message had come from his temporary replacement. Perhaps partly because of this, Dad refused the order and sent the runner back. Another message came up soon afterwards, complete with replacement officer in a vehicle. Reluctantly, Dad did as he was ordered. He explained the layout of the company to the new man and went back to B Echelon, where he slept. The next day, he awoke to find that his entire company had been killed or captured, a fate from which he believed he might have saved them. In retrospect, it's doubtful that any single officer could have made a difference. The men were outflanked on both sides and were being pressed by German tanks and pounded by artillery and Nebelwerfers, a sort of multi-barrelled mortar. Had he disobeyed the order for a second time, I don't think I would be writing these words.

Shortly afterwards, on 9 February, still mourning the loss of his company, Dad emerged from a trench near Carroceto and was shot in the head. 'The major's a goner' were the last words he remembered hearing as they waited for the stretcher-bearers.

By this stage Brian Webb-Carter had lost all his company commanders, either dead or wounded. The forward companies were under constant German bombardment, in slit trenches half-filled with water and excrement, conditions as bad as those endured by their fathers at Ypres. These men did not take kindly to their efforts later being referred to by ignorant people at home as their having 'dodged' the fighting in Normandy.

While he was waiting to be evacuated from the beachhead hospital, Dad was hit in the shoulder by further shrapnel. The medical staff were not much concerned, as it was thought that he would probably not survive the head wound anyway. But he did survive, somehow, and from his bed in Sorrento watched Mount Vesuvius erupt on the far side of the bay. Uncle Neville, in Italy with the Eighth Army, hurried south in the belief that his younger brother was dead or dying. At the nursing home, however, he looked up to see a familiar figure at the turn of the stairs, in a dressing gown, smoking a cigarette. Thinking he had seen a ghost, Neville leaned against the banister and wept.

Dad, almost incredibly it seems to me, returned to action a few weeks later. Or as he put it, 'Some sort of operation was carried out to my head and I emerged wearing a plaster cast, but didn't feel too bad.' If you had been wounded three times you could go home, but he thought it would be feeble to 'count' the shrapnel in the shoulder. The orderly said it was a 'nice clean wound', though I can remember him going into the local hospital in about 1960 to have a piece of the metal removed from his arm, where it had worked its way down to his elbow and was inhibiting his tennis.

His fractured skull was thought to be no bar to his leading his new men (C Company) in the long overdue and successful breakout from the beachhead in May. At Anzio the 1st Dukes had lost 39 officers and 921 other ranks; their brigade companions, the 2nd Sherwood Foresters and the 1st King's Shropshire Light Infantry, had fared even worse. In June the Allies marched into Rome, and there is a photograph of Dad taking the salute from the American General Mark Clark at the head of C Company. In August they were among the troops that captured Florence, and Dad walked through the Arno, near the Ponte Vecchio, which was the only bridge the Germans had not blown. While his battalion continued to fight further north, Dad was sent to run an infantry training school nearby, though I think he would have liked to have been with the others, especially when Private Burton won a VC in the mountains by taking out two German machine-gun posts single-handed. When

Burton was told of the award by his commanding officer, his response was, 'Well, bugger me, sir.'

In February 1945 it was decided that the First Division should leave Europe and be switched to peacekeeping duties in Palestine, where the British mandate, issued by the League of Nations in 1923, still had three years to run. Jewish terrorist groups, which included two future Israeli Prime Ministers, had lost faith in all promises and viewed the British peacekeepers as enemies preventing them from inhabiting their promised land.

British soldiers arriving from the battlefields of Europe were not impressed by this terrorist activity, which they thought cowardly. However, their sympathies were divided. As Belsen was liberated, news was reaching them of the extent of Nazi atrocities. The Jewish settlers, it was clear at once, farmed in a more productive way than the Arabs; they were more energetic and better equipped. If the Arabs could not organise themselves politically, their future looked grim.

For most British soldiers, life was enjoyable. The weather, the landscape, the lack of real fighting and the Sunday School associations of so many places were a balm to them. Dad was not there long, because the battalion was moved to Beirut, which they liked very much, and later to Syria, where they were required to put down a revolt by native soldiers against their French officers in a desert fort. When Dad arrived, he found six dead French officers laid out in the sand; the seventh had been spared because he was married to a local woman. With the help of a French liaison officer who spoke Arabic, Dad managed to disarm the Syrian men and restore order. He was not demobilised until the following year. On his return to London he found that his widowed father had sold the family house and moved into a small residential hotel nearby, so Dad had nowhere to live and had to lodge with his married sister, Lorna. He had written many long letters home, describing his experiences in different theatres of war, but found that his father had not bothered to keep them. Instead, to mark his return, he took Dad to a Gilbert and Sullivan show. After seven years under arms, an MC and three wounds, one almost fatal, it was not much of a homecoming.

Brian Webb-Carter used to refer to his company commanders as 'the Barons', independent powers under his benevolent kingship. Fred Huskisson was one, an international rugby player who won two MCs, but a gentle man in peace and godfather to Edward. Tony Randall was my godfather, another brave soldier of the most kind and modest manner in real life. They had respectively led A and B companies of the 1st Duke's in the breakout from Anzio. We met them when they, and Bruce Hindley, the dapper adjutant, occasionally came to stay; and others, like Jim Sills, Tony Peel and 'Brainy' Benson (killed at Anzio), were known to us by name. And these names were spoken always with a joshing amusement that never quite concealed the profound nature of the attachment. No friends that Dad made in peacetime would equal them. I was delighted to be invited to lunch in London one day by Brian Webb-Carter's son, Evelyn, who was the last colonel of the regiment (the Duke's amalgamated with the Yorkshire Regiment in 2006). Evelyn was tall and military while I can't help but look a bit scruffy, even in my best suit, but we got on well and I like to think our fathers would have smiled when we raised a glass to them.

That's all. Those are the facts. And an entire generation had similar stories to tell. Not that they told them often, and never to strangers, for fear that someone would accuse them of 'spinning a line'. The men who did talk openly tended to be those who — usually through no fault of their own — had not seen much action. People who had witnessed killing at close quarters tended to be more focused on how they could provide a peaceful future for their children, as Europe tried to put itself together again.

In 1947, Dad set about looking for a job, but the country was awash with young men recently returned from the War to a drained economy with few openings. He was shortlisted for positions in the Diplomatic Service and ICI but narrowly missed both; perhaps it was the brown demob suit he picked up from Olympia that put them off. Reluctantly, he decided his best chance of making a living was to use his degree to go into the law, which in those days involved paying a firm to take you on as an articled clerk while you did further exams. He found such a place in Reading and at the age of twenty-nine resumed his life.

And so a few years later at our crossroads in Donnington, Dad was happy to mow the lawn, build bonfires, grow vegetables, play the occasional game of tennis or cricket and work five and a half days a week to pay for it all. While he had the most humorous and friendly manner, he was not a pushover. He had a layer of self-discipline that could verge on the ascetic. For instance, he would never take an aspirin 'because then I wouldn't know if the headache's gone away'. He had been granted a 13 per cent disability pension by the army medical board, but he never complained about his wounds; he was simply amused by the fact that this odd figure had been plucked from the air by a one-legged doctor. He didn't give in to Edward's homesickness when he was sent away at the age of eight, nor to his deep unhappiness at his next school. I don't think Dad expected anyone to be happy, as if it were a right, and he was suspicious of too much talk about emotions or psychology as being a failure to confront the fact that life was innately hard and/or unfair. The dividend of this stoical view was that when things did go right – with his wife or friends or children – he was innocently delighted. 'I say. I think this calls for a small celebration.'

It took me a long time to be reconciled to the fact that he was dying. I used to tell myself that I just wouldn't be seeing him — and that in any event *not* seeing Dad had been the pattern of my life since the age of eight. After all, I'd done a whole term without seeing either parent when I was quarantined with mumps. So it'll be like that, I told myself as I walked to the Tube each morning, only with a longer term.

When I look back at my mother's loveless childhood, makeshift education, her loneliness and constant fear of being broke, 'found out' or let down by other people — and all the scars these experiences left her to battle with as an adult . . . When I consider my father's life, his beloved mother dying when he was twenty-three and absent at war, losing his two best friends from university and countless army colleagues in combat, persevering through his own near-fatal wounds, then for decades doing a job he never much wanted to do, losing his money and almost his livelihood to a criminal colleague, then gritting his teeth through the 75 per cent taxation of the 1970s to try to make a life for his family . . . Well, I feel as if by contrast I've lived in some absurd cocoon of undeserved good fortune. I have tried to tell myself that this was what that generation fought for — there on the beaches, in the skies, on the seas and in the slit trenches of the malarial marsh: the chance for a son to sit on his backside inventing fictional worlds and swan about literary festivals in far-off places in the winter sun. Occasionally, I can even convince myself that this was their aim; but on other days it seems like almost everything else in life, both inexplicable and unfair.

Dad made his last visit to London in late 1997, when he took Edward and me out to lunch in Covent Garden. He drank wine and ate well; he was jovial and without self-pity, if a little frail. After lunch, Edward had to go for a conference with a client, but I had nothing planned so said I would accompany Dad on the Tube back to Paddington. We had a bit of a fight about it when he protested he was perfectly able to manage, but I prevailed and, at the other end, went up with him into the main station. We said goodbye, and I walked across the width of the concourse and down Platform 1, past Jagger's bronze of the First World War soldier reading a letter from home. I suppose it was a distance of about a hundred yards, but as I was on the point of going out on to the taxi rank, something made me stop.

I swung round and looked back across the concourse, past the news-stand and the fast-food stalls and the milling people, all the way to the top of the steps up from the Tube. Dad was still standing there, motionless, and had been watching me all the time. I lifted my hand and waved. He raised his arm in response. Then I went out into the London afternoon, where it was starting to grow dark.

Acknowledgements

With additional thanks to:

Christopher Beharrell, Mark Lanyon, Robert Colquhoun, Martin Winch, Alistair Troughton, Max Baker, Richard Lanyon, Henry Porter, Ronald Herring, Heather Letts, David Malvern, Joanna Pine, Bernard Briquet, Hilary Clark, Kevin Davis, Roya Hajiani, Jon Spiteri, Nooshin Abderabbani, John Tribe, Jill Dinnage, Rose Krzyz, Anne Rickwood, Keith Rubidge, Richard Pearce, Gail Sagman, Fiona Bonham-Carter, Karen Russo, Anna Immanuel, Rita Carter, Uta Frith, Chris Frith, Simon Wessely.

Harbourne Stephen, Bill Deedes, Morrison Halcrow, Charles Moore, George Evans, Carla Dobson, Peter McKay, Ivo Dawnay, Ed Steen, Simon Carr, Jamie Fergusson, Sabine Durrant, Giles Smith, Hermione Davies, Penny Lewis, Carrie Donald, Mark Lawson, Mark Steyn, Georgina Brown, Crispin Simon, Phil Shaw, Jonathan Keates, Jonathan Fenby, Roya Nikkhah, Andrew Holgate, Max Hastings.

Robert Easton, Simon Palethorpe, Adam Jay, Trudi Charles, Mark Charles, Barbara Kimber, Jacky Constantin, Adam Brett-Smith, Julian Turton, Mark Bicknell, Tom Knox, Tanya Roussel, Jane Moore, Sarah Delaney, Stephen Moore.

Liz Sich, Najma Finlay, Robyn Sisman, Caroline Gascoigne, Jocasta Hamilton, Venetia Butterfield, Richard Cable, Susan Sandon, Frances Coady, Caroline Michel, Tom Weldon, Joanna Taylor, David Milner, Mary Chamberlain, Alex Clark, Sally Riley, Lisa Baker, Susannah Porter, LuAnn Walther, Steve Rubin, Deb Futter, Patrice Hoffman, Marco Tropea, Jessica Terrier, Caroline Hutton, Sharon Zohar, Lisa Rozova.

Elizabeth Clough, Jeremy Paxman, Phil Cairney, David Vincent, Basil Comely, Simon Delaney, Genevieve O'Reilly, Trevor Nunn, Alastair Whatley, Julian Barnes, Ed Roussel, Georgiana Gibbs, Emily Read, Jackie Jones-Parry, Artemis Cooper, Charles Alexander, Molly Dineen, Antony Beevor, William Sieghart, Lynn Dennison, Tai-Shan Schierenberg, Piers Paul Read, Simon Schama, William Boyd, Anuradha Roy.

I first came across the quotation from Scott Fitzgerald (page 261) in *Behold America* by Sarah Churchwell (London, Bloomsbury, 2018), a persuasive book which does little to support my jet-lagged take on its author's homeland.

If anyone wants to know more about life in the Fifties, I recommend *Austerity Britain* and *Family Britain*, by David Kynaston (both published by Bloomsbury), from which I learned more than I could remember from actually living through the period.

A few details in the final essay have been taken from the Duke of Wellington's regimental history and many from an informal memoir my father wrote for the benefit of his grandchildren.

One of the best reader's letters (in the shape of a forwarded email) I have ever received began something like this:

I was interested to read in Mr Faulks's novel *Engleby* the main character's account of a concert given by Procol Harum at the Rainbow, Finsbury Park and his comments on Mick Grabham's guitar playing. Lead guitar that night was in fact played by Dave Ball. I know this because I was myself playing bass and Hammond organ . . .

The writer was Chris Copping and we have been in email correspondence ever since. I met Keith Reid briefly once, in Bristol in 1975, and I regret that I never got to say hello to Gary Brooker, who died in 2022. I wrote a short appreciation of the band in a biography that came out a few years back (*Procol Harum* by Henry Scott-Irvine, Omnibus Press, 2012) and was happy to see that a fellow fan-boy essayist was Martin Scorsese.

Text Acknowledgements

Page 4: 'Champion the Wonder Horse', lyrics by Marilyn Keith/Norman Luboff

Page 5: 'Bronco Theme Song', lyrics by Mack David/Jerry Livingston

Page 7: '*J'ai perdu le "doh" de ma clarinette*', Virginie Laban

Page 32: 'A Little Song of Life', Lizette Woodworth Reese

Page 36: 'It's Over', lyrics by Bill Dees/Roy Orbison

Page 50: 'Torches', lyrics by John Joubert/Barrie Carson Turner

Page 65: 'Shine on Brightly', lyrics by Keith Reid/Gary Brooker

Page 71: 'Magdalene (My Regal Zonophone)', lyrics by Gary Brooker/Keith Reid

Page 82: The Great Gatsby, F. Scott Fitzgerald

Page 98: 'White Rabbit', lyrics by Grace Wing Slick

Page 118: 'At Grass', Philip Larkin

Page 134: 'Fires (Which Burnt Brightly)', lyrics by Gary Brooker/Keith Reid

Page 178: 'Kid Charlemagne', lyrics by Donald Jay Fagen/ Walter Carl Becker

Page 250: 'Bad Neighbour Sam' (*Cheers*), written by Glen Charles, Les Charles, James Burrows, Cheri Steinkellner, Bill Steinkellner, Dan Staley, Rob Long
'Norman's Conquest' (*Cheers*), written by Glen Charles, Les Charles, James Burrows, Lissa Levin

Page 252: 'Spirit of '76', *Endpoint*, John Updike

Page 254: 'The Art of Fiction No. 22', *Paris Review* (Issue 19, Summer 1958), Henry Green interviewed by Terry Southern

Page 261: 'The Swimmers', F. Scott Fitzgerald

Page 273: 'Babylon Sisters', lyrics by Walter Becker/Donald Fagen

Page 274: 'Wouldn't It Be Nice', lyrics by Brian Douglas Wilson/Tony Asher